The Fabulous Originals

THE
Fabulous Originals

Lives of Extraordinary People

Who Inspired Memorable

Characters in Fiction

by Irving Wallace

NEW YORK

Alfred · A · Knopf

1955

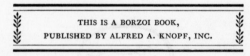

L. C. CATALOG CARD NUMBER: 55–9293

© IRVING WALLACE, 1955

THIS IS A BORZOI BOOK,
PUBLISHED BY ALFRED A. KNOPF, INC.

PUBLISHED OCTOBER 17, 1955
SECOND PRINTING, NOVEMBER 1955

FOR SYLVIA

Preface

The basic research for this book took place over a period of seven years in the libraries of Rome, Paris, London, New York City and Los Angeles. Compilation of material demanded the combined talents of biographer and detective. The task was exotic drudgery and was great fun.

Information on the novelists discussed, on the tracing of their inspirations to real persons, on the prototypes themselves, was drawn from many sources—from books, periodicals, places, and people.

I read, and re-read, all of the works of fiction mentioned in my pages. Often, the prefaces or introductory essays to these novels, so frequently ignored by readers, proved useful for their perception and scholarship. Among the many prefaces I read, I should like particularly to acknowledge those written by John Hampden, Montagu Slater, J. Cuthbert Hadden, Andre Maurois, and Edmund Gosse for the novels of Stevenson, Poe, Defoe, Flaubert, and Dumas *fils*.

For material on the prototypes discussed, I went to biographies, autobiographies, diaries, journals, memoirs, letters and histories. I consulted contemporary newspapers, pamphlets and periodicals, as well as manuscripts, documents and pertinent papers of every sort. Among the great mass of books and magazines consulted in my researches on obscure personalities, I inevitably found a small number that proved indispensable for their aid in furnishing background and guidance. I should like to record my obligation to these works and their authors, specifically to the following—

Leigh Hunt by Edmund Blunden, London, 1930; *Memories and Adventures* by Sir Arthur Conan Doyle, Boston, 1924; *Claire Clairmont* by R. Glynn Grylls, London, 1939; *The Life and Adventures of Alexander Selkirk* by John Howell, Edinburgh, 1829; *Lord Cochrane* by Christopher Lloyd, London, 1947; *The Real Robinson Crusoe* by R. L. Megroz, London, ND; *Portrait of Ianthe* by E. M. Oddie, London, 1935; *The Case of Constance Kent* by John Rhode, London, 1928; *The Trial of Deacon Brodie* edited by William Roughead, London, 1921; *The Prodigal Father* by Edith Saunders, London, 1951; *Joseph Bell, An Appreciation* by Jessie Saxby, Edinburgh, 1913; *Lives of Twelve Bad Men* by Thomas Seccombe, New York, 1894; *Flaubert and Madame Bovary* by Francis Steegmuller, London, 1947; *Literary Characters Drawn From Life* by Earle Walbridge, New York, 1936; an article by Dr. Harold Emery Jones, *Collier's Magazine*, New York, January 9, 1904; an article by William Kurtz Wimsatt, Jr., *The Publications of the Modern Language Association*, March, 1941.

In three trips to Europe, between 1946 and 1953, I visited, whenever possible, the actual sites that served as backdrops to the dramas enacted by the various prototypes. During these travels I interviewed and corresponded with a great number of persons who had first-hand knowledge of, or whose interests touched upon, the lives of the originals. Among these persons, I am especially indebted, for information and suggestions, to Hesketh Pearson, of London; Professor Sydney Smith, of Edinburgh; Dr. Douglas Guthrie, of Edinburgh; Dr. E. P. Scarlett, of Calgary; Mrs. Lilias Gordon Wilson, of Old Bennington, Vermont; Vincent Starrett, of Chicago; Edgar W. Smith, of New York; and the late William Roughead, of Edinburgh. Also, I owe my thanks to Mrs. Cecil Stisted, of Egerton, Kent, England, for personal reminiscences, and the use of scrapbooks and letters, relating to Dr. Joseph Bell.

Preface

I am grateful to the publishers of the *Reader's Digest* and the *Saturday Review* for permission to reprint those portions of "The Real Sherlock Holmes" that originally appeared in their pages. My thanks, also, to Charles Scribner's Sons, of New York, for permission to use excerpts from Henry James' *The Art of the Novel*, 1934, and from Henry James' *The Aspern Papers*, 1908, and to the Oxford University Press, of New York, for permission to quote from *The Notebooks of Henry James*, edited by F. O. Matthiessen and Kenneth B. Murdock, 1947.

And finally, I cannot conclude without a nod of gratitude to those sturdy novelists of years past who so fearlessly and openly acknowledged the sources of their heroes and heroines. It was their frankness that made my work easier, and, perhaps, in the end, made it possible.

IRVING WALLACE

Los Angeles, California

(ix)

Contents

(xi)

Contents

The Fabulous Originals

I

The Anatomy of Inspiration

On the early morning of July 11, 1906, a group of summer tourists, hiking around the shore of Big Moose Lake, in Herkimer County, New York, spotted an overturned rowboat in the shallow waters. When they saw a woman's cape and a man's straw hat floating near by, they summoned the authorities.

Within a few hours the lake was dragged and the dead body of an attractive twenty-year-old brunette dredged up. She was identified as Grace Brown, of South Otselic, New York. She had arrived two days earlier with a tall, blond young man, who had registered for both of them in the neighboring Glenmore Hotel under the name Carl Graham, of Albany, New York.

Before the police could dismiss the drowning as another resort accident, the physicians examining Grace Brown's corpse discovered two astounding facts. Miss Brown had been killed, not by drowning, but by a blow on the skull struck with great violence. In short, she had been murdered. And—possible motivation—she was pregnant.

The police, who had been dragging the lake further for the body of her male companion, abruptly abandoned their watery search. Hastily, they began to hunt for Carl Graham on land.

From distraught relatives of the murdered girl, the police learned that Miss Brown had worked the three years past in the

Gillette Shirt Factory, located in Cortland, New York. She had been dating her employer's nephew, a tall, blond young man named Chester Gillette. She had hinted to her parents that she was going to be married.

The police were prompt in locating a sample of Chester Gillette's handwriting. They compared his signature to the signature of "Carl Graham" on the Glenmore Hotel register. The handwriting matched. Gillette and Graham were one and the same man.

Chester Gillette was found and arrested for murder. He went on trial November 16, 1906, doggedly insisting that Miss Brown's drowning had been an "accident." The prosecution, to put it mildly, demurred. The prosecution accused Gillette of premeditated murder, and trotted out 106 witnesses to back the accusation.

According to the evidence presented, Chester Gillette had met Grace Brown in his uncle's factory. He had visited her regularly, eventually made love to her, and from time to time had spoken vaguely of marriage.

But the marriage did not occur. Through his influential uncle, Chester Gillette was beginning to be invited into rich homes. There he met wealthy, more socially attractive young ladies. When he tried to disencumber himself of Grace Brown, he suddenly found he could not. She was pregnant. Desperately anxious to dispose of her, he resolved upon homicide. He suggested an idyllic week-end. He took her to Big Moose Lake, rowed her out onto the lake, smashed her on the head with a tennis racket, and dumped her overboard.

The jury needed only four hours to find Chester Gillette guilty of murder in the first degree. Four months later he died in the electric chair.

Chester Gillette died—and yet he did not die.

Something about his life, his entanglement, his motivation, his violent act, and his fate rings a familiar chord, even among those totally unfamiliar with American crimes of the last half-century. The explanation is simple. Chester Gillette is familiar because he lives on, among us, under a different name—under the name of Clyde Griffiths, the fictional hero of Theodore Dreiser's moving, realistic novel *An American Tragedy*.

Dreiser was thirty-five years old when Chester Gillette went on trial in 1906. He followed the case closely in the press, and he remembered it. When he was ready to write a documentary novel showing how the American dream (the desire "to rise in the world, to be a success as measured by money and social position . . . stimulated and sanctioned by twentieth-century capitalist society," as F. O. Matthiessen has described it) could finally victimize a weak, sensitive, underprivileged youth, he remembered the case of Chester Gillette.

And so Dreiser wrote *An American Tragedy*, a book that gave him his largest audience. He freely and publicly admitted his debt to the prototype. The fictional travail of Clyde Griffiths was born of the real-life tragedy of Chester Gillette. There was more to Dreiser's hero, of course. There was Dreiser himself. For, while the living Gillette had been raised middle-class, the make-believe Griffiths was poor, savagely poor as Dreiser himself had once been. Further, the details of the first half of the book differed from fact, though in the latter chapters Dreiser drew heavily from Gillette's correspondence with Grace Brown and from his courtroom ordeal. But one thing is certain. While Dreiser might have penned *An American Tragedy* without ever hearing of Gillette, he could not have created Clyde Griffiths, as we know him, without the living model he followed.

The method Dreiser employed to develop his torn and sensitive hero is nothing new. For centuries other novelists as great as Dreiser—greater, even—have fashioned unforgettable fictional characters in the images of persons who actually lived.

Yet, though the Clyde Griffiths are enshrined in world literature, living on and on through generations of readers, their human prototypes remain neglected and forgotten. There are none to sing of the Chester Gillettes, who often lived lives as thrilling as the fiction they inspired.

For years my fascination has been with the unsung, with the

unique who lived, died, disappeared into oblivion, yet live forever in the wonderland of story-telling. Who, after all, was really Sherlock Holmes? And Dr. Jekyll and Mr. Hyde? And Robinson Crusoe?

Who were they in the flesh?

It is a question I have tried to answer in these pages. For, to put it as simply as possible, this is a book about unusual or interesting people in real life who inspired great characters of fiction.

How do novelists invent their fictional characters?

The anatomy of inspiration is complex, and difficult to dissect. Some writers have based their creations on legends, songs, dramas, sculpture, paintings. Gustave Flaubert wrote *The Temptation of St. Anthony* after gazing upon Brueghel's *Temptation* in Genoa. Other writers, however, have insisted that their heroes and heroines were completely figments of the imagination. Whether any character has ever been, or could ever be, entirely imaginary is still debatable.

The case for those who have claimed that their fictional folk were born full-grown out of their fantasies—dreamed up, so to speak—has been impressively documented by the creators themselves. Goethe spoke for these artists in discussing the creative experience with Eckermann in 1828: "No productiveness of the highest kind, no remarkable discovery, no great thought that bears fruit and has results, is in the power of anyone; such things are above earthly control. Man must consider them as an unexpected gift from above."

The origin of inspiration, of course, can depend upon the limitations given the word *imagination*. Some contend, with psychologists like Professor S. S. Sargent, that "imagination means forming new combinations or patterns out of past experiences, resulting in an original product." Or, as Helen Hull put it: "Imagination is the faculty of rearranging the known, of transmuting it into a new and sometimes wonderful piece of creation."

The Anatomy of Inspiration

According to these definitions, it would be extremely difficult for any so-called fictional character to be wholly dreamed up, since the character must have its genesis in "the known," in "past experiences." For, after all, almost all thought—perhaps the entire act of creation itself—must depend on some sort of pre-knowledge.

But modern psychiatry contends that inspiration may have deeper roots. Artistic creation need not stem only from "past experiences." An author may, indeed, be born with impressions that precede knowledge. Or receive impressions that cannot be accounted for. Dr. Beatrice Hinkle speaks of that "mysterious inner union, which takes place in the unconscious at the moment when the artist feels himself possessed and lost in the mystic embrace." Dr. Edmund Bergler elaborates on this point: "The writer's pen is guided by subterranean forces. The more understanding writers have often given expression to this fact and have described the creative act as being composed of two phases: the appearance of the ideas which 'something' within them has brought into being, and the working out of these ideas. The former, whatever it be called—inspiration, intuition, the favor of God—infuses the artist and appears independent of any voluntary act."

There is no denying that some writers have more nearly, more completely, made up their characters than others. It would appear that their invented people were not so readily identifiable, to themselves or to others, and more scrambled as to appearance, characteristics, attitudes, histories, than is usually the case. Possibly their invented people came from the deep recesses of the unconscious, rather than from the conscious.

I think it would be safe to say that when Cervantes thought up Don Quixote in his prison cell in 1597 and finally put the mad knight's adventures to paper and published them in 1605, he was creating a character that owed more to the unconscious imagination than to reality. There is no record that Cervantes based his anachronistic knight on anyone. The idea for this classical character, used by Cervantes as a mouthpiece to satirize the flowery tomes on chivalry he had read, may indeed have been a bolt from the blue. Yet there are critics who still believe that the knight may have had some ancestor in actuality, someone or something that Cervantes knew, which he embellished with fantasy. Gerald Brenan has suggested that "one of the sources of Don Quixote's power to move us comes from his being a projection of a discarded part of Cervantes himself; that is to say, of the noble intentions and failure of his life."

Similarly, Leo Tolstoy created Anna Karenina without employing a recognizable model. He long wished to tell a tale, we are informed by Professor Ernest J. Simmons, of "a married woman in high society who had lapsed morally." He mulled the idea for three years and then, one day, inspired by an utterly unrelated Pushkin story, began putting Anna and Vronski to paper. Only Anna's tragic end was taken fully from fact. Tolstoy had heard that the despondent mistress of a neighbor had thrown herself beneath the wheels of a train. Tolstoy had his own fictional mistress die the same way.

Probably the most fascinating example of a writer pulling a character out of the dim depths of the imagination occurred on a rainy summer's night in Switzerland during 1816. Lord Byron, his young, excitable physician, Dr. John W. Polidori, Percy Shelley, and Mary Shelley were discussing the supernatural. Suddenly Lord Byron spoke up. But let Mary Shelley recall it in her own words. "We'll each write a ghost story, said Lord Byron, and his proposition was acceded to. There were four of us. The noble author began a tale, a fragment of which he printed at the end of his poem Mazeppa. Shelley . . . commenced one founded on the experiences of his early life. Poor Polidori had some terrible idea about a skull-headed lady. . . . I busied myself to think of a story—a story to rival those which had excited us to this task. One which would speak to the mysterious fears of our nature, and awaken thrilling horror."

Inspiration did not come easily. Mary pondered until one night she overheard Lord Byron and Shelley discussing "the nature of the principle of life." The two poets talked about the experiments of Dr. Erasmus Darwin, "who preserved a piece of vermicelli in a glass case till by some extraordinary means it began to move with voluntary motion." In bed that night, the experiment stayed with Mary, and she began to picture a human corpse "re-animated." And thus was born *Frankenstein, or the Modern Prometheus.*

Victor Frankenstein and his Monster may have been completely products of the Freudian unconscious. Or they may have owed more to reality than Mary Shelley realized. I have read somewhere that Mary Shelley had, in London or in Scotland, become acquainted with a young medical student who enjoyed constructing strange skeletons out of stray bones. Whether that is true or not, it is true that Mary met many singular people through her eccentric father, William Godwin, and through Shelley himself, and the personalities and conversations of these guests may have remained with her, been digested, been elaborated upon, until the highly imaginative Frankenstein emerged.

But more often, in creating their characters, authors have fashioned their puppets after actual human beings, rather than after unexplained fantasies. And it is this type of creativity, the conscious kind, the kind that can be clearly identified, that I have concerned myself with in these pages.

Countless novels, especially early novels, are known to be autobiographical. When Mme de la Fayette published *La Princesse de Clèves* in 1678—which tells of a married princess who falls in love with a duke in the court of King Henry II, and confesses her love to her husband, though she will not betray him (her confession eventually breaks and kills her husband)— the married authoress was drawing upon herself and her own emotions when she fell in love with La Rochefoucauld.

With the same relentless sense of expiation, Dostoevsky recounted his personal adventures and feelings at the gaming-tables of Baden-Baden in *The Gambler*. Charles Dickens was himself *David Copperfield*. Samuel Butler assumed the guise of

Ernest Pontifex in *The Way of All Flesh*. Thomas Wolfe portrayed himself as Eugene Gant in *Look Homeward, Angel*, and H. G. Wells masked himself as Mr. Britling in *Mr. Britling Sees It Through*.

Wearying of themselves, many writers have turned to carbon-copying, in fictional characters, those very near at hand and very familiar—parents, sisters and brothers, wives, mistresses, friends, enemies.

Tolstoy nominated his grandfather, father, and mother for leading roles in *War and Peace*. Louisa M. Alcott mirrored her entire family in *Little Women*. Dickens employed both his mother and sister in *Nicholas Nickleby*. Of his own mother, Dickens said: "Mrs. Nickleby, sitting bodily before me, once asked whether I really believed there ever was such a woman." In fact, few people in Dickens's circle ever escaped the immortality of his pen. Even his first love, Maria Beadnell, a banker's daughter who rejected him for his poverty, found her way into *David Copperfield* as Dora. Years later, when Dickens was married, wealthy, celebrated, he met his first love again, found her "fat, commonplace, stupid," and transformed her into Flora Finching in *Little Dorrit*. James Joyce, while projecting his own personality into the character of Stephen Dedalus, copied the characteristics of his onetime schoolmate Oliver St. John Gogarty for Buck Mulligan in *Ulysses*.

And Gabriele D'Annunzio broke Eleanora Duse's heart—some say he sent her into retirement—when he sketched her as the aging actress La Foscarina in *The Flame of Life*. When Duse's manager, Schurmann, obtained advance proofs of the book, he was appalled at the ruthless detailing of Duse's sex life with D'Annunzio. One passage in particular offended him. It read: "The woman lay heavily on top of him, bringing down her whole weight; she embraced and enveloped him, hiding her face and brow against his shoulder, with the unrelenting pressure of a corpse grown rigid while clutching a living body." Schurmann rushed to Duse with the book. Sadly she replied to him the following day with a little note: "I knew about the novel you brought me. I even gave the author permission to publish it, since, regardless of my reaction to it, I am forty—and in love."

But the most fascinating character inspirations have come from those outside the authors' intimate circle. Writers have met these bizarre and intriguing personalities everywhere—in person, in print, in gossip—and used them openly, without permission, often without disguise, for their fiction.

The classics abound in *romans à clef*. François Rabelais, it is generally agreed, borrowed heavily from François Villon for his fictional Panurge in *Pantagruel*. Anatole France reflected one of his country's foremost poets, the ugly, sniveling, alcoholic, and homosexual pimp Paul Verlaine, in *The Red Lily*, confessing to a friend: "Yes, Choulette is Verlaine." George du Maurier, when he serialized *Trilby* in *Harper's Magazine* in 1894, described the painter Joe Sibley as "an idle apprentice, the king of bohemia . . . always in debt, like Svengali . . . vain, witty, and a most exquisite and original artist. . . . The moment his friendship left off, his enmity began at once." James McNeill Whistler took offense at this and castigated du Maurier in a letter to *Harper's* for his "mendacious recollection and poisoned rancour." Needless to add, Trilby appeared between hard covers with the character of the offending Sibley rewritten.

In locating and studying these *romans à clef*, in examining hundreds of others, I soon enough realized that their number was too great to document in detail. To do the job thoroughly, I decided to limit myself to a select group. But how to settle upon a method of choice?

Immediately a literary measuring-stick presented itself, one which I might hold up against each prototype. I would not, I determined, write about character models who were too well known. I could not write about those who were too obscure. And I had no desire to write about those who had inspired great characters, simply because they had done so; in other words, I demanded that my prototypes be interesting in themselves, as interesting as their fictional stepchildren.

I confined my investigations to the field of the novel. There were countless plays whose heroes and heroines had been based on real persons. These ranged from Marlowe's *Dr. Faustus*, which drew upon a real Dr. Faustus, a friend of Paracelsus who practiced necromancy, to W. S. Gilbert's *Pinafore*, which satirized the publisher W. H. Smith, who became First Lord of the Admiralty, to Lillian Hellman's *The Children's Hour*, which Miss Hellman admitted was based on an actual girls'-school scandal in Edinburgh during 1810.

Then there were poems, verse after verse, based on real people. There was Whittier's "The Man with the Branded Hand," drawn from the *cause célèbre* surrounding Jonathan Walker, who was branded with a red-hot iron for helping seven slaves escape from Florida in 1844. There was Longfellow's "Evangeline," founded on Hawthorne's factual notes about a young couple in Acadie who were separated on the eve of their wedding and reunited years later when the bridegroom was on his deathbed. There was Browning's "Mr. Sludge, the Medium," a searing portrait of the celebrated medium Daniel Dunglas Home, whose ability to move inanimate objects without touching them had impressed Czar Alexander II of Russia and the Empress Eugénie of France, and whose influence over Elizabeth Barrett Browning incited the poet's resentment.

With some reluctance I discarded the prototypes who inspired poems and plays in favor of those who had inspired novels and novelettes. This, largely because I felt the heroes and heroines of novels were better known.

Further, I confined myself to authors who had already passed into history. Contemporary writers who had made use of recognizable prototypes were plentiful. But the departed seemed safer. So it was with regret that I passed up Norman Douglas's *South Wind*, in the foreword of which he stated: "Bashakuloff, for example, is obviously derived from Rasputin and another holy Russian impostor whose name I cannot recall." I passed up Aldous Huxley's *Point Counter Point*, which drew upon D. H. Lawrence for Mark Rampion, and Katherine Mansfield and her husband for Beatrice and Denis Burlap. And I passed up the characters of W. Somerset Maugham—especially the painter Charles Strickland in *The Moon and Sixpence*, inspired by Paul Gauguin.

In assessing, for inclusion in this work, my vast number of living inspirations, I was most firm in eliminating those whose backgrounds were too familiar. Though authors like Dickens and Tolstoy drew heavily upon their own personalities for characters, I felt they could not be re-examined again in a work of this kind. They had literarily done themselves to death. As to other prototypes, such as those I mentioned—François Villon, Paul Verlaine, James Whistler—they were indeed intriguing, but again too well known and too oft belabored by biographers in full-length treatments.

The greatest difficulty was not in eliminating the too familiar, but in abandoning the too obscure. Some of the most fascinating prototypes—cases where the association was not denied, where the inspiration itself was well documented—had to be left in the limbo of the past simply because of their anonymity. These prototypes had sparked the fire of inspiration in certain artists, but had left no light by which to reveal themselves.

I cannot resist citing at least one example of regrettable obscurity. I refer to the case of a young Frenchman—not unlike Chester Gillette—who inspired Stendhal to create Julien Sorel for *The Red and the Black*.

Stendhal, a brilliant writer, an incredibly honest and introspective diarist, a fat and timid lover who daydreamed of being a dashing rake, was leafing through some old issues of the *Gazette des Tribunaux* in October 1828 when he stumbled upon Julien Sorel. The *Gazette*, ten months old, carried the account of an unusual murder trial in Grenoble. It appeared that a young man named Antoine Berthet, the ambitious son of a Grenoble artisan, had inveigled a priest into helping him obtain a job tutoring in the household of a wealthy attorney named Michaud. While educating Mme Michaud's children, Berthet seduced the Madame herself. Finally, bored, Berthet left the Michaud household and entered a near-by seminary. While training for the priesthood, he took another job tutoring in the home of a Grenoble aristocrat named De Cordet. Again Berthet became amorously involved. He fell in love with his employer's daughter and in a short time seduced her. One day he was exposed, promptly fired from his job, and expelled from the seminary. Enraged and frustrated, positive that his former mistress, Mme Michaud, had jealously given away his second affair—actually, it had been revealed by a maid—Berthet determined to have his revenge. He went after Mme Michaud, found her attending Mass in church, fired two pistol shots into her, then tried to kill himself, and failed. Shortly after, the court fulfilled his wish for extinction. Despite his argument that his mistresses had "corrupted his youth," he was found guilty and guillotined. Two years after reading about Berthet's adventures and trial, Stendhal reproduced them in *The Red and the Black*.

But if I had to relinquish Antoine Berthet for lack of material, I had to relinquish many more prototypes for lack of color. An excellent case in point was Sir Walter Scott's "beautiful Jewess" Rebecca in *Ivanhoe*, who was fashioned after a living American model.

In 1817 Sir Walter Scott was working on his story of the disinherited Wilfred of Ivanhoe, Lady Rowena, and a pious Jewish girl. Scott, who knew no Jews, was stumped when he tried to portray the devout daughter of Isaac, the Jewish moneylender. Luckily, as he was wrestling with his problem, Scott was also playing host for four days to Washington Irving at Abbotsford. Irving remembered a Jewish girl he knew in Philadelphia. She was Rebecca Gratz, the beautiful and religious daughter of a wealthy merchant. She had fallen in love with a young man of another faith. After a long inner battle, she decided to give him up. Feeling she could never fall in love again, she determined to devote the rest of her days to charitable works.

When *Ivanhoe* was published in December 1819, Scott dispatched a copy to Washington Irving with a letter which read: "How do you like your Rebecca? Does the Rebecca I have pictured compare well with the pattern given?" The real Rebecca Gratz died in 1869, at the age of eighty-eight, after helping to found the Philadelphia Orphan Society and the Philadelphia Hebrew Sunday School Society. When in her later years people asked her if she was really Scott's heroine, she would smile, pleased, and reply: "They say so, my dear."

She served Sir Walter Scott well, and her charities even better, but in examining her life I did not feel I could reward virtue further. She had been a perfect inspiration to a great novelist. But in herself, in the detail, she lacked sustaining interest.

In the end, when my researches were done, I found I had settled upon six people who deserved full inquiry, and six more who deserved somewhat briefer biographies.

But even when they were selected, I had to be doubly certain of one basic thing: had each living person I was writing about positively inspired a memorable character of fiction?

In three out of six cases it seemed simple enough. In these cases the authors admitted openly the sources of their fictional characters. A. Conan Doyle told his old instructor, Dr. Joseph Bell, that he was indeed the model for Sherlock Holmes; Henry James noted in his journals that he had got the idea for Juliana Bordereau by hearing an anecdote about Lord Byron's onetime mistress Claire Clairmont; and Edgar Allan Poe wrote friends that the murder of Mary Cecilia Rogers had inspired the creation of Marie Roget.

In the remaining three cases the evidence was secondhand—circumstantial, yet overwhelming and irrefutable. While Robert Louis Stevenson never actually stated in so many words that he had based Dr. Jekyll and Mr. Hyde on Deacon William

Brodie, his friends assured the world that he had, and, as a matter of fact, his preoccupation with Brodie lasted his entire life. Honoré de Balzac did not publicize his infatuation with the remarkable and scandalous Lady Ellenborough, any more than he admitted using her under the name Lady Arabella Dudley in *The Lily of the Valley*, but use her he did, with almost no disguise. And while Daniel Defoe never actually recorded that London's nine-day wonder Alexander Selkirk had been the prototype for Robinson Crusoe, the fact remains that Defoe probably met Selkirk and certainly read about the castaway Scotsman's desert-island adventures.

Understandably, most authors prefer not to admit that they have drawn upon life for their fiction. There are the minor question of vanity and the major question of legality. The average fiction-writer prefers the distinction of being an imaginative creator and dislikes being regarded as a parrot of fact. More important, open confession that a living person has been portrayed invites embarrassment, physical injury, and court action involving possible slander, libel, invasion of privacy.

A typical case where court action seemed likely, and was finally averted, involved George Meredith's use of the beautiful Caroline Norton for the model of his Diana Warwick in *Diana of the Crossways*. In 1836 Mrs. Norton, a granddaughter of Richard Brinsley Sheridan, was accused by her husband of immoral relations with Lord Melbourne, Prime Minister of England, and acquitted. In 1845 she was accused of obtaining a Cabinet secret from a lover and selling it to *The Times*. In 1884 Meredith, who had known her briefly, published *Diana of the Crossways*, using these incidents with little disguise, while admitting to Robert Louis Stevenson that his heroine was "partly modelled upon Mrs. Norton. But this is between ourselves." With the publication of the novel, the wrath of Mrs. Norton's influential relatives descended upon the nervous Meredith. Fearful of a slander suit, he hastily created an apology for the flyleaf of all subsequent editions. It read: "A lady of high distinction for wit and beauty, the daughter of an illustrious Irish house, came under the shadow of a calumny. It has latterly been examined and exposed as baseless. The story of *Diana of the Crossways* is to be read as fiction."

Finally, most authors insist, and with justification, that few characterizations are ever excavated wholly from actual persons. Sometimes, as we have seen, authors will cannibalize the living completely—background, appearance, habits, ideas. But more often they will borrow only one of these—something of the prototype's early life, perhaps, or something of his particular talents, or something from a unique accomplishment in his life—and, for the rest, add remnants from relatives, friends, reading, parlor talk, and, if you will, from the imagination. As W. Somerset Maugham told the *New York Times* in 1949: "More often I have taken persons I know, either slightly or intimately, and used them as the foundation for characters of my own invention. To tell you the truth, fact and fiction are so intermingled in my work that now, looking back, I can hardly distinguish one from the other."

One of the principal reasons authors do not transpose actual persons entire into fiction—beyond the automatic desire to be creative—is that authors simply do not know enough about their models. Real people may furnish the springboard, even the frame, but the novel must be more fully furnished. E. M. Forster outlined the necessity clearly in a lecture delivered at Cambridge in 1927: "In daily life we never understand each other, neither complete clairvoyance nor complete confessional exists. We know each other approximately, by external signs, and these serve well enough as a basis for society and even for intimacy. But people in a novel can be understood completely by the reader, if the novelist wishes; their inner as well as their outer life can be exposed. And this is why they often seem more definite than characters in history, or even our own friends."

Still, neither the necessity to embellish and expand, nor the threat of libel when the embellishment is not sufficient, will ever make the prototype extinct. Authors insist that they create from the imagination or the composite, and yet rarely do they resist drawing recognizable portraits. And, somehow, both subjects and readers understand this. Consequently, from Restoration days to the present, authors have been sorely beset.

Charles Lamb once complained: "Write—and all your friends will hate you—all will suspect you. Are you happy in drawing a character? Show it not for yours. Not one of your acquaintance but will surmise that you meant him or her—no matter how discordant from their own. Let it be diametrically different, their fancy will extract from it some lines of likeness. I lost a friend—a most valuable one—by showing him a whimsical draught of a miser. He himself is remarkable for generosity, even to carelessness in money matters; but there was an expression in it, out of Juvenal, about an attic—a place where pigeons are fed; and my friend kept pigeons. All the waters in the Danube cannot wash it out of his pate to this day, but that in my miser I was making reflections upon him."

More recently, and more bitterly, H. G. Wells wrote: "Cannot those who criticize books and write about books cease to pander to that favorite amusement of the vulgar, half-educated, curious, but ill-informed people, the hunt for the imaginary originals of every fictitious character?" Yet, despite his irritation, H. G. Wells continued, in his novels, to base a variety of his characters on "imaginary originals" like Winston Churchill, Arthur Balfour, Mr. and Mrs. Sidney Webb, and G. K. Chesterton.

It is plain that so long as authors cannot resist, prototypes will persist. But while the majority of writers, fearful or annoyed, refuse to publicly acknowledge their sources, there remain those who happily give credit where credit is due. Yet even an author's frank confession is often not enough. For when he is gone, his relatives or friends will sometimes repudiate what has already been acknowledged.

A case in point is the one involving Dr. Joseph Bell of Edinburgh. As I have remarked, Dr. Bell's student Sir Arthur Conan Doyle acknowledged in letters, in press interviews, in his own books that Dr. Bell had been the inspiration for Sherlock

The Anatomy of Inspiration

Holmes. Yet, since Doyle's death in 1930, his eldest son, Adrian Conan Doyle, has taken it upon himself to repudiate his father's words. Adrian Doyle doubtless feels that any credit given Dr. Bell only detracts from his father's genius. In the years since, Adrian Doyle has waged a persistent, unrelenting campaign to prove that his own father, and not Dr. Bell, was the original for the great detective.

Early in 1944 Adrian Doyle jousted with Mrs. Cecil Stisted, the surviving daughter of Dr. Bell. When Mrs. Stisted displayed letters to her father from Doyle, crediting her father with being the prototype, Adrian Doyle wrote to the Edinburgh *Evening News:* "It is neither my wish nor my intention to belittle the remarkable characteristics of Dr. Bell, nor to question the attributes of the doctor's influence upon my father. But it is my intention to rectify a most fallacious impression that Sherlock Holmes was, in fact, merely a literary reflect of Dr. Joseph Bell. My father's letters quoted by Mrs. Stisted open no fresh ground whatever, for as my father's old friends will agree, one of his most marked and lovable characteristics was the genuine pleasure that he derived in placing the major part of the credit for any of his successful adventures upon the shoulders of others rather than upon his own."

A short time later, when Hesketh Pearson brought out an unauthorized biography of Doyle in which he questioned the author's deductive prowess and gave much credit to Dr. Bell, Adrian Doyle returned to the wars with a little booklet in which he replied: "Dr. Bell's remarkable characteristics brought to their full growth the deductive propensities latent in Conan Doyle. They did that, and they did no more. If the good doctor had been endowed with the power to create extraordinary gifts that were not already innate, then the Edinburgh University course of 1876–81 would have produced, among the many hundreds of students that passed under his ægis, a spate of incarnated Sherlock Holmes! What, then, is the alternative conclusion? That my father himself had those very gifts, probably to an even greater degree than Dr. Bell."

The Fabulous Originals

As recently as 1948 Adrian Doyle was still serving as sentinel over his father's renowned character. When I published in a literary periodical a small portion of my chapter on Dr. Bell, Adrian Doyle wrote the magazine from England: "I have in my possession the inside facts of the correspondence and friendly association that linked my father and his old professor, Dr. Bell. I wish to place it on record that there is not a word of truth in Mr. Irving Wallace's statement that Dr. Bell made an assertion that he was Sherlock Holmes. On the contrary, he denied it most flatly, while on the other hand in 1918 my father put on record the fact that Sherlock Holmes was none other than himself."

Despite the continued indignation of the heir, the final word on the genesis of Sherlock Holmes must belong to the creator of Holmes. Only he knew who inspired him to invent the Baker Street detective. And if he hadn't already told us, and told us again, that it was Dr. Bell—we should know so, anyway, by simply acquainting ourselves with Dr. Bell's incredible talents, which I have set down in a full chapter.

Though the obstacles in the path of anyone who attempts to trace the actual sources of character inspiration are many, I have nevertheless attempted to bring to life, or into focus, the forgotten faces of literature. For these were the little-known originals, fascinating and bizarre in themselves, who gave so many of us so much pleasure and entertainment in the heroes and heroines they inspired.

Though I have undertaken the biographies in this book because I think that any examination of the mechanics of inspiration is of value, and because I feel that the persons who did the inspiring deserve acknowledgment, I think my main purpose has been to entertain. It is my hope that the prototypes, improbable as many of them may seem, will divert and interest others as much as they have myself.

I have but one misgiving. I fear that the whole idea of even discussing some of the processes of inspiration may be annoying to certain persons in the writing craft. Yet, I tell myself that dissections such as these are justified. For by constant and flagrant use of the defenseless living, authors invite gossip and discussion. And if they resent being embarrassed by having their sources publicly recalled, they must be made aware that they embarrass others by poaching on privacy.

I am reminded of the character-assassination in W. Somerset Maugham's *Cakes and Ale*, when he displayed Thomas Hardy to the public gaze, drawn and quartered, as the fictional "Grand Old Man of Letters," Edward Driffield. Somewhat surprised and deeply pained by the subsequent outcry—though I cannot imagine why—Mr. Maugham stiffly replied: "This practice of ascribing originals for the creatures of the novelist's fancy is a very mischievous one."

True enough. Nevertheless, let us be mischievous this once. . . .

II

The Real Sherlock Holmes

"Can this be my old friend Joe Bell?"
R. L. STEVENSON

One evening, about the turn of the century, after a week-end shoot in Scotland, a dozen guests sat around a dinner table discussing human monsters, famous murders, and unsolved crimes. One of the guests, Dr. Joseph Bell, the eminent surgeon and medical instructor, had the others wide-eyed with his deductive acrobatics.

"The trouble with most people," he said, "is that they see, but do not observe. Any really good detective ought to be able to tell, before a stranger has fairly sat down, his occupation, habits and past history through rapid observation and deduction. Glance at a man and you find his nationality written on his face, his means of livelihood on his hands, and the rest of his story in his gait, mannerisms, tattoo marks, watch chain ornaments, shoe laces and in the lint adhering to his clothes."

The guests were fascinated but skeptical. One challenged Dr. Bell to give an example of applied observation. Happily, Dr. Bell obliged.

"A patient walked into the room where I was instructing the students, and his case seemed to be a very simple one. I was talking about what was wrong with him. 'Of course, gentlemen,' I happened to say, 'he has been a soldier in a Highland regiment, and probably a bandsman.' I pointed out the swagger in his walk, suggestive of the Highland piper; while his short-

(22)

ness told me that if he had been a soldier, it was probably as a bandsman. But the man insisted he was nothing but a shoemaker and had never been in the army in his life. This was rather a floorer, but being absolutely certain, I told two of the strongest clerks to remove the man to a side room and strip him.

"Under his left breast I instantly detected a little blue D branded on his skin. He was an army deserter. That was how they used to mark them in the Crimean days. You can understand his evasion. However, this proved my first observation correct. He confessed having played in the band of a Highland regiment in the war against the Russians. It was really elementary, gentlemen."

Most of the guests were impressed. But one listener chidingly remarked: "Why, Dr. Bell might almost be Sherlock Holmes."

To which Dr. Bell snapped: "My dear sir, I *am* Sherlock Holmes."

Dr. Bell was not jesting. He was, indeed, the original Sherlock Holmes, the real-life inspiration for the immortal detective of fiction. In fact, A. Conan Doyle, in a letter to Dr. Bell dated May 7, 1892, frankly acknowledged the source. He admitted that he owed the creation of Holmes to his old instructor's teachings and to his demonstrations of deduction, inference, and observation.

When Dr. Bell, in his correspondence with Doyle, once ventured to repeat the anecdote of the Highland regiment bandsman, the author gratefully accepted it for a future Sherlock Holmes mystery. Though Doyle felt that the anecdote needed a secondary plot, as well as added character suspects to throw readers off the trail of the deserter-bandsman, he also felt that it contained the nucleus for an intriguing tale. He requested Dr. Bell's permission to employ it, and added that he wished he had a dozen more cases like it. In 1924, thirteen years after Dr. Bell's death, Doyle confessed: "I used and amplified his methods when I tried to build up a scientific detective who solved cases on his own merits."

In recent years, when Doyle's heirs loyally insisted that their father and not Dr. Bell was the model for the celebrated sleuth, one of Doyle's biographers retorted that this was unlikely, since Doyle was "singularly unobservant." Further refutation of the Doyle family contention was an early Sherlock Holmes book, which Doyle had dedicated to Dr. Bell with the words: "It was my own good fortune to have found the qualities of my hero in actual life."

As a matter of fact, few of the qualities of Doyle's hero, and little of his mode of living, were derived from Dr. Joseph Bell. For, unlike the detective, Dr. Bell wore neither deerstalker cap nor ankle-length cape coat, and used neither magnifying-glass nor cocaine. Where Sherlock Holmes was the eccentric bachelor in his cramped room at 221B Baker Street, Dr. Bell was entirely the family man with a son, two daughters, and two sprawling gabled homes of his own, one located on the slopes of the Pentlands. Where Sherlock Holmes dwelt in a shadow world bound by Moriarty and Watson, Dr. Bell was a surgeon whose courage won compliments from Queen Victoria, whose crusades for nurses earned the friendship of Florence Nightingale, whose classroom wizardry influenced five decades of Edinburgh University undergraduates from Conan Doyle to Robert Louis Stevenson and Sir James Barrie.

The detective and the doctor were also different at the core. "Sherlock Holmes, the subtle, callous man-hunter, tracking a criminal with cool and sleuth-hound persistency, had little, indeed, in common with the kind-hearted doctor," insisted Jessie Saxby, whose own mystery stories were often inspired by her friend Dr. Bell. With this opinion, Dr. Bell's only surviving offspring, elderly, aristocratic Mrs. Cecil Stisted, who dwells in Kent, concurs. "My father was altogether unlike Sherlock Holmes. The detective was hard and stern, while in striking contrast my father was gentle and kind."

However, the one unique thing the detective and the doctor did have in common overshadowed all differences. Just as Sherlock Holmes was the foremost fictional practitioner of what he termed "the science of deduction and analysis," so his real-life model, Dr. Joseph Bell, was perhaps the most brilliant master of observation the world has seen in the last one hundred years.

Dr. Bell's occupation was that of consulting surgeon to the Royal Infirmary of Edinburgh. His avocation, and most spectacular skill, involved meeting total strangers and, by merely glancing at them, deducting their nationalities, habits, trades, and backgrounds. Besides inspiring the creation of what the late Grant Overton has called "the most famous character in English literature," this hobby helped Dr. Bell successfully investigate numerous murder cases, helped him produce several generations of remarkable M.D.'s with talent for diagnosis, and, finally, helped Dr. Bell himself become a legend in international literary and police circles.

Many of Dr. Bell's views on the science of observation became household words when the character Sherlock Holmes mouthed them in sixty classic stories. "Let the inquirer begin," advised Sherlock Holmes, "by mastering more elementary problems. Let him, on meeting a fellow-mortal, learn at a glance to distinguish the history of the man, and the trade or profession to which he belongs. By a man's fingernails, by his coat-sleeve, by his boots, by his trouser-knees, by the callosities of his forefinger and thumb, by his expression, by his shirt-cuffs—by each of these things a man's calling is plainly revealed."

In story after story Sherlock Holmes reiterated his rules for deduction and analysis. "It is a capital mistake to theorize before one has data. Insensibly one begins to twist facts to suit theories, instead of theories to suit facts. . . . You know my method. It is founded upon the observation of trifles. . . . It is a curious thing that a typewriter has really quite as much individuality as a man's handwriting. . . . I have frequently gained my first real insight into the character of parents by studying their children. . . . I always put myself in the other man's place, and, having first gauged his intelligence, I try to imagine how I should myself have proceeded under the same circumstances."

These rules merely echoed the real-life gospel of Dr. Joseph

Bell. "Every good teacher, if he is to make his men good doctors, must get them to cultivate the habit of noticing the little apparent trifles," Dr. Bell once told a reporter. "The great majority of people . . . resemble each other in the main and larger features. For instance, most men have apiece a head, two arms, a nose, a mouth, and a certain number of teeth. It is the little differences, in themselves trifles, such as the droop of the eyelid or what not, which differentiate men."

In an essay on crime penned a half-century ago, Dr. Bell wrote: "The importance of the infinitely little is incalculable. Poison a well at Mecca with the cholera bacillus, and the holy water which the pilgrims carry off in their bottles will infect a continent, and the rags of the victims of the plague will terrify every seaport in Christendom."

What were some of these "infinitely little" factors Dr. Bell regarded as important in observation? "Nearly every handicraft writes its sign-manual on the hands," contended Dr. Bell. "The scars of the miner differ from those of the quarryman. The carpenter's callosities are not those of the mason. . . . The soldier and sailor differ in gait. Accent helps you to district and, to an educated ear, almost to county. . . . With a woman, especially, the observant doctor can often tell, by noticing her, exactly what part of her body she is going to talk about."

While Dr. Bell felt that the development of observation was a necessity to doctors and detectives, he felt as strongly that it was a thrilling sport for laymen. The vain Sherlock Holmes disagreed, holding little hope for the common man. "What do the public, the great unobservant public, who could hardly tell a weaver by his tooth or a compositor by his left thumb, care about the finer shades of analysis and deduction?" bemoaned Sherlock Holmes. But Dr. Bell felt that the unobservant public might care a good deal, once let in on the game.

Every man, argued Dr. Bell, can transform his world from one of monotony and drabness into one of excitement and adventure by developing his faculty of observation. For this reason—though once he complained in exasperation: "I am haunted by my double, Sherlock Holmes!"—Dr. Bell heartily approved of Conan Doyle's detective stories which popularized his ideas. "Doyle shows how easy it is, if only you can observe, to find out a great deal as to the works and ways of your innocent and unconscious friends, and, by an extension of the same method, to battle the criminal and lay bare the manner of his crime. . . . His stories make many a fellow who has before felt very little interest in his life and daily surroundings think that, after all, there may be much more in life if he keeps his eyes open."

Throughout his life Dr. Bell continued to amaze his circle with the observation game. "When the family travelled in a train," his surviving daughter recently recalled, "he would promise the children a treat, and when we got out of the carriage he would tell us where all the other passengers in the carriage were from, where they were going to, and something of their occupations and their habits. All this without having spoken to them. When he verified his observations, we thought him a magician."

His students also thought him a magician. Years after Dr. Bell's death, Conan Doyle told an interviewer: "Dr. Bell would sit in his receiving room, with a face like a red Indian, and diagnose people as they came in, before they even opened their mouths. He would tell them their symptoms, and even give them details of their past life, and hardly ever would he make a mistake."

Inside the spired Royal Infirmary of Edinburgh, in the packed amphitheater beneath the flickering gaslight, Dr. Bell daily tried to prove to his pupils that observation was not a magic but a science. His standard demonstration of this, given in a voice full of dry humor before each new class of medical students, involved taking up a tumbler filled with an amber-colored liquid. "This, gentlemen, contains a very potent drug," Dr. Bell would explain. "To the taste it is intensely bitter. Now I want to see how many of you have educated your powers of perception. Of course, we might easily analyze this chemically, but I want you to test it by smell and taste, and, as I don't ask anything of my students which I wouldn't be willing to do myself, I will taste it before passing it around."

Dr. Bell would then dip a finger into the liquid, put his finger to his mouth, suck it, and grimace. He would then pass the tumbler around. Each student would dip a finger into the vile concoction, suck it, and make a sour face. When the tumbler had made the rounds, Dr. Bell would gaze at the assembly and begin laughing. "Gentlemen, gentlemen," he would say, "I am deeply grieved to find that not one of you has developed this power of perception, which I so often speak about. For, if you had watched me closely, you would have found that, while I placed my forefinger in the bitter medicine, it was the middle finger which found its way into my mouth!"

In the Royal Infirmary wards, in the dispensaries, especially in the out-patient department where ailing citizens were brought forward by student-clerks, Dr. Bell practiced what he preached. Glancing at a newcomer, Dr. Bell remarked: "A cobbler, I see." He explained to his students "that the inside of the knee of the man's trousers was worn; that was where the man had rested the lapstone, a peculiarity only found in cobblers." Another time, when a laborer appeared with a spinal complaint, Dr. Bell said to him: "Your back must ache badly, but carrying a heavy hod of bricks won't improve it." The laborer was astounded, and cannily inquired: "I'm no' saying ye're wrang, but wha tell't ye I was a bricklayer to trade?" Dr. Bell replied by pointing to the laborer's peculiar, rough, horny hands. On yet another occasion Dr. Bell studied his visitor a moment, then announced to his students: "Gentlemen, I am not quite sure whether this man is a cork-cutter or a slater. I observe a slight callus, or hardening, on one side of his forefinger, and a little thickening on the outside of his thumb, and that is a sure sign he is either one or the other." The visitor quickly admitted he was a cork-cutter.

Once when a tall, weather-beaten patient entered the ward, Dr. Bell looked at him and said to his students: "Gentlemen, a fisherman. It is a very hot summer's day, yet the patient is wearing top-boots. No one but a sailor would wear them in this season. The shade of his tan shows him to be a coast sailor. A knife scabbard beneath his coat, the kind used by fishermen. And to prove the correctness of these deductions, I notice several minute fish-scales adhering to his clothes and hands."

Students of Dr. Bell's would remember for years some of the master's deductive feats. One former student, Dr. Harold E. Jones, recalled that Dr. Bell would summon his charges up front to try their own hand at observing. "What is the matter with this man, sir?" Dr. Bell once asked a quaking student. "No, you mustn't touch him. Use your eyes, sir, use your ears, use your brain, your bump of perception, and use your powers of deduction." At sea, the confused student blurted: "Hip-joint disease, sir." Dr. Bell scowled, shook his head. "Hip-nothing! The man's limp is not from his hip, but from his foot. Were you to observe closely, you would see that there are slits, cut by a knife, in those parts of the shoes where the pressure of the shoe is greatest against the foot. The man is a sufferer from corns, gentlemen, and has no hip trouble at all. But he has not come here to be treated for corns, gentlemen. His trouble is of a much more serious nature. This is a case of chronic alcoholism, gentlemen. The rubicund nose, the puffed, bloated face, the bloodshot eyes, the tremulous hands and twitching face muscles, with the quick, pulsating temporal arteries, all show this. These deductions, gentlemen, must however be confirmed by absolute and concrete evidence. In this instance my diagnosis is confirmed by the fact of my seeing the neck of a whiskey bottle protruding from the patient's right-hand coat pocket. . . Never neglect to ratify your deductions."

Another former student, the late Dr. J. Gordon Wilson, witnessed many similar exhibitions in the Infirmary. One feat in particular made a lasting impression on Dr. Wilson. "While Dr. Bell was seated at a table in the well of the amphitheatre with his internes and dressers, the patients were shown in by the out-patient clerk. On this occasion, awaiting his advice, was an old lady dressed in black and carrying over her arm a black bag which had seen service of many years. Bell gave her a quick glance and to our amazement said to the woman, 'Where is your cutty pipe?' [A cutty pipe is a clay pipe with a short stem.] Her bag was on her left arm and instinctively she grasped it with her right hand.

"This act did not pass unnoticed by Bell. 'Don't mind the students,' said Bell to the woman, much embarrassed, 'show me the pipe.' After a few minutes she put her hand into the bag and produced an old short-stemmed, much used clay pipe. Bell quickly noticed the embarrassment of the old lady and whispered to his ward nurse, 'Let her lie down in the waiting room and see she does not faint.' As the patient was being led away, she whispered to the nurse, 'I began to feel faint.'

" 'Now,' said Bell, turning to the students, 'how did I know she had a cutty pipe?' No answer. 'Did you notice the ulcer on her lower lip and the glossy scar on her left cheek indicating a superficial burn? All marks of a short-stemmed clay pipe held close to the cheek while smoking—the characteristic attitude of a peasant woman smoking a clay pipe as she sits by her fireside.' "

This talent for observation encouraged many of the nurses and students to bring their problems to Dr. Bell. Often he was able to solve them. One afternoon an Irish lad, terribly agitated by a letter he had received from his girl friend, came to see the doctor. He explained that his girl's previous letters had been affectionate. Now, suddenly, in her own hand she was telling him that they were not for each other, and that he must never see her again. The boy was too shattered to return to his studies, and, in desperation, he had come to Bell for advice. Dr. Bell requested the letter, examined it carefully. At last he returned it. "Pay no attention to this letter," Dr. Bell said cheerfully. "There's nothing to worry about. She still loves you." The boy was speechless, but Dr. Bell quickly explained. His knowledge of graphology enabled him to deduce, from the wavering feminine handwriting, that the letter had not been spontaneous. Further, from the construction of the sentences, from the general approach and psychology of the note, it was clear that the letter had been penned under pressure. "The writing may be hers," said Dr. Bell, "but the letter is not. It was dictated by her mother. I would suggest you keep in touch with your girl." The boy did, and was overjoyed to learn that the letter had indeed been dictated by a disapproving mother.

But of all the Edinburgh undergraduates, it was Conan Doyle who was the most deeply impressed by his incredible mentor. One time when the young Doyle was working as Dr. Bell's student assistant, a patient entered and sat down. "Did you like your walk over the golf links today, as you came in from the south side of the town?" inquired Dr. Bell. The patient replied: "Why, yes, did your honor see me?" Dr. Bell had not seen him. "Conan Doyle could not understand how I knew," Dr. Bell related later, "but on a showery day such as that had been, the reddish clay at bare parts of the golf links adheres to the boot, and a tiny part is bound to remain. There is no such clay anywhere else." Years later, writing "The Five Orange Pips," Conan Doyle had Sherlock Holmes say to a visitor: "You have come up from the southwest, I see." The visitor replied: "Yes, from Horsham." And Holmes explained: "That clay and chalk mixture which I see upon your toe caps is quite distinctive."

But the most famous example of Dr. Bell's skill was the one Conan Doyle retold in his autobiography. A civilian out-patient, a total stranger to Dr. Bell, came into his ward. In silence Dr. Bell studied the visitor, then spoke.

"Well, my man, you've served in the army."

"Aye, sir."

"Not long discharged?"

"No, sir."

"A Highland regiment?"

"Aye, sir."

"A non-com officer?"

"Aye, sir."

"Stationed at Barbados?"

"Aye, sir."

Dr. Bell turned to his students. "You see, gentlemen, the man was a respectful man, but he did not remove his hat. They do not in the army, but he would have learned civilian ways had he been long discharged. He has an air of authority and he is obviously Scottish. As to Barbados, his complaint is elephantiasis, which is West Indian and not British."

Years after, Conan Doyle was still sufficiently impressed by this incident ("very miraculous until it was explained," he admitted) to closely parallel it in his Sherlock Holmes story "The Greek Interpreter." In that tale, Sherlock Holmes and his portly, more brilliant brother, Mycroft, were seated at the bow window of the Diogenes Club, looking out upon Pall Mall. Two men stopped opposite the window, on the street below. Sherlock and Mycroft studied the smaller, darker of the two men.

"An old soldier, I perceive," said Sherlock.

"And very recently discharged," remarked the brother.

"Served in India, I see."

"And a non-commissioned officer."

"Royal Artillery, I fancy," said Sherlock.

"And a widower."

When the dumfounded Watson sought an explanation, Sherlock Holmes answered: "Surely it is not hard to say that a man with that bearing, expression of authority, and sun-baked skin is a soldier, is more than a private, and is not long from India." To which Mycroft added: "That he has not left the service long is shown by his still wearing his ammunition boots as they are called." Then Holmes went on: "He has not the cavalry stride, yet he wore his hat on one side, as is shown by the lighter skin on that side of his brow. His weight is against his being a sapper. He is in the artillery." And Mycroft concluded: "Then, of course, his complete mourning shows that he has lost someone very dear. The fact that he is doing his own shopping looks as though it were his wife."

Thus, Conan Doyle's five years as a struggling medical stu-

dent—and his months serving his uncanny Scotch instructor—
gave him both the idea for the character and much of the material that helped make him a world-famous author. But actually,
when he graduated from Edinburgh University in 1881, Doyle
intended to be a doctor. He nailed up his oculist shingle in a
suburb of Portsmouth and waited for patients. Six years later he
was still waiting. Lacking a practice, desperate for any kind of
income, Doyle turned to writing. After one false start, and
under the influence of Gaboriau and Poe, he decided to try a
detective story. And for it he wanted a new kind of detective.
Perhaps he looked at the photograph of Dr. Bell which he kept
on the mantelpiece of his study. At any rate, he thought of Bell,
and, thinking of him, hit upon his detective.

"I thought of my old teacher Joe Bell, of his eagle face, of his
curious ways, of his eerie trick of spotting details," Doyle recollected in his autobiography. "If he were a detective, he would
surely reduce this fascinating but unorganized business to something nearer to an exact science. . . . It was surely possible in
real life, so why should I not make it plausible in fiction? It is
all very well to say that a man is clever, but the reader wants
to see examples of it—such examples as Bell gave us every day
in the wards. The idea amused me. What should I call the
fellow?"

He called him Sherlock Holmes after an English cricketer and
Oliver Wendell Holmes.

In describing the detective, Doyle again remembered his old
instructor. Dr. Bell had been aged forty-four when Doyle saw
him last. "He was thin, wiry, dark, with a high-nosed acute
face, penetrating grey eyes, angular shoulders, and a jerky way
of walking. His voice was high and discordant." With this as
his model, Sherlock Holmes became the familiar, tall, stooped,
hawk-faced, intense, and inscrutable human bloodhound. His
first appearance, in *Beeton's Christmas Annual*, with *A Study in
Scarlet* in 1887, was inauspicious. But as a result an American
editor two years later ordered more Sherlock Holmes stories—

and *Strand Magazine* published the memorable "A Scandal in Bohemia," and the detective was on his way to literary immortality.

Sherlock Holmes's deductive tricks thrilled readers on both sides of the Atlantic. Each Holmes stunt was discussed and repeated by fans everywhere. In "The Adventure of the Norwood Builder," when a frantic young man burst into the room on Baker Street and announced himself as John McFarlane, Sherlock Holmes lazily replied: "You mention your name as if I should recognize it, but I assure you that, beyond the obvious facts that you are a bachelor, a solicitor, a Freemason and an asthmatic, I know nothing whatever about you."

In "The Adventure of the Blue Carbuncle," after studying an unknown's seedy, hard-felt hat, Holmes concluded that its owner was a sedentary, middle-aged gentleman who had lost his wife and his fortune and taken to drink. Again, in *The Sign of Four*, the detective, challenged by Watson, studied his Boswell's old watch and deduced from it that Watson had had an older brother, that the watch had belonged to that brother, and that the brother had been a careless and untidy person who had fallen into poverty.

This fictional witchcraft, made so plausible by Doyle's deft pen, became an international fad. But very often an Edinburgh grad would recognize from whom Doyle had derived this strange aptitude. In 1893, the year before his death, Robert Louis Stevenson, after meeting the "ingenious and very interesting" Sherlock Holmes in print for the first time, asked Conan Doyle in a letter from Samoa: "Only one thing troubles me. Can this be my old friend Joe Bell?" Conan Doyle was quick to tell Stevenson, the press, and the world that the prototype for Sherlock Holmes was indeed Dr. Bell. After informing a reporter from *Strand Magazine* that Dr. Bell's "intuitive powers were simply marvelous" and giving some graphic examples of the professor's skills, Doyle could not resist dashing off a teasing letter to his onetime teacher. Cheerfully, he warned Dr. Bell that soon he would be deluged under lunatic letters from

Constant Readers who would request his assistance in rescuing maiden aunts from certain starvation in sealed attics at the hands of homicidal neighbors and who would inquire as to his opinions on the identity of Jack the Ripper.

At first Dr. Bell labeled pestering reporters "fiends" and pretended annoyance with Conan Doyle. But he was secretly pleased at being regarded as the original of Sherlock Holmes and at the wide publicity given his methods.

In 1924 Conan Doyle wrote: "Bell took a keen interest in these detective tales and even made suggestions which were not, I am bound to say, very practical." But surely, when he made that statement, the years had dimmed Doyle's memory. For, in letter after letter, written three decades earlier, Doyle may be found asking Dr. Bell for plots and incidents and thanking him for the ones used.

True, when Dr. Bell suggested in 1892 that Holmes pit himself against a germ murderer, and hinted at knowledge of one such case, Doyle was quick to question if a bacteriological killer might not be too complex for the average reader. Nevertheless, Doyle was sufficiently intrigued to request more information. He implored Dr. Bell to find ten minutes, one day, to jot down any details he could remember of the bacteriological slayer. And, as always, Doyle reminded Dr. Bell to send along anything else that had a Sherlock Holmesy flavor.

As a matter of fact, Dr. Bell had many ideas of a Sherlock Holmesy flavor and faithfully sent them along. Conan Doyle gobbled up most of the suggestions, including the anecdote about the bandsman in the Highland regiment who insisted he was a shoemaker to hide the fact that he was a deserter.

Though, in speaking of his Edinburgh mentor, Conan Doyle pointed out that "it was toward the detection of disease rather than of crime that his remarkable talents were directed," Dr. Bell could never resist dabbling in a first-class murder. If he was Sherlock Holmes, he would have the fun of playing Sherlock Holmes. This was his primary extra-curricular activity. And, indeed, the Crown welcomed Dr. Bell's detecting genius.

As an amateur detective without official status, Dr. Bell worked hand in hand for twenty years with Sir Henry Littlejohn, Professor of Medical Jurisprudence and Police Surgeon to the city of Edinburgh. Sir Henry, slight, dapper, nicknamed "Little John" by his students, was almost as perceptive and caustic in his observations as his friend Bell. Together the pair investigated and testified in case after case for the Crown. Dr. Bell's greatest personal success, in the years before he became known as Sherlock Holmes, was the part he played in the sensational Chantrelle murder.

Eugene Chantrelle, a onetime Paris medical student, was a powerful, handsome man with muttonchop whiskers. He had come to Edinburgh in 1866 to teach languages, and within a year had seduced a fifteen-year-old pupil named Elizabeth Dyer and been forced to marry her.

The marriage was a singularly unhappy one. Constantly resentful, Chantrelle, in moments of anger, would wave a gun in his young wife's face, curse her, beat her black and blue, and boast that he would poison her in such a way as to baffle even the Edinburgh University faculty. Regularly he flaunted his extra-marital affairs. He made love to his wife's servants under the family roof. He openly visited the city's most notorious bordellos.

In October 1877, fearing that his fragile mate might meet with an accident, Chantrelle thoughtfully insured her life for $5,000.

Early one morning, about ten weeks later, the housemaid heard a moaning sound from one of the upstairs bedrooms. Rushing to Mme Chantrelle's room, the maid found her unconscious. Beside her bed were a glass partially filled with lemonade and some orange slices and leftover grapes. After calling Chantrelle, the maid ran out for a doctor. Returning, the maid found Chantrelle hurriedly stepping away from the window. The lemonade glass was empty, the orange slices and grapes were gone. When the doctor arrived, Chantrelle told him he thought his wife had been overcome by a gas leakage. At once the doctor sent a note to Sir Henry Littlejohn: "If you would like to see a case of coal-gas poisoning, come up here at once."

Littlejohn, accompanied by Dr. Bell, studied the bedroom and the ailing woman, and then removed her to the Royal Infirmary. There, after several hours, she died. Chantrelle was told that she had died of narcotic poison. He protested: "But you know we have had an escape of gas!" Nevertheless, he was arrested for murder.

Littlejohn and Dr. Bell had indeed found evidences of poison. There were many green-brown vomit spots on her pillow, and two on her nightgown. These contained opium in solid form mingled with grape-seed fragments—matching a smaller portion of the same found in her alimentary canal. Checking chemists, Dr. Bell found Chantrelle had recently purchased thirty doses of opium.

Chantrelle loudly insisted that his wife had died accidentally from leaking gas. Investigating, the gas company located a broken gaspipe behind Madame's window shutter. The maid claimed that there had been no smell of gas in the room when she discovered the body, but a faint smell when she returned to find Chantrelle moving away from the window; she thought Chantrelle himself had wrenched the pipe loose to make the death appear accidental. To this, Chantrelle replied that he could not have broken the pipe, since he did not know it existed.

Suspicious, Dr. Bell began snooping about, and finally located a gasfitter who admitted repairing the pipe behind the shutter for Chantrelle only a year before while "Chantrelle watched with interest the operation." With this evidence, plus proof that Chantrelle had been in serious financial difficulties, the Crown brought the French schoolmaster to dock. The trial lasted four days. The jury was out one hour and ten minutes. The verdict: "Guilty of murder as libelled."

On May 31, 1878, Chantrelle, gay dog to the last, started his long march. Recalling the scene, a former student of Dr. Bell's, Z. M. Hamilton, reports: "The morning of the execution, Chantrelle appeared on the scaffold beautifully dressed and smoking an expensive cigar. Dr. Littlejohn was there in accordance with his duty. Just before being pinioned, Chantrelle took off his hat, took a last puff on his cigar and, waving his hand to the police physician, cried out, 'Bye-bye, Littlejohn. Don't forget to give my compliments to Joe Bell. You both did a good job in bringing me to the scaffold!' "

A far more spectacular affair, if a less satisfactory one for Dr. Bell, was the celebrated Monson case. This case had its beginnings in 1890, when a London financier, Major Dudley Hambrough, hired a bankrupt young Oxford graduate named Alfred Monson to tutor his seventeen-year-old son, Cecil, for the Hants Militia. Three years later Monson leased Ardlamont House in Scotland, in young Cecil Hambrough's name, for a season of shooting.

In August 1893, after twice being refused insurance for his charge, Monson met the Glasgow manager of the New York Mutual Assurance Company, advised the manager that he was guardian of a boy coming into $1,000,000, that Mrs. Monson had advanced the boy considerable money against that inheritance, and that to protect this advance the Monsons wanted to insure Cecil for $100,000. The company agreed, and after Cecil passed the medical examination, Monson paid a premium of $1,000.

Two days later Monson, who could swim, took Cecil, who could not swim, out fishing in a rowboat at dusk. Suddenly the boat sprung a leak, flooded, capsized. Fortunately for young Cecil, they were near shore and he was able to hold on to a rock until rescued.

Early the next morning, as if to relax from the near-drowning, Monson, carrying his 12-bore gun, and Cecil, carrying his 20-bore, and an unarmed mustached man named Scott whom everyone thought to be an engineer, went hunting in the near-by woods. A few hours later Monson returned to calmly announce that Cecil Hambrough was dead. Monson claimed that they had separated, he had heard a shot, and had gone in its direction. "I then saw Hambrough lying at the bottom of the sunk fence on his left side, with his gun beside him. We lifted him up, and he was quite dead."

Everyone agreed that the killing was accidental, that Cecil had stumbled and shot himself. The mysterious Scott left town, not to be heard from again for over a year. After a brief lull Monson applied for the $100,000 insurance. The company replied that Cecil was a minor and the policy invalid. Monson said he knew that, and had only been trying to bluff payment out of them. Nevertheless, the company became suspicious, and a month later Sir Henry Littlejohn and Dr. Bell exhumed the body and re-examined the remains.

The two doctors found that the skull had suffered a triangular wound, that it was shattered only locally, that there was no blackening or scorching from gunpowder. Re-enacting the crime, Dr. Bell showed that to produce such a wound the shot had to be fired nine feet from the body. Had Cecil killed himself, by intent or accident, the gun would have been but two or three feet from his skull, would have blown his head apart, and blackened and scorched him.

Monson was indicted for murder. The Crown, using 110 witnesses, tried to show that Monson had earlier attempted to drown Cecil by boring a hole in a rowboat and removing the plug, and failing in this, had shot him from behind. In support of this contention, Dr. Bell, who was receiving much fanfare as the living Sherlock Holmes, went to the witness stand and testified: "Mr. Hambrough died in consequence of a gunshot wound, and I have not been able to make out any way by which the injury could have been done either designedly or accidentally by Mr. Hambrough himself."

However, the presiding judge, Lord Kingsburgh, was sitting at his first trial. In his reminiscences, later, he admitted lying awake nights in "dull perspiration, turning things over and over." In his final charge, preferring a safe and sure verdict, he reminded the jury not to be swayed from justice by Monson's bad character. In a little over an hour the jury announced: "Not proven on both charges"—a quaint Scottish verdict meaning acquitted.

To his last days Dr. Bell remained convinced that Monson was guilty. "He got off because it was Kingsburgh's first case," Dr. Bell told his wife. "Kingsburgh was afraid to start off with a death sentence." It pleased Dr. Bell to learn that Monson eventually wound up in prison for again attempting to defraud an insurance company.

Dr. Bell went after a baffling crime as others attack difficult crossword puzzles. In 1888, when the fiendish, insane butcher, Jack the Ripper, was prowling London's sidestreets, Dr. Bell co-operated with the police. Receiving copies of all the clues, Dr. Bell did most of his work at long distance.

But clues were extremely scarce. It was not even known for certain whether Jack the Ripper was male or female. Popular belief held that the Ripper was a doctor who sought vengeance on harlots for having given him, or a member of his family, syphilis. A few insisted that the Ripper was a psychopathic mid-wife who, carrying a kit of instruments, wandered the dark streets disguised as a man. But all agreed that, man or woman, the criminal was the greatest monster of modern times. His surgical slaughters, since celebrated in play, film, and novel, began in August of 1888, when a prostitute was found in a Whitechapel gutter with her throat slit and her body cold-bloodedly mutilated. The next month three more prostitutes were dissected. Miss Chapman, her head almost off, was discovered in the back yard of a tenement, organs extracted and neatly laid at her feet. Miss Stride, affectionately known as Long Liz, was killed on the lawn of a house in which a party was taking place (a man riding a pony cart interrupted the dissection, the pony shied, and the Ripper ran). Miss Eddowes was cut down in an alley, and when the killer finished he wiped his hands on her dress. The fifth was the worst. Mary Kelly, aged twenty-four, a beautiful and pregnant prostitute, was found naked on her bed, her ears, nose, and vital organs removed and arranged neatly around her corpse, with her bleeding heart placed on the pillow. "The operator must have been at least two hours over his hellish job," stated Scotland Yard. "The madman made a bonfire of some old newspapers, and by this dim irreligious light, a scene was enacted which nothing witnessed by Dante, in his visit to the infernal regions, could have surpassed."

These were the five certain murders. There may have been three others. London was terrified, and it seemed that everyone possessing a long-handled knife and a knowledge of anatomy was suspected. There was a Polish barber, seen running from the vicinity of a Ripper murder (coincidentally, the killings ceased when he moved to Jersey City). There was an insane Russian physician. There was an American sailor. There was an English doctor, who was found floating in the Thames after the last crime.

Among the firsthand material sent to Dr. Bell, there existed only one eyewitness description of a possible suspect. For it appeared that alongside Miss Stride's corpse there had been found a bag of grapes. These were traced to a vendor named Parker, who recalled selling them, shortly before Miss Stride's demise, to her and a male escort, a young man "about thirty, approximately five feet seven inches tall, stockily built, and of dark complexion." At the insistence of Scotland Yard, the fruit-vendor, Parker, closed down his business and devoted his waking hours to patrolling the Whitechapel district in search of the late Miss Stride's escort. On the evening of his eighth day of search the vendor saw his man. Before the police could be summoned, the suspect had ducked into a tenement building and disappeared from sight.

When Dr. Bell had accumulated all the available evidence, he called a friend of his into the investigation to help him sift and evaluate the facts. "There were two of us in the hunt," Dr. Bell said later, "and when two men set out to find a golf ball in the rough, they expect to come across it where the straight lines marked in their mind's eye to it, from their original positions, crossed. In the same way, when two men set out to investigate a crime mystery, it is where their researches intersect that we have a result."

Dr. Bell and his friend made independent investigations. From the suspects brought in, Dr. Bell deduced the murderer, wrote his name on a strip of paper, placed it in a sealed envelope. His friend did likewise. They exchanged envelopes. In both, the same name occurred. At once Dr. Bell communicated with Scotland Yard. A week later the murders ended. If this was coincidental or if Dr. Bell was in any way responsible, no one will ever know. But the murders did end—and Jack the Ripper was never arrested.

Despite all his publicity as the original of Sherlock Holmes, Dr. Bell abhorred the spotlight. He was a reticent man, and interviewers learned little about his background or his private life.

Joseph Bell was the product of five generations of surgeons. "It is interesting to note," Dr. J. Gordon Wilson observed, "that from 1771, for 140 years without a break, there was always on the Roll of Fellows of the Royal College of Surgeons, either a Benjamin or a Joseph Bell." As the eldest son of a devout and renowned physician, Dr. Bell entered Edinburgh University at sixteen and took his medical degree before he was twenty-one. For a year he worked as a surgeon under the great instructor Professor Syme, whose son-in-law was Joseph Lister. The following year Dr. Bell became house surgeon in the Royal Infirmary, and by the time he was twenty-six he was lecturing in the extra-mural medical school.

As a physician, Dr. Bell's courage was amazing. On one occasion, at a time when diphtheria was a little-known disease, an ailing child suffering diphtheria was operated upon. After the operation, poison accumulated, and since there were no instruments for suction, the child was given little chance to survive. Without a moment's hesitation, Dr. Bell placed his lips to the child's lips, sucked the poison from its throat, and saved its life. As a result, Dr. Bell himself caught diphtheria and permanently impaired his voice. When elderly Queen Victoria, visiting Edinburgh, heard the story, she personally congratulated Dr. Bell. "The dear old lady was so friendly," he reported afterwards, "and I was not one bit flustered."

Dr. Bell devoted much of his medical career crusading for nurses, and through this crusade he won Florence Nightingale and Robert Louis Stevenson as two of his closest friends. At a time when nurses were little better than street women, with no interest whatsoever in their patients ("quite often a drunken nurse would turn a patient out of bed, and get in the bed herself," Bell once told his daughter), Dr. Bell fought to dignify the profession. Later, when nursing became fashionable, Dr. Bell fought equally hard to keep out pretty girls who were only interested in wearing uniforms. Dr. Bell's only published book, in 1906, was *Notes on Surgery for Nurses*.

Dr. Bell's wedded life was idyllic but short-lived. He married at the age of twenty-eight, and his wife, Edith, died nine years later. On her tombstone he had carved: "I thank my God upon every remembrance of you."

He immersed himself in work, filled his home at Melville Crescent with friends, and grew into old age a crusty widower. He lost the Sherlock Holmes look, and a student remembers him toward the end as "a brisk Scotsman, rather under middle height, of compact but not stout build, and of energetic manner. He had a weathered, rather red, full face and iron grey hair and eyebrows, with little tufts of iron grey whiskers on each cheek." He walked with a limp, due to an old hunting fall, and his eye was so keen he could spot the species of any bird on the wing. He liked to drive fast, never drank, and felt that cigarettes made his feet grow cold.

He was unswervingly loyal to those who had studied under him. When Conan Doyle ran for Parliament in the central division of Edinburgh, and was derisively called "Sherlock Holmes" by some hecklers and "a Papist conspirator" by others, Dr. Bell immediately came to his aid. Much as Bell hated public appearances, he felt his old student was being unjustly manhandled. Dr. Bell stood beside Doyle on the platform of the

Literary Institute in Edinburgh and advised the audience to vote for Doyle. He assured his listeners that if Doyle did half as well in Parliament as he had done in the Edinburgh Royal Infirmary, he would make an unforgettable impression on English politics. But Dr. Bell's endorsement was not enough. Doyle lost to his opponent, a publisher, by 2,459 votes to 3,028 votes.

Dr. Bell was as loyal to his opinions as to his friends. In company he had very definite notions on all matters. "Hysterical people are generally liars," he would say. Or: "I have no patience with bigots. There is always some hypocrisy in conjunction with bigotry." Or, after visiting the remains of Wellington and Nelson: "I should not have liked to know them. One should not see a hero too near." He was Empire-minded, defending the Boer War to a friend: "You surely don't want us to be kicked out of South Africa. Once a nation begins to give in, it is a dying nation, and soon will be a dead one." He liked parables and Sir Walter Scott, and pitied "poor Dreyfus." He was extremely frank with mystery-writers who sent their manuscripts to the real Sherlock Holmes for criticism, often scribbling "gush" or "high falutin' " in the margins of the stories. Like all amateur detectives, he regarded policemen as flatfoots. "You cannot expect the ordinary policeman to stand eight hours on his legs and then develop a great mental strength."

Most of all, he had a sense of humor. When visitors begged him to recount tales of his deductive prowess, he liked to relate the story of his visit to a bedridden patient. "Aren't you a bandsman?" Dr. Bell asked, standing over the patient. "Aye," admitted the sick man. Dr. Bell turned cockily to his students. "You see, gentlemen, I am right. It is quite simple. This man had a paralysis of the cheek muscles, the result of too much blowing at wind instruments. We need only inquire to confirm. What instrument do you play, my man?" The man got up on his elbows. "The big drum, doctor!"

Dr. Bell died in October 1911, at the age of seventy-four. His funeral was impressive, attended by a deputation of nurses, by the Seaforth Highlanders, by a great number of influential medical men, and by swarms of poor people he had once treated. He was dead, but he did not rest long.

Conan Doyle, who had once killed Sherlock Holmes and brought him back to life, now attempted to resurrect the prototype. Doyle, before dying in 1930, became intensely interested in spiritualism. One night at a seance he announced that Dr. Bell had appeared to him and spoken to him. As proof, Doyle produced a spirit photograph of Dr. Bell attired in flowing hair and long gown. When Dr. Bell's daughter, Mrs. Stisted, saw the photograph, she was furious.

"It looked nothing at all like Father," she said. "And anyway, if he was going to return and appear before anybody, I am most sure he would appear before me!"

III

The Real Juliana Bordereau

By 1879 Percy Bysshe Shelley, drowned near Viareggio, Italy, had been dead fifty-seven years, and Lord Byron, taken by fever in a bed at Missolonghi, Greece, had been dead fifty-five years. With them had been buried the age of the romantics.

By 1879 the world had entered the era of the industrial, the scientific, the realistic, and names that would stir the twentieth century were already in existence. John D. Rockefeller was forty years old, Thomas Edison thirty-three, George Bernard Shaw and Sigmund Freud twenty-three, Henry Ford and William Randolph Hearst sixteen. H. G. Wells, André Gide, and Arturo Toscanini were active youths.

Yet in the first part of that year, in the busy, bewildering new period, there dwelt still in Florence, Italy, obscurely, half forgotten, one of the few survivors of the misty, legendary, romantic past. Her name was Claire Clairmont, aged eighty-two, a little English lady with white curls and black silk dress—as incredibly out of date, in 1879, as Lord Byron making an assignation on the newly invented telephone or Percy Shelley penning a poem supporting the railroad strikes in the United States. Yet the elderly Miss Clairmont was one of the few persons alive who had known those romantics at all—in fact, one of the few humans who had known them well; for she had been

(46)

both friend and inspiration to Shelley and been the mother of an illegitimate child by Lord Byron.

Only a handful of the growing cult of Shelley-Byron worshippers knew she was still alive. One of the few was a retired Salem, Massachusetts, seaman named Captain Edward Augustus Silsbee. His hobby was Shelleyana. He was a fanatic about anything Shelley had written, owned, or touched. He hungered to possess every Shelley manuscript fragment, letter, or relic in existence. When he learned that a human relic still lived—a woman who had dwelt with Percy and Mary Shelley almost their entire married life—he scurried off to Italy to meet her.

It was not easy. Claire Clairmont in her last years was no longer the gregarious, aggressive hellion who had pursued Byron to his bed. She had become an ailing, crotchety recluse. She shared rooms at 43 Via Romana, in Florence, with her brother's daughter, Paula Clairmont, her somewhat plain, attentive, middle-aged companion.

In the more than half-century since Claire Clairmont had last set eyes on Shelley, the spell of his persuasion and example had almost evaporated. In his presence, and for years after, she had been an atheist. Now she was a Roman Catholic convert, having written her friend Edward Trelawny eight years before: "My own firm conviction after years and years of reflection is that our Home is beyond the Stars, not beneath them"—to which Trelawny testily replied: "Dissatisfied with this world, you have faith in another—I have not." In the old days she had subscribed to free love. Now she began making notes for a book she intended to write, but which she never completed, to "illustrate from the lives of Shelley and Byron the dangers and evils resulting from erroneous opinions on the relations of the sexes."

Nevertheless, though she finally rejected Shelley's philosophy, she still loved him dearly, loved his memory as much as she hated Byron's. Beside the crucifix that hung in her quaint bedroom at 43 Via Romana, she kept a portrait of Shelley. She retained also two precious notebooks in which Percy and Mary Shelley had copied his poems, more than two dozen personal letters written to her by Shelley, and a lock of Shelley's hair preserved in a small red morocco box.

These were the mementoes that brought Captain Edward Augustus Silsbee from his native Massachusetts to Italy. It was the determination to beg, borrow, or steal these items, as well as to set eyes upon the eyes that had actually seen Shelley, that made Captain Silsbee take up the last watch in Florence. He had set for himself the difficult task of not only meeting the old lady, but of winning her complete confidence. This he accomplished, finally, in a devious manner. He went to 43 Via Romana and asked to rent rooms. There happened to be a vacancy. He promptly moved in and became Claire Clairmont's neighbor.

Soon enough Captain Silsbee met Claire and her niece, and was on intimate terms with them. Silsbee and the Clairmonts must have made a remarkable threesome. Claire, according to her relatives, was "small, distinguished, very English." John Singer Sargent, who was born in Florence, recalled that he first met her when he was thirteen. According to Evan Charteris, Sargent was attending dancing-classes. "He told me that on one occasion the usual pianist was unable to attend, and the class was on the point of being dissolved when it was remembered that someone who played and might be willing to fill the vacancy lived on the floor above. Presently a handsome old lady dressed in black silk came into the room. He noted a certain faded elegance about her as she took her place at the piano. The lady was Jane [Claire] Clairmont."

Claire's niece, Paula, who had been born in Vienna, where her father taught English to royalty, was in her fifties and a spinster when Captain Silsbee arrived in Florence. Once there had been prospects, apparently. Claire disclosed to a friend in 1869: "I am troubled by circumstances. My niece during and after her Mother's sickness and death was very much assisted by an elderly Austrian retired Major—he wishes to marry her; he cannot leave Austria or he would lose his pension—if they marry I must either go to Austria or live on here without one

relation near me. . . . I have told Pauline to do exactly what
she thinks will be best for her happiness. I will give no advice
or take any responsibility on myself in her affairs." Here one
detects the tyranny of the old. For Paula, timid and unsure,
docilely agreed to pass up her prospect, and to stay on as her
aunt's companion.

Alongside these two retiring women, Captain Edward Augustus Silsbee was something else again. A veteran of the merchant marine, he looked like an uncouth pirate. He was much
given to tall stories of his adventures in the China seas, and
once told the youthful, wide-eyed Sargent "of a fall, when in
command of a steamer, into an oil tank, and of his being left so
long to struggle in that medium before he was pulled out that
his hair positively refused ever to curl again."

After his retirement, Captain Silsbee's one passion was
Shelley. At the drop of his idol's name, in parlor or in public,
he would boom forth the verses of "The Cloud." Violet Paget,
the English novelist who wrote under the name Vernon Lee,
remembered how Silsbee would "come and sit gloomily in an
armchair, looking like some deep-sea monster on a Bernini
fountain, staring at the carpet and quoting his favorite author
with a trumpet-like twang quite without relevance to the conversation."

Another ardent Shelleyite, Dr. Richard Garnett, thought
Captain Silsbee "a most remarkable man . . . amiable and
gracious." According to Dr. Garnett: "He has traveled far and
thought much. A grizzled, weather-beaten veteran of fine
physique, his discourse was mainly of poetry and art, on both
of which he would utter deeper sayings than are often to be
found in print. He was the most enthusiastic critic of Shelley
the present writer had known, but also the most acute and dis-
criminating."

In his hunt for Shelley fragments, Captain Silsbee had shown
persistence and patience. He had already tracked down the
grandson of the beautiful, lightheaded Jane Williams, whose
husband had died with Shelley, and from the grandson had ob-

tained the very guitar Jane used to strum for the poet. Now, in Florence, he applied the same persistence and patience to Claire Clairmont. He pumped her for Shelley and Byron anecdotes. She had much to recount of Shelley, but usually refused to discuss Byron.

Meanwhile, Captain Silsbee kept his eye on the Shelley treasures in Claire's rooms. As Sargent told Charteris: "It was even said that he never ventured far from the house lest the owner of the manuscripts should die during his absence." For her part, Claire liked Captain Silsbee, perhaps even saw in him one who might take care of her niece after she was gone. At any rate, she permitted him to see and read her letters from Shelley and Trelawny and to borrow one of the Shelley notebooks. But she gave no indication of permanently parting with the treasures while she lived.

Captain Silsbee watched and waited. The old lady lived on. To Silsbee it seemed she would live forever. Discouraged, yet secure in the knowledge that the treasures were safe, Silsbee decided to briefly abandon his watch and take a short trip to the United States.

On March 19, 1879, while Captain Silsbee was vacationing in America, Claire Clairmont finally died. The moment Silsbee heard the news, he caught a ship and hastened back to Florence. Claire was already buried in the cemetery of S. Maria, in the Commune of Bagno a Ripoli, three miles outside Florence. But the spinster niece, Paula, was still at 43 Via Romana, surrounded by the Shelley treasures.

Captain Silsbee begged Paula to sell him her aunt's mementoes. "Then arose an unfortunate complication," according to the tale Sargent told his biographer. "The niece, mature in years and gifted with few of the graces which appeal to buccaneers, had long nourished a secret flame for the Captain. She declared her passion and proposed a bargain; the manuscripts should be the Captain's, but he must take her in marriage as a term of the deal."

Undoubtedly Captain Silsbee was stunned. He had, he

thought, been prepared to undergo anything to obtain the Shelley treasures. He had moved to Florence, invaded Claire Clairmont's home, spent long evenings charming the two elderly women. And, failing to obtain what he wanted in Claire's lifetime, he was positive he would attain his objective after her death. But suddenly the price was too high. The last of his limited funds, yes; but marriage to the spinster, never.

After Paula's proposal, Captain Silsbee left Florence in haste. But not entirely empty-handed. He still had the 150-page notebook in which Percy and Mary had written Shelley's poems. This he presented to Harvard University eight years later. And he had a single letter Shelley had written Claire, which he retained.

When dealers approached Paula and found some items missing, they were furious with Silsbee. They accused him of every disgraceful device. Thomas J. Wise charged Silsbee with having obtained the precious notebook by agreeing to marry Paula and then backing down on his word.

Four months after Claire's death and Silsbee's flight, H. Buxton Forman bought the entire pack of treasures from Paula —including twenty-four letters from Shelley to Claire, sixty-five letters from Trelawny to Claire, and a miniature portrait of Allegra, Claire's child by Lord Byron. But Forman was bitter about losing the notebook, which he implied Silsbee had stolen. As Forman reported later: "Of the mutilated manuscript volume, containing fair copies of many of his [Shelley's] published poems . . . there is a sad tale to tell. An American who had been residing in the same house at Florence with the Clairmonts had been bidding against me for the collection; but as his free bids turned out to be only in bills at long date, the executrix decided to accept my cash rather than his paper, in which she lacked confidence. This man, however, had 'borrowed' and not restored the precious manuscript book—which now graces the classic precincts of Harvard College."

In June 1887, a year after the Shelley Society was formed in London, Captain Silsbee lectured to many of its four hundred members on the subject of Shelley, exciting them with first-hand anecdotes he had heard from Claire. In 1900, still basking in the reflected glory of having known Claire, Silsbee sat for a charcoal portrait by Sargent, which was presented to the Bodleian Library. In 1904 Captain Silsbee died. As to Paula, the spinster niece, she suffered a dizzy spell while mountain-climbing one day, slipped, and fell to her death in the river below.

But if neither Paula nor Captain Silsbee got quite what they wanted from each other in their fencing over Claire's legacy, there was one other in Florence at that time who eventually profited the most from the curious drama. This person was Henry James, a small, pale, shy writer, bearded and formal, who had been born in New York and settled in England when he was thirty-three. He was living, off and on, in Florence while Claire Clairmont was still alive. He never met her. As he reflected later: "Had I happened to hear of her a little sooner, I might have seen her in the flesh. The question of whether I should have wished to do so was another matter. . . . The thrill of learning that she had 'overlapped,' and by so much, and the wonder of my having doubtless at several earlier seasons passed again and again, all unknowing, the door of her house, where she sat above, within call and in her habit as she lived, these things gave me all I wanted."

Eight years after Claire's death, in January of 1887, Henry James was again in Florence. One afternoon he went to visit at the home of the poet Eugene Lee-Hamilton, a half-brother of Violet Paget, who had known Silsbee. During the afternoon there were other visitors, among them the Italian Countess Gamba. Her husband was the nephew of Teresa Guiccioli, with whom Byron had had his last affair before his death in Greece. After the Countess left, Lee-Hamilton told Henry James that she possessed many letters written by Byron to Mme Guiccioli. She felt that the letters were disgraceful, refused to publish them, and had already burned one. After indignantly relating this, Lee-Hamilton went on to tell James another story concerning another packet of valuable letters. He told James the story, which had been making the rounds of Florence for some years, about Captain Silsbee's siege of the Clairmont household.

Back in his quarters, Henry James sat down to his notebook and jotted the following:

"Florence, January 12th, 1887. Hamilton (V. L.'s brother) told me a curious thing of Capt. Silsbee—the Boston art-critic and Shelley-worshipper; that is of a curious adventure of his. Miss Claremont, Byron's ci-devant mistress (the mother of Allegra) was living, until lately, here in Florence, at a great age, 80 or thereabouts, and with her lived her niece, a younger Miss Claremont—of about 50. Silsbee knew that they had interesting papers—letters of Shelley's and Byron's—he had known it for a long time and cherished the idea of getting hold of them. To this end he laid the plan of going to lodge with the Misses Claremont—hoping that the old lady in view of her great age and failing condition would die while he was there, so that he might then put his hand upon the documents, which she hugged close in life. He carried out this scheme—and things se passerent as he had expected. The old woman *did* die—and then he approached the younger one—the old maid of 50—on the subject of his desires. Her answer was—'I'll give you all the letters if you will marry me!' H. says that Silsbee court encore. Certainly there is a little subject there: the picture of the two faded, queer, poor and discredited old English women—living on into a strange generation, in their musty corner of a foreign town—with these illustrious letters their most precious possession. Then the plot of the Shelley fanatic—his watchings and waitings—the way he couvers the treasure. The denouement needn't be the one related of poor Silsbee; and at any rate the general situation is in itself a subject and a picture. It strikes me much. The interest would be in some price that the man has to pay—that the old woman—or the survivor—sets upon the papers. His hesitations—his struggle—for he really would give almost anything . . . "

Six months later Henry James was at work on the story. He finished it in Venice—it ran to a short novel, about thirty-six thousand words in length—and he mailed it off to the *Atlantic Monthly*. They published it in March–May 1888, under the title *The Aspern Papers*.

Henry James's fictionization hewed close to the facts. The hero-narrator of his tale, that "publishing scoundrel," is "a critic, a commentator, an historian" who, with a partner, specializes in the life and works of a great romantic American poet, Jeffrey Aspern, long dead. Constantly on the hunt for information concerning Aspern's life, the critic is surprised to learn that Aspern's onetime mistress, Juliana Bordereau, is living in Venice. "The strange thing had been for me to discover in England that she was still alive: it was as if I had been told Mrs. Siddons was, or Queen Caroline, or the famous Lady Hamilton, for it seemed to me that she belonged to a generation as extinct. 'Why she must be tremendously old—at least a hundred,' I had said."

Determined to lay his hands on some of the immortal Aspern's remaining papers and relics, the critic makes his way to Venice and succeeds in renting a room in the "dilapidated old palace" owned by Juliana Bordereau and her niece, Tina. The critic worms his way into the confidence of the "tremulous spinster" Tina, and through her manages finally to set eyes on the legendary Juliana Bordereau. "I was really face to face with the Juliana of some of Aspern's most exquisite and most renowned lyrics. . . . She had over her eyes a horrible green shade which served for her almost as a mask. . . . She was very small and shrunken, bent forward with her hands in her lap. She was dressed in black and her head was wrapped in a piece of old black lace. . . . I could see only the lower part of her bleached and shrivelled face."

The critic makes every effort to locate the precious Aspern papers. But neither he nor Tina can find them. Frustrated, the critic departs on a twelve-day trip through Italy. When he returns he finds Juliana has died in his absence. He asks Tina for the papers. She has indeed found them, hidden in the old lady's mattress. When he presses her for them, she hesitates. She feels she can give them only to a "relation." With shock, the critic realizes the price Tina has set on the Aspern papers. "What in the name of the preposterous did she mean if she didn't mean to offer me her hand? That was the price—that was the price!" The critic, horrified, rushes out to think it over. At last he returns to Tina. "It seemed to me I *could* pay the price." But it is too late. Tina has destroyed the papers.

" 'Destroyed them?' I wailed.

" 'Yes; what was I to keep them for? I burnt them last night, one by one, in the kitchen.'

" 'One by one?' I coldly echoed it.

" 'It took a long time—there were so many.' "

When *The Aspern Papers* appeared between book covers in 1908, Henry James publicly, if cautiously, admitted the precise source of inspiration in a detailed preface. Juliana Bordereau was indeed Claire Clairmont. "I saw it somehow at the very first blush as romantic," wrote James, "that Jane Clairmont, the half-sister of Mary Godwin, Shelley's second wife and for a while the intimate friend of Byron and the mother of his daughter Allegra, should have been living on in Florence, where she had long lived, up to our own day."

Limited though he was to the small canvas of a short novel, Henry James's portrait of Juliana Bordereau followed closely the original model. In the story Juliana is given a French ancestry, was once a governess, was in her youth "perverse and reckless," possessed of a "terrible" temper and an inherited income from America. In actual life Claire Clairmont was of French ancestry, served as a governess in Austria, Russia, and England, admitted to Byron that she was "imprudent and vicious" though insisting she could "love gently and with affection," and the recipient of a twelve-thousand-pound inheritance from the Shelley estate in England.

Though she lived to be eighty-one, Claire Clairmont was really alive only until her twenty-fourth year, when she lost both her daughter by Byron and her friend Shelley. In those brief years she lived tremendously, and among giants, and the long decades after were blurred and anti-climactic.

She was born Clara Mary Constantia Jane Clairmont, on April 27, 1798, the second child of a shrewish, business-minded mother and a Swiss merchant father. Her name changed as she grew, from Clara to Clare to Claire, though her mother persisted in calling her Jane. Some time after her father's death, her widowed mother, Mary Clairmont, moved into Skinner Street in London. Their next-door neighbor was a stocky, almost bald bookseller and publisher named William Godwin.

Godwin, a onetime preacher, had become famous less than a decade before for his radical work *An Enquiry Concerning Political Justice*. In 1796 he had met Mary Wollstonecraft, authoress of *A Vindication of the Rights of Women*. She had had an affair with an American, Gilbert Imlay, who deserted her and left her with a child named Fanny Imlay. Godwin and Mary Wollstonecraft lived together, without the sanction of marriage, until she became pregnant. The couple then married. Six months later Mary Godwin, the future wife of Shelley, was born, and ten days after her birth Mary Wollstonecraft died.

When the widow Clairmont moved next door, the widower Godwin was unsuccessfully searching for a stepmother to care for his adopted daughter, Fanny Imlay, and his own daughter, Mary. He set his sights upon the widow Clairmont, wooed and won her. Thus, in 1801 Claire Clairmont and her older brother, Charles, moved into 41 Skinner Street. To this overcrowded menage was added, in 1803, a newborn son named William.

Life at the Godwins' was about as reposeful as the French Revolution. Amid the clatter of the brood and the comings and goings of visitors, Godwin wrote two books, quarreled with his critics, fended off creditors. Claire's mother, constantly vocal and angry, pecked away at the nerves of all. Still, Claire found the intellectual atmosphere stimulating. Once she hid in the octagon-shaped library to hear Samuel Taylor Coleridge recite "The Ancient Mariner."

The Real Juliana Bordereau

In the early summer of 1814 occurred the event that was to shape Claire's life. Percy Bysshe Shelley appeared. He had been to visit his hero, Godwin, two years before, accompanied by his wife, Harriet. But Claire, as well as her stepsister Mary, had been out of town. Now, in London on business, Shelley appeared almost daily for supper.

Claire was stirred by him. In a shrill voice he held forth on Mary Wollstonecraft, revolution, poetry, vegetarianism, free love, and atheism. Claire's mother was less impressed. As she told a friend later: "I remember Mr. Godwin telling him once that he was too young to be so certain he was in the right—that he ought to have more experience before being so dogmatic and then he said some Saint, St. Cyril I think, but I know the name began with a C., had spoken most wisely that Humility was Truth. Mr. Shelley laughed and said he would listen to Socrates or Plato but not to a Saint."

Soon Shelley was directing most of his talk to Mary Godwin. He talked less of books and politics as his secret love for Mary grew. But it was she who used the word first. It was on a Sunday evening in June of 1814, before her mother's grave in Saint Pancras churchyard, with Claire standing near by, trying not to eavesdrop. Mary's declaration sent Shelley into an ecstasy of excitement.

There was one minor detail. Shelley had a wife. But before he told Harriet of his new love, he told Godwin. The old philosopher was furious. He denounced Shelley as a "seducer." When Shelley summoned Harriet to London and told her of Mary, she called Mary the seducer. As Harriet wrote a friend: "Mary was determined to seduce him. She is to blame. She heated his imagination by talking of her mother, and going to her grave with him every day, till at last she told him she was dying in love for him."

When Mary realized how badly Harriet was taking it, she went with Claire Clairmont to call on Shelley's wife. As Claire remembered it years later, Mary "went at the end of June with me to see Harriet in Chapel Street at her father's house. I was

(57)

present at the whole interview and heard Mary assure Harriet that she would not think of Shelley's love for her."

When Shelley heard of this, he raced to Skinner Street, burst into the house, elbowed past Mrs. Godwin and Claire toward Mary. "They wish to separate us, my beloved, but Death shall unite us," he shouted. He handed her a bottle of laudanum, and pulled a pistol from his pocket for himself. Claire screamed and Mrs. Godwin ran for help. Mary burst into tears, sobbing: "I won't take this laudanum, but if you will only be reasonable and calm, I will promise to be ever faithful to you."

Terribly agitated, Shelley left. His friend of two years, the satirist Thomas Love Peacock, tried to calm him, reminding him of Harriet's virtues. Shelley replied: "Everyone who knows me must know that the partner of my life should be one who can feel poetry and understand philosophy. Harriet is a noble animal, but she can do neither." Shortly after, Shelley took poison, but was saved. Distressed, Mary and Claire met with him, and while Claire stood off at a distance, Mary listened to his proposal that they elope to the Continent. Shelley argued that Harriet did not love him, was in fact having an affair with a Major Ryan she had met in Dublin. This convinced Mary. She consented to run off, and both she and Shelley agreed that Claire, who knew French and deserved to be liberated, must accompany them.

At four in the morning of July 28, 1814, Claire and Mary, loaded under packages, crept down the stairs of their home and out into Skinner Street. They hurried off, found Shelley restlessly waiting with chaise and horses. They started for Dover. When they reached Dover in late afternoon, the Channel boat had already left. All were fearful that Godwin would catch them. At last they hired a sailboat and two sailors, and started through the swells toward Calais. A storm came up. The two-hour crossing took almost twelve hours. But they arrived safely.

That evening, while resting at Dessein's Hotel, Shelley received word that "a fat lady had arrived who claimed that he had run away with her daughter." It was Mrs. Godwin. Claire promised to pacify her, and tried to do so through the night by promising to return to London. But by morning, after consulting Shelley, Claire changed her mind again and refused to return. Defeated, Mrs. Godwin waddled back to her boat. Shelley accidentally passed her in the street. They did not speak.

The three spent six weeks in Europe. With little money, they traveled through France and Switzerland on foot, on mule back, and in a two-wheeled cabriolet. They spent six days in Paris studying Notre Dame, sitting in the Tuileries, walking through the Louvre, and visiting an old friend of Mary Wollstonecraft's. Hiking across the war-ravaged countryside toward Switzerland, they made a curious sight—Claire and Mary in long silk dresses and Shelley in open-collar shirt and tight trousers. Claire sang a good deal, and began to keep a journal in a used notebook Shelley had given her. Mary read; Shelley told stories and wrote. They ate in open meadows, once slept in beds Napoleon and his officers had recently vacated, and were terribly impressed by the Alps. They started home by the cheapest means possible, taking a variety of filthy Rhine passenger boats to Rotterdam.

In London, Shelley and Mary rented quarters in Cavendish Square. Claire, learning that her mother wanted to place her in a convent, remained with the fugitive couple. Also, Claire was briefly intrigued by Thomas Love Peacock. She thought him handsome, even if he did eat and drink too much. Peacock, in turn, was extremely impressed with Claire's vivacity, candor, intellect. He used her as the model for Stella in *Nightmare Abbey*, and paraphrased her speech when he had Stella remark: "If I ever love, I shall do so without limit or restriction. I shall hold all difficulties light, all sacrifices cheap, all obstacles gossamer."

Soon Claire was to put her unrestricted feelings about love into practice. She was becoming restless under Shelley's roof, where life was as hectic as it had ever been at the Godwins'. Shelley was daily pawning possessions for rent and vegetables.

Then, hounded by Harriet's creditors and the threat of imprisonment, he fled into hiding for sixteen days. And finally, when Harriet gave birth to a child, Mary was deeply hurt by Shelley's satisfaction. She angrily noted he was mailing "a number of circular letters of this event, which ought to be ushered in with the ringing of bells, etc., for it is the son of *his wife*." Mary, thus irritated, and Claire, suffering liver trouble and ennui, began quarreling.

Claire took up temporary lodgings elsewhere, and turned her gaze upon England's greatest celebrity.

George Gordon Noel Byron, at twenty-seven, was the talk of London. Three years before, with the publication of "Childe Harold's Pilgrimage," he had, in his own words, "woke one morning and found himself famous." His incredibly attractive appearance—brown curly hair, gray-blue eyes, feminine mouth, milky complexion, and a muscular body—had attracted women by the droves. His affairs with Lady Caroline Lamb and Lady Oxford, his rumored incest with his wedded half-sister, Augusta Leigh, and his marriage to Anne Milbanke, as well as their spectacular separation the month after his daughter was born, heightened his notoriety.

It is no wonder Claire Clairmont fell in love with him. She was alone. She envied Mary her poet. She wanted someone, and she wanted adventure. Years after, she explained: "I was young and vain and poor. He was famous beyond all precedent—so famous that people, and especially young people, hardly considered him as a man at all, but rather as a god. His beauty was as haunting as his fame, and he was all powerful in the direction in which my ambition turned. It seems to me almost needless to say that the attentions of a man like this, with all London at his feet, very quickly completely turned the head of a girl in my position; and when you recollect that I was brought up to consider marriage not only as a useless but absolutely sinful custom that only bigotry made necessary, you will scarcely wonder at the result."

The result was that Claire, though she may have conveniently forgotten this in her later years, set out to seduce Lord Byron. She had the equipment, too. She was uninhibited, impulsive, charming. Once when she asked Shelley what he thought of her, he said there were two Claires—the bad Claire was sarcastic, irritable, gloomy, and the good Claire "the most engaging of human creatures." On another occasion, discussing her character, Claire told Lord Byron: "I may appear to you imprudent and vicious, my opinions detestable, my theories depraved but one thing at least time shall show you, that I love gently and with affection, and that I am incapable of anything approaching to the feeling of revenge or malice." As to her appearance, she felt she was physically attractive. At eighteen, she was tall, shapely, vivacious, with sleek black hair, dark eyes, and Latin complexion.

In March of 1816 Claire sat down and addressed the following letter to Lord Byron:

> An utter stranger takes the liberty of addressing you. . . . If a woman whose reputation has yet remained unstained, if without either guardian or husband to control her, she should throw herself on your mercy, if with a beating heart she should confess the love she has borne for you for many years, if she should secure to you secrecy and safety, if she should return your kindness with fond affection and unbounded devotion, could you betray her, or would you be silent as the grave? I am not given to many words. Either you will or you will not. Do not decide hastily, and yet I must entreat your answer without delay. . . . E. Trefusis.

She mailed the letter to Lord Byron. He did not reply. Undaunted, she wrote a second letter:

> Lord Byron is requested to state whether seven o'clock this Evening will be convenient to him to receive a lady to communicate with him on business of peculiar importance. She desires to be admitted alone and with utmost privacy. If the hour she has mentioned is correct, at that hour she will come; if not, will his lordship have the goodness to make his own appointment, which shall be readily attended to though it is hoped the

interview may not be postponed after this Evening. . . .
G.C.B.

Claire dispatched this note by hired messenger. She did not
have to wait long. The messenger returned with an answer:

> Ld. B. is not aware of any "importance" which can be at-
> tached by any person to an interview with him, and more par-
> ticularly by one with whom it does not appear he has the honour
> of being acquainted. He will however be at home at the hour
> mentioned.

They met that night at seven o'clock. Precisely what transpired we shall never know. Claire knew that Lord Byron was
on the Board of Management of the Drury Lane Theatre. She
was seeing him, presumably, to solicit his suggestions and help
in furthering an acting career. She asked his advice. "Is it
absolutely necessary to go through the intolerable and disgusting drudgery of provincial theatres before commencing on the
boards of a metropolis?" He offered to help her with a letter of
introduction to Drury Lane.

Then she changed her mind. She didn't want to be an actress,
after all. She wanted to be a writer. She had half a novel done
and desired his opinion. Soon that subterfuge was discarded
and she revealed plainly what she really wanted. "Have you
then any objection to the following plan?" she asked him. "On
Thursday Evening we may go out of town together by some
stage or mail about the distance of ten or twelve miles. There
we shall be free and unknown; we can return early the following morning. I have arranged everything here so that the
slightest suspicion may not be excited. Pray do so with your
people. Will you admit me for two moments to settle with you
where? Indeed I will not stay an instant after you tell me to go."

Lord Byron thought the intrigue of the coach and travel out
of town a lot of nonsense, and suggested the use of a house near
by. Long after, Claire admitted that the house was in Albemarle
Street and said Byron's wife saw them entering it together.

The affair progressed. Though she slept with him, Claire was in awe of the great man. "Do you know I cannot talk to you when I see you? I am so awkward and only feel inclined to take a little stool and sit at your feet." For a short time Byron seemed to love her. As she told him: "Much to my surprise, more to my happiness, you betrayed passions I had believed no longer alive in your bosom." One morning, after leaving Byron, she burst into Shelley's home shouting: "Percy! Mary! The great Lord Byron loves me!" Byron loved her enough, apparently, to show jealousy toward her friend Shelley, whom he had not met. For on one occasion she sent some of Shelley's letters to him with the note: "Pray compare them and acquit me, I entreat you, from the list of those whom you suspect."

But Lord Byron was soon bored by her, as he was eventually bored by most of his mistresses. He tired of her temper, her possessiveness, her indiscretions, her feminist views. He began to break dates, and when he kept them, he was often rude. When Claire prepared to bring Mary Godwin to meet him, she first demanded that he show some politeness. "I say this," she wrote him, "because on Monday evening I waited nearly a quarter of an hour in your hall, which though I may overlook the disagreeableness, she is not in love and would not."

Claire's love for Byron persisted in spite of his growing coldness. There is evidence her love was not mainly sexual. She told him frankly that his looks did not make her passionate. "First, I have no passions; I had ten times rather be your male companion than your mistress." It would appear that she was much more excited by his fame and genius.

He was preparing to leave England, and this troubled her. He had to leave. His life was a chaos. The newspapers hammered at his morals and his politics. The fact that his wife had left him amid the gossip of incest, that he had defended Napoleon as "Freedom's son," turned the tide against him. When he went to the House of Lords, only one member spoke to him. When Lady Jersey gave a party for him and he arrived with his sister, the guests walked out en masse. And all the while his creditors pressed for cash.

He sailed from England on April 25, 1816, never again to return alive. He left with a customed Napoleonic coach, containing built-in library and dining-accessories, taking along three servants and his personal physician. Claire hoped he would take her, too. This he refused to do. He was still married and wanted no more scandal. When Claire asked if she could visit him in Geneva, Byron was agreeable, as long as she was properly chaperoned.

Realizing that Shelley and Mary were considering a trip to Italy, Claire pleaded with them to stop over in Geneva. When she poured out her entire involvement with Lord Byron, Shelley consented. Shelley, Mary, and Claire left England on May 3, 1816, and reached Geneva ten days later. Byron, visiting Waterloo, had not yet arrived. When he finally did, he infuriated Claire by not looking her up at once. But at last, as Dr. Newman White has described it: "When he lounged into Shelley's hotel on May 25, with the slightly mortifying limp that could never be quite fully concealed, Claire Clairmont had brought about a junction of literary influences that was to have an important effect upon both men and upon English public opinion."

Although Byron and Shelley took to each other at once, Shelley was not completely overwhelmed. "Lord Byron is an exceedingly interesting person," he wrote Peacock, "and as such is it not to be regretted that he is a slave to the vilest and most vulgar prejudices, and as mad as the winds?" When Shelley, Mary, and Claire rented a bungalow called Mont Alègre across the lake, Lord Byron leased the Villa Diodati, which was separated from them only by a vineyard.

For three months Claire continued to see Lord Byron and sleep with him, though he worried about gossip that might get back to London. Her indiscreet notes and impulsive visits annoyed him, since English tourists across the lake were observing every movement through telescopes. Once, leaving his villa at daybreak and hurrying through the vineyard, she lost a shoe.

The Real Juliana Bordereau

The vineyard workers found it and turned it over to the town mayor.

She was making copies of "The Prisoner of Chillon" and several other poems for Byron, and using this as an excuse to be with him. "I am afraid to come, dearest, for fear of meeting anyone," she said in one note. "Can you pretext the copying?" She had more and more difficulty in seeing Byron alone. Often his cocky, obnoxious physician, Dr. John William Polidori, was about. She demanded Byron get the meddlesome doctor out of the way, pack him off "to write a dictionary, or visit his lady·· love."

Once when Claire had Byron alone in his villa, a curious incident occurred. "I went up to copy out Childe Harold as was my wont," she recorded, "and he asked me whether I did not think he was a terrible person—I said No I won't believe it— and I don't. He then unlocked a cabinet and spread a number of his sister's letters upon a table; he opened some and showed them: the beginning was ordinary enough—common news of their friends, her health and then came long spaces written in cyphers which he said only he and she had the key of—and unintelligible to all other people." When he gathered up the letters, he found that one was missing. He became terribly agitated, accused Claire of concealing it. Then he found it and apologized.

Claire discussed the incident with Shelley. Why ciphers in letters between brother and sister? Shelley thought that this was used to disguise discussion of Byron's illegitimate children. This half satisfied Claire. The thought always remained that the ciphers were used by brother and sister to discuss their love affair.

The issue of incest hung over Byron's head throughout his life. In the more than century since his death it has violently split his biographers. Richard Edgcumbe and John Drinkwater have denied or doubted incest; Lord Lovelace and André Maurois have been certain it occurred. True, Byron was always touchy about the subject. A few days after his marriage, his wife pointed at their reflection in the mirror and laughingly said: "We are as like as if we were brother and sister." Angrily, Byron grabbed her wrist and shouted: "When did you hear that?" After the incident in Geneva, Claire apparently never gave the subject another thought. That is, not until her old age, when she told Trelawny: "There is no positive proof that the connexion between L. B. and Mrs. Leigh existed; but his verses to Augusta, by a Brother to a Sister—then his fit of hysterics at Bologna when he witnessed the performance of Myrrha [Alfiere's *Myrrha* depicted the love of a girl for her father]—then Manfred and Cain—all form presumptive evidence against him."

During August, Claire learned that she was pregnant. Shelley, who had to be back in London on business, insisted that Claire have the child in England. Lord Byron wanted the baby raised by his sister. Claire vehemently refused. Byron then agreed that Claire could pose as the child's aunt, to avoid scandal, and that either of them would look after it until the age of seven.

When Claire wanted to see Byron again, he refused. His old friends—John Cam Hobhouse, Monk Lewis, Scrope Davies— were visiting. He didn't want any scenes in their presence. And he was pleased when Hobhouse, writing Lady Melbourne of life in Byron's villa, remarked: "In spite of all ridiculous rumors, none of its apartments receive any more disreputable guests than Mr. M. Lewis and myself."

Nevertheless, rumors of Byron's affair with Claire had reached London, been exaggerated into many affairs, and provoked Augusta Leigh to write and inquire if the rumors were true. Byron replied cheerfully: "As to all these 'mistresses,' Lord help me—I have had but one. Now don't scold; but what could I do?—a foolish girl, in spite of all I could say or do, would come after me, or rather went before—for I found her here—and I have had all the plague possible to persuade her to go back again; but at last she went. Now, dearest, I do most truly tell thee, that I could not help this, that I did all I could to prevent it, and have at last put an end to it. I was not in love, nor have any love left for any; but I could not exactly play the Stoic with a woman, who had scrambled eight hundred miles to unphilosophize me."

For Lord Byron it was over. For Claire Clairmont it was not. She wrote him a letter as she left with Shelley and Mary for London. "When you receive this, I shall be many miles away; don't be impatient with me. I don't know why I write unless it is because it seems like speaking to you. Indeed I should have been happier if I could have seen and kissed you once before I went. . . . My dreadful fear is lest you quite forget me—I shall pine through all the wretched winter months whilst you, I hope, may never have one uneasy thought. One thing I do entreat you to remember—beware of any excess in wine. . . ."

Much happened the following year in England, where Claire lived with Mary in Bath and Marlow. A sensation was caused by the appearance of a novel, *Glenarvon*, written by Lady Caroline Lamb, which portrayed a fictional Lord Byron as a scoundrel. The psychotic, pretty Caroline Ponsonby had been Byron's mistress for three months before he tired of her indiscretions and dropped her. The novel *Glenarvon* was her revenge.

When Claire returned to London, the book was a sell-out. Teasingly, she wrote Byron: "Well, I have read it all through. You wretched creature to go about seducing and stabbing and rebelling. . . . I really am ashamed to hold communion with you. Some of the speeches are yours—I am sure they are; the very impertinent way of looking in a person's face who loves you, and telling them you are very tired and wish they'd go. But why so gentle a creature as you are should be transformed to such a fierce, mysterious monster as Glenarvon is quite inconceivable."

Lord Byron reacted to the book with disgust. According to Hobhouse: "*Glenarvon* has been read with appropriate indignation, not unmixed with contempt." Later, for the tag of a poem he sent Hobhouse, Byron concluded:

I read Glenarvon, too, by Caro. Lamb,
God damn.

During Claire's stay in England, two tragedies struck close. Claire's stepsister, Fanny Imlay was found in a hotel at Swansea, a suicide, with a bottle of laudanum by her bed. Then, on December 10, 1816, Shelley's legal wife, Harriet, was fished out of the Serpentine in Hyde Park. She had apparently committed suicide at the age of twenty-one.

Less than two weeks later Shelley legalized his union with Mary. Though he disapproved of marriage, he wanted to make Godwin happy, wanted to legitimize his own offspring by Mary, and wanted to improve his chance to win possession of his two children by Harriet.

On January 12, 1817, Claire gave birth to a girl. The next day Mary wrote Lord Byron: "She sends her love to you and begs me to say she is in excellent spirits and as good health as can be expected." Lord Byron determined his daughter's name. "I mean to christen her Allegra, which is a Venetian name." Claire, though she adored the child, was anxious that Byron have a hand in her upbringing. Byron's position and wealth, Claire felt, would help Allegra's future. The idea did not displease Byron. As he wrote his sister: "They tell me she is very pretty, with blue eyes and dark hair; and though I never was attracted nor pretended attachment to the mother, still it may be as well to have something in my old age, and probably circumstances will render this poor little creature a great, and perhaps my only, comfort."

Meanwhile, Shelley had gone before the Court of Chancery to fight for his two children by Harriet. However, his writings on religion and marriage counted against him. Guardianship of the children was awarded Shelley's father and Harriet's grandfather. Tired, at last, of London, Shelley weighed the idea of a trip to Italy. His doctors encouraged him to seek a warmer climate. But what finally decided him was Claire's Allegra. He felt, with Claire, that the little girl needed Byron's support. And Byron was in Italy.

On March 11, 1818, Claire and Allegra left England with Shelley, Mary, their two youngsters, and two nurses. Three weeks later the party arrived in Milan, Italy. Byron was not there to meet them. He wanted nothing more to do with Claire. He had sent a messenger to pick up Allegra. Though angered by his rudeness and by the gossip about his wild new Italian mistress, Claire relented. Allegra was shipped off to Byron with the Shelley's Swiss nurse, Elise.

As Claire traveled through northern Italy with the Shelleys, she bombarded Byron with inquiries about their child. "How is my Allegra?" she wrote him. "Is she gay? And has she given you any knocks? I sincerely hope she has, and paid you all your unkindness to me in very innocent coin. Whenever I think of the little creature I feel myself smile. She is so funny. . . ."

Lord Byron, though he liked animals, frequently said he despised children, and once informed his sister: "I don't know what Scrope Davies meant by telling you I liked Children. I abominate the sight of them so much that I have always had the greatest respect for the character of Herod." ("Then Herod . . . was exceeding wroth, and sent forth, and slew all the children that were in Bethlehem." Matthew 2:16.) However, Byron seemed to like Allegra more than most, though he turned her care over to friends, the British Consul in Venice, Richard Belgrave Hoppner, and his Swiss wife. Hoppner thought Allegra much quieter and colder than his own boy Rizzo, and some time later admitted: "She was not by any means an amiable child, nor were Mrs. Hoppner or I particularly fond of her, but we had taken her to live with us, not thinking Lord Byron's house . . . a very proper one for the infant." But Shelley adored her—

A lovelier toy sweet Nature never made
A serious, subtle, wild yet gentle being. . . .

Once Shelley took Claire to Venice to visit the child. Claire was upset by what she saw. "She is pale and has lost a good deal of her liveliness, but is as beautiful as ever." At Shelley's request, Byron permitted Allegra to remain with Claire several months.

After being forced to return Allegra, Claire accompanied the Shelleys on a sightseeing tour of Rome and Naples. It was in Naples that Mary learned her Swiss maid, Elise, was pregnant by the Shelleys' manservant Paolo Foggi. Mary forced them to wed, then packed them off to another job. Paolo, angry with the Shelleys, determined to get even. He did so by making Elise tell the Hoppners in Venice, who in turn told Lord Byron, about a scandal that had occurred in Naples. The scandal involved an alleged affair between Shelley and Claire which resulted in the birth of a girl.

Hoppner broke it wide open in a letter to Byron dated September 16, 1820. He asked Byron to keep the news secret, then went on: "I therefore proceed to divulge to you, what indeed on Allegra's account it is necessary that you should know, as it will fortify you in the good resolution you have already taken never to trust her again to her mother's care. You must know then that at the time the Shelleys were here Clare was with child by Shelley: you may remember to have heard that she was constantly unwell, and under the care of a Physician, and I am charitable enough to believe that the quantity of medicine she then took was not for the mere purpose of restoring her health. . . . This account we had from Elise, who passed here this summer. . . . She likewise told us that Clara does not scruple to tell Mrs. Shelley she wishes her dead, and to say to Shelley in her presence that she wonders how he can live with such a creature."

A year later, when Shelley was visiting Byron at Ravenna, Byron broke his pledge of secrecy. Though Byron had earlier told Hoppner: "Of the facts, however, there can be little doubt; it is just like them," he now assured Shelley that he didn't believe the rumor at all. But Shelley was disturbed enough to spill it out to Mary, who promptly wrote the Hoppners a passionate denial:

"She [Elise] says Clare was Shelley's mistress . . . but I had rather die than copy anything so vilely, so wickedly false, so beyond all imagination fiendish. . . . It is all a lie—Clare is timid; she always showed respect even for me—poor dear girl! She has some faults—you know them as well as I—but her heart is good, and if ever we quarrelled, which was seldom, it was I, and not she, that was harsh, and our instantaneous reconciliations were sincere and affectionate."

Did Claire actually have a love affair with Shelley and a child by him? The truth has never been discovered. We know that Claire was curiously ill in Naples. We know that Shelley had a baby baptized Elena in Naples, a little girl who was placed in an orphanage and later died of fever. And we know that Lord Byron, despite his denials to Shelley, believed not only that Claire had a daughter by Shelley in Naples, but that Allegra herself might have been Shelley's child. Once when Elise was playing with little Allegra in the nursery, Byron came in and watched. Suddenly, indicating Allegra, he said: "She will grow up a very pretty woman and then I will take her for my mistress." Elise was not amused. "I suppose, my lord, you are joking, but even as a joke, it is a very improper one." Byron insisted that he was not joking at all. "I'll do it," he said. "I can very well do it—she is no child of mine—she is Mr. Shelley's child."

All of this made it more difficult for Claire to keep in touch with Allegra, and rendered her helpless when Byron finally placed their child in the austere Convent of Bagnacavallo, twelve miles outside Ravenna. Earlier, Claire had pleaded with Byron to send the child to her in Pisa. Byron did not bother to answer, but instead wrote Hoppner: "Clare writes me the most insolent letters about Allegra; see what a man gets by taking care of natural children! Were it not for the poor little child's sake, I am almost tempted to send her back to her atheistical mother. . . . If Claire thinks that she shall ever interfere with the child's morals or education, she mistakes; she never shall. The girl shall be a Christian and a married woman, if possible. As to seeing her, she may see her—under proper restrictions; but she is not to throw everything into confusion with her Bedlam behavior. To express it delicately, I think Madame Clare is a damned bitch. What think you?"

When Claire learned that Allegra had been placed in the convent, she was enraged. Convents were impersonal, she felt, and Italians "unnatural mothers, licentious and ignorant." On Claire's behalf, Shelley traveled to Ravenna to plead her case with Byron. But Byron was interested only in discussing his fight for Italian freedom and his latest mistress, Teresa Guiccioli, a married noblewoman. According to André Maurois: "Count Guiccioli was sixty when he married Teresa, who was sixteen. From the first they had occupied separate rooms, and she had not ceased to address him as 'Sir.' He was quite a pleasant old man, although reported to have poisoned his first wife and to have been the murderer of Manzoni." Though Byron would talk about Teresa—whom Shelley thought "pretty, sentimental, innocent, superficial"—he would not talk about Claire. As to little Allegra, Byron had not seen her since he had placed her in the convent.

Shelley went out to the convent on his own. He found Claire's Allegra, at four and a half, thinner, taller, extremely pale. He presented her with a little gold chain and a bag of candies. Excitedly she showed him about the convent grounds. When it was time to depart, Shelley wondered if there was any message for her mother. "I want a kiss and a beautiful dress," the little girl said. Shelley asked if there was any special kind of dress. "All of silk and gold." And what did she wish from her father? "To make me a visit and bring mammina with him."

Shortly after, when Byron followed Teresa up to Pisa, Shelley continued to intercede for Claire. One evening he told Byron that Claire's health was being affected by worry over her child. Byron wasn't interested. Women liked to make scenes, he said. His callousness infuriated Shelley, who admitted to others that it was the one time he wanted to punch Byron in the nose. Meanwhile, a lady friend of Claire's had visited the convent and reported that it was poorly run and dangerously unhealthy. Claire became frantic. She demanded that Shelley help her kidnap Allegra. He refused on the grounds that it wouldn't work, and if it did, it would only involve him in a duel with Byron. He begged Claire to let him continue trying to persuade Byron.

While Claire waited and hoped, there were diversions. Many new visitors were joining Shelley's Pisa circle, and Claire was busy with them as well as with the society of the town. Shelley's cousin, Tom Medwin, was attentive. Two others, very close to the Shelleys, Captain Edward Williams and his wife, Jane, became friends of Claire's. Williams had been an army officer in India, where he met and married Jane, who had been abandoned by her sailor mate. Then there arrived Edward John Trelawny, a towering, dramatic figure, who had been a pirate six years, and would in years to come escape assassination in Greece, swim Niagara, and marry four wives (one an Arab girl, another the daughter of a Greek guerrilla leader). Trelawny fell deeply in love with Claire, and immediately had in common with her a love for Shelley and a dislike for Byron. A half-century later, when someone asked Claire why Trelawny seemed to resent Byron, she replied: "Well, Byron snubbed him, you know. He said, 'Tre was an excellent fellow until he took to imitating my Childe Harold and Don Juan.' This got to Trelawny's ears, and he never forgave Byron for it."

On April 20, 1822, while Claire and Jane Williams were out hunting for a summer house near Spezzia, word reached Shelley that Allegra, aged five, had died of typhus in her lonely convent.

Shelley tried to keep the news from Claire, fearing she might attempt to murder Byron, who was living near by. Then, while Shelley discussed the child's death with Mary, Trelawny, and Williams, Claire walked in on the group. From their faces, their sudden silence, she sensed at once what had happened. "You may judge of what was her first burst of grief and despair,"

Mary reported. But she calmed quickly, and asked only to see Allegra's body, and to have a portrait of her and a lock of her hair. Byron obliged at once, delivering both miniature and hair. When Claire had no heart to see the body, Byron shipped Allegra back to England for burial. However, since she was illegitimate, the Harrow Church refused to bury her inside, but laid her to rest outside its entrance.

At first Lord Byron himself seemed deeply moved. "He desired to be left alone and I was obliged to leave him," said Teresa. "I found him on the following morning tranquillized and with an expression of religious resignation on his features." When Teresa started to console him, he interrupted. "She is more fortunate than we are. It is God's will. Let us mention it no more." But he mentioned it in a letter to London, and Thomas Moore noted in his diary: "A long letter from Lord Byron today; he has lost his little natural daughter . . . and seems to feel it a good deal. When I was at Venice, he said, in showing me this child, 'I suppose you have some notion of what they call the parental feeling, but I confess I have it not.' This, however, was evidently all affected; he feels much more naturally than he will allow." Yet when a priest brought Allegra's body from Bagnacavallo to Leghorn, Byron would neither receive the man nor listen to the story of Allegra's last illness. The priest returned to the convent "greatly mortified." And when the convent sent Byron his last bill, he haggled with them over the funeral costs and insisted that the apothecary's charge was exorbitant, arguing that enough spices had been used on Allegra to embalm a full-grown adult.

In his entire relationship with Claire Clairmont, it is only in his handling of the Allegra affair that Lord Byron, erratic, moody, mercurial, yet somehow always attractive, comes out badly. It is perfectly true, of course, that he did not seduce Claire. It is perfectly true, too, that he was cornered, badgered, and pestered by Claire, and that she, so to speak, asked for it. But the fact remains that, once he accepted her love and reciprocated, once he gave her a child, he might well have shown a little more of human understanding. This he did not possess. And his biographer Harold Nicolson possessed even less in failing to grasp Claire's later hatred of Byron and in rudely referring to her as "that untruthful and, by then, senile wanton."

Allegra's death was followed, two and a half months later, by another tragedy of more far-reaching consequences. Shelley and Williams had sailed in their boat, the *Don Juan*, across the Bay of Spezzia to visit the newly arrived Leigh Hunt and his family. On the return trip, the pair and a boy companion disappeared. Trelawny and a navy friend, Captain Dan Roberts, searched the coast for them while the women nervously waited. Then, after ten days, Claire intercepted a letter from Roberts. In it he said he had heard that two bodies had been washed ashore and he was investigating. Claire could not tell Mary. She sent for Hunt. But before he arrived, Trelawny appeared. He had seen the bodies and his expression was enough.

While the three women, each with her loss, remained behind —"We have one purse, and joined in misery, we are for the moment, joined in life," said Mary—Trelawny, Byron, Hunt, and several others went by carriage to cremate the bodies. It was high noon, and sweltering, when the brushwood atop Shelley's remains was set blazing. Byron watched a moment. "Is that a human body?" he suddenly asked. "Why, it's more like the carcass of a sheep, or any other animal, than a man; this is a satire on our pride and folly." He started toward the water with Trelawny, exclaiming: "Let us try the strength of these waters that drowned our friends." After a brief swim, Trelawny returned to the beach in time to rescue Shelley's heart from the embers of the cremation. He gave the heart to Leigh Hunt, who finally surrendered it to Mary. Throughout her life she kept it in a silken shroud and carried it along on her travels. When her son, Sir Percy, died in 1889, the heart, enclosed in a silver case, was buried with him.

After the cremation, Captain Roberts salvaged the *Don Juan*. It was never known if the vessel had capsized in the storm or been rammed by Italian fishing-boats who hoped Byron was aboard and intended to rob and murder him. Captain Roberts auctioned off the shell of the *Don Juan* for $200 and distributed the personal effects he found in the hull. He presented Shelley's soggy books to Lord Byron, but turned Captain Williams's private journal over to Leigh Hunt because it contained "many severe remarks on Lord Byron."

In the years following Shelley's drowning, Trelawny remarked, "we all degenerated apace." In a sense, this was true of Claire Clairmont. Two months after the final tragedy she set out alone, with ten pounds in her purse, to meet her older brother, Charles, who had promised to find her a job as governess in Vienna. But as she left Italy for Austria, her mind was not on the journey. "During the first part of the road," she noted, "I was too occupied with my own thoughts to attend the scenery. I remembered how hopelessly I had lingered on the Italian soil for five years, waiting ever for a favorable change, instead of which I was now leaving it, having buried there everything that I loved."

Though Charles, an extrovert who taught English for his keep, was kind, Claire found Vienna impossible. The Habsburgs and Metternich had transformed Austria into a police state, and all speech was censored. When Charles spouted his opinions publicly, an anonymous letter reported the indiscretion, as well as his family background. He and Claire were given five days to leave the country. But his contacts with the Esterhazys and other noble families finally enabled him to have the expulsion order shelved. Claire did not like this any more than she liked the weather of Vienna. When an opportunity came to serve as governess with a wealthy Russian family who lived near Moscow, she decided to accept.

But before Moscow, there was one other choice. Trelawny wrote, offering her money to return to Florence and become his wife or mistress, as she preferred. "Remember, Clare," he remonstrated, "real friendship is not nice-stomached or punctilious—we are too far apart for tedious negotiation—give me these proofs of your attachment."

Claire would not have him. When Mary Shelley wrote to Moscow later, advising her to marry Trelawny, Claire replied that it could not work. "He likes a turbid and troubled life, I a quiet one; he is full of fine feelings and has no principles, I am full of fine principles but never had a feeling; he receives all his impressions through his heart, I through my head."

After eight years Claire assumed the female prerogative of changing her mind. Tired of manhandling little brats—"I never thought children could be so hideous or vicious, they never cease brawling, squabbling and fighting"—she wrote Trelawny and proposed that they live together. But Trelawny's passion had descended into friendship, more comfortable, less threatening. Tactfully as possible he declined.

In the summer of 1824 Claire reached Czarist Russia. She went to work in a large house outside Moscow for a well-connected lawyer named Zachar Nikolaevitch, his wife, Marie, and their two youngsters, John and Dunia. Claire was wide-eyed at the black-robed priests in Red Square, at single aristocratic families who possessed fifteen thousand serfs, at the acres of dark pines in the countryside.

She had brief romances. She became enamored of a German named Harmonn, and told Mary: "What you felt for Shelley, I feel for him." Then there was a pianist named Genichsta. "He is a divine musician and the first that, as a man, pleased me." And finally there was an Englishman, a professor, but one too easily shocked for her tastes. When a gossipy Miss Frewin, who had met Claire's mother in London, appeared in Moscow and revealed Claire's background to the professor, Claire wrote Jane Williams: "I can see that he is in a complete puzzle on my account. He cannot explain how I can be so extremely delightful and yet so detestable."

But mostly she vegetated. As she noted in her journal: "No talk of public affairs, no discussion of books—nothing save cards, eating, and the different manners of managing slaves." She read the Russian papers daily at breakfast, and in them, one morning, she learned of Lord Byron's death in the pesthole of

Missolonghi, Greece, on April 19, 1824. Letters from England soon told her the rest of the story. Byron's body, preserved in a large cask filled with spirits, was returned to England by boat. Viewing the body, Hobhouse recognized the corpse as Byron's only by his clubfoot. Augusta Leigh thought his face looked "serene." His body lay in state for a week in a candle-lit, black-draped room in Great George Street. Mary Shelley went to see it. Byron's faithful valet, Fletcher, was there. Mary listened to Fletcher and then reported: "It would seem from a few words he imprudently let fall, that his Lord spoke of Clare in his last moments and of his wish to do something for her, at a time when his mind, vacillating between consciousness and delirium, would not permit him to do anything." In Russia, Claire heard of this, and heard also that Byron's last will and testament made a provision for Allegra, but made none for her mother.

At last Claire tired of Russia. Her little charge, Dunia, had died of an ear ailment. Claire shifted from job to job in Moscow, bored with Russian "ill humour," resentful of the gossip about her background, uncomfortable with the climate. She thought of going to India, but finally went to Germany with a family named Kaisaroff.

In 1828, after a decade's absence, she returned to England. For the next twenty years, excepting occasional side trips to Dresden, Paris, Nice, Pisa, Vienna, usually as a governess, she was in London. She trudged from home to home, tutoring rich pupils in Italian, toiling from nine in the morning until seven at night, "condemned for life," as Trelawny put it, to "this vile servitude."

Her relationship with her stepsister, Mary Shelley, was a mixture of affection and envy. In England or out, she kept in touch with Mary, and was never shy about advice. "I hope you are all well," she said in closing one letter, "leave off your stays—eat no potatoes—take ginger and you will be well." Mary, in turn, reciprocated Claire's affection, though Mary always secretly resented the attraction Claire had held for Shelley. In fact, once when Claire was expected to drop by to visit and Mary's daughter-in-law tried to duck out, Mary exclaimed: "Don't leave me alone with her! She has been the bane of my life ever since I was three years old!"

Before Shelley's death, he had written Claire into his will to the sum of twelve thousand pounds. Mary always insisted that Shelley had intended to leave Claire only six thousand, and that through a clerical error the amount had been written in twice. The inheritance meant much to Claire, but she was told she could not receive it until Shelley's father, Sir Timothy, died. When Claire first left Italy, the old man was seventy and was given only five years to live. He crossed the physicians, and Claire, by remaining alive twenty-two more years. But in 1844 he died at last and Claire was in possession of her twelve thousand pounds. She lost most of it investing in a Lumley Opera House box and in foolish Austrian speculation that Charles had suggested. With what remained, she decided to retire to Florence, Italy, where living was cheaper.

She spent the last thirty years of her life secluded in Florence. Eventually she was joined by her old-maidish niece, her brother Charles's daughter, Paula, a plain woman regarded by her family as "gifted, original, high-tempered, somewhat eccentric."

Throughout the years Claire's opinions of Shelley and of Byron never changed. She felt Shelley's genius "the greatest that was ever known." For Lord Byron she kept only contempt and hatred. She never forgave him for Allegra's death. When she thought she might die of cholera, she wrote Mary: "You might be curious to know whether, in leaving life, my sentiments experience any change with regard to Lord Byron. Not at all; so far from it, that were the fairest Paradise offered to me upon the condition of his sharing it, I would refuse it. . . . For me there could be no happiness, there could be nothing but misery in the presence of the person who so wantonly, wilfully, destroyed my Allegra." Even when Byron's death in the cause of Greek independence had been glorified, Claire would not relent. She told a visiting Englishman: "He simply invested a great deal of money in the Greek cause with the idea of being made a King."

When she was seventy-one, there was a brief flurry of excitement in her life. A rumor reached her that Allegra had not died in the convent. Hopefully she investigated, though Trelawny warned her: "If I was in Italy I would cure you of your wild fancy regarding Allegra. . . . I cannot conceive a greater horror than an old man or woman that I had never seen for forty-three years claiming me as Father." But Allegra was not alive, and Claire resumed her routine.

She did not mind old age. When she heard that Shelley's son was about to start school, she pitied him and all young people for what they had ahead. As she told Mary: "It is not much praise to the supreme Lord of Life what I am going to say, which is, Thank God I can never be young again. At least that suffering is spared me."

Friends, and the curious, often came to her dark, old-fashioned rooms at 43 Via Romana. After her conversion to Catholicism, priests dropped by to chat. Once an awed twenty-year-old English tourist, William Graham, came calling and found her "a lovely old lady; the eyes still sparkled at times with irony and fun; the complexion was as clear as at eighteen." And finally Captain Edward Silsbee of Salem, Massachusetts, seeking romantic relics, appeared, and anxiously listened to her speak of an old passion that "lasted ten minutes, but these ten minutes have decomposed the rest of my life."

On March 19, 1879, Paula Clairmont opened her diary, took pen in hand, and made one last entry:

"This morning my Aunt died at about 10, calmly, without agony, without consciousness—as she had predicted herself, she went out like a candle. . . . She was buried as she desired, with Shelley's little shawl at the Cemetery of the Antella."

IV

The Real Lady Arabella Dudley

Late in the autumn of 1829 the beautiful twenty-two-year-old wife of Great Britain's Lord of the Privy Seal, Lady Ellenborough, fled her estranged husband, her agitated family, and her gossiping friends in London, and arrived in Paris to meet her Austrian lover.

Six months later, while Lady Ellenborough, preparing to bear an illegitimate child, remained in complete seclusion in her Paris apartments, the English House of Lords began a pitiless public debate on a scandal that had long titillated London society. For on March 9, 1829, Lord Ellenborough presented to his fellow peers a Bill entitled "An Act to dissolve the Marriage of the Right Honourable Edward Baron Ellenborough with the Right Honourable Jane Elizabeth Baroness Ellenborough, his now Wife, and to enable him to marry again; and for other Purposes therein mentioned."

Since, at the time this Bill was presented, the consent of both houses of Parliament and the King was required to obtain a divorce—an average of two divorces being granted annually—the indiscretion committed by Lady Ellenborough was aired openly, not only in England, but throughout the continent of Europe.

The marriage between Lord Ellenborough and Jane Elizabeth

Digby—"a noble lord and his faithless lady," Lord Ellenborough's counsel called them—had prevailed four years. In that time Lord Ellenborough, an unpopular, imperious, and ambitious man, had devoted most of his energies to Tory politics. With his encouragement, his youthful mate had busied herself with the frivolities of London's most sophisticated set. Man and wife had not, according to Lady Ellenborough's governess and companion, "slept together for a very long time." When Prince Felix Schwarzenberg, a dashing attaché in the Austrian Embassy, came along, it surprised no one that Lady Ellenborough was soon involved in an illicit love affair. What did surprise everyone, however, was Lady Ellenborough's indiscretion. According to the witnesses who appeared before the House of Lords, and later the House of Commons, Lady Ellenborough had made little effort to keep her unfaithfulness a secret.

On April 8, 1829, Lord Ellenborough was granted his divorce. He did not, however, emerge unscathed. In the House of Commons, Joseph Hume, the highly moral member from Montrose, had voiced a minority opinion. "Ought not the charge be read as one of criminality against Lord Ellenborough, who had permitted and even encouraged his wife's association with the persons responsible for her downfall, rather than one of marital infidelity against an unfortunate lady whose youth and immaturity ought to have been safeguarded by her natural protector?"

But in the end the real sufferer was Lady Ellenborough. The scandal became her cross for life. It branded her easy game for years thereafter. This, combined with her incredible beauty, her impulsive, emotional nature, her never-ceasing desire for sexual satisfaction and security, started her on a romantic career seldom matched in modern times. In seven decades she is known to have acquired at least four husbands, and possibly as many as nine, each married in a different capital of Europe and the Near East. As to her affairs, there is documentary evidence of at least twelve lovers—French, German, Italian, Greek, and

Arab—though more likely she had enjoyed three times that number.

While many of Lady Ellenborough's lovers were men of great renown, wealth, and title, perhaps the most gifted was the massive, red-faced Honoré de Balzac, regarded by enthusiasts in the century since (among them Henry James and W. Somerset Maugham) as literature's foremost novelist.

At the time she was publicly divorced and disgraced, Lady Ellenborough was living with Prince Schwarzenberg in Paris, awaiting the birth of their child. She hoped to marry the Prince, but there were difficulties. His dominant sister in Vienna, as well as his rigidly Catholic family, objected to a union with a divorcee, and his political mentor, Prince Esterhazy, indicated that the marriage would be harmful to his future. While the Prince went about his career, both diplomatic and social, Lady Ellenborough continued to be confined by her pregnancy and the scandal. Among the few friends the couple had in common were the De Thurheins. And it was through the Countess De Thurhein that Jane Ellenborough became acquainted with Balzac.

The affair between the Prince and the Lady, which had lasted a year and a half in London and continued another year and a half in Paris, began to fall apart just before Lady Ellenborough gave birth to their daughter. Lady Grenville, wife of the English Ambassador to France, wrote friends across the channel: "Poor Lady Ellenborough is just going to be confined. Schwarzenberg going about flirting with Madame Oudenarde."

Early in 1831, probably because Lady Ellenborough was making scenes about his philandering, Prince Schwarzenberg secured a transfer back to Vienna, and thence to a post in Berlin. In short, he deserted her completely. "Felix avenged most awfully Heaven's outraged laws," she wrote years later. The Austrian Embassy in Paris, in an effort to protect Schwarzenberg's name, let it be known that the good Prince abandoned his lady with sufficient provocation. According to a member of the Embassy staff, twenty-seven-year-old Count Rudolf Apponyi, "Milady was receiving in her house an Ancien of the Garde du Corps [a former bodyguard of the King's]."

Jane Ellenborough was deserted in a Paris seething with revolution. Mobs marched through the streets, stormed the Bishop's Palace, in reaction against the unpopular King Charles X. In the midst of this national discontent and her personal loneliness, Lady Ellenborough turned to one of the few friends she truly admired. She turned to Honoré de Balzac.

Their love affair was brief in duration—no more than two months—but it produced one offspring. For through the union Balzac gave birth in 1835, four years later, to a magnificent brain-child—Lady Arabella Dudley, beautiful and scandalous English nymphomaniac of *Le Lys dans la vallée*.

At first glance, Lady Ellenborough and Honoré de Balzac made an unlikely couple. She was tall and stately, with firm breasts and willowy legs. Her hair was a soft, golden blond, her eyes large and blue, her complexion creamy and flawless. "One of the most beautiful women I ever saw," Count Apponyi reported when he first met her. Count Walewski concurred. She was the most "divinely beautiful" woman he had ever laid eyes upon.

Balzac, on the other hand, was physically repulsive. He was short and fat—at a single meal he once consumed twelve cutlets, one duck, two partridges, one sole, one hundred oysters, twelve pears, and several desserts. His hair was black, his nose wide, and his lips thick. He affected blue coats with gold buttons, pleated trousers, patent-leather shoes, and a turquoise-studded cane.

Where Lady Ellenborough actually lived her adventures, in reality, from London to Munich, Athens, Damascus, Balzac sublimated his adventures in his creative work. He had quit the practice of law to take up the writing of historical pot-boilers in a Paris garret, publishing many under anagrams of his name. The very year he met Lady Ellenborough, he launched his first serious novel and his sensuous study of French life which he called *La Comédie humaine*.

The Real Lady Arabella Dudley

Balzac was a Spartan for work. Daily, twelve to twenty hours at a stretch, his raven's quill scratched out his fiction, and in this fiction he lived an entire second life. For the characters he created were as real to him as his friends—George Sand, Victor Hugo, Alexandre Dumas—or his mistresses. Once while immersed in the novel in which he portrayed Lady Ellenborough and which was narrated by its anemic hero, Félix de Vandenesse, Balzac startled his family with the announcement: "Do you know who Félix de Vandenesse is marrying? A Mlle de Grandville. The match is an excellent one. The Grandvilles are rich, in spite of what Mlle de Belleville has cost the family." On his deathbed, it is said, he cried over and over again: "Send for Bianchon—he can save me!" Bianchon was the fictional doctor Balzac had invented for his *Comédie humaine*.

This complete immersion in his work, among other reasons, may account for the brevity of Balzac's romance with Lady Ellenborough. During their few months she must have pleased him. She was witty, intelligent, attractive. And, apparently, she was passionate enough to encourage the creation of what one biographer has called "the most erotic heroine in the whole *Comédie humaine*."

Yet it is quite possible that he did not fully please her. In the search for peace of mind and body which characterized Lady Ellenborough's first fifty years, she demanded a man who could supply full-time emotional security. This need Balzac was not capable of fulfilling.

She needed days of affection. Balzac had only hours to give. Further, she wanted to escape from the painful memories of Paris and the nearness of London. She was restless for fresher, more vitalizing scenes. In the spring of 1831 she acted. She moved on to Munich, there to become the mistress of that lovable classicist, King Ludwig I of Bavaria, and there to eventually regularize the royal affair by marrying a wealthy court official, the redheaded Baron Carl Venningen. It was in the third year of her second marriage, at a time when she had briefly settled down as Baroness or Mme Venningen, that

Honoré de Balzac finally decided to include her in his *Comédie humaine*.

Of the ninety-seven books, totaling over four million words, Balzac would write in two decades, more than half were planned as part of *La Comédie humaine*, and each of these was classified under one of eight headings. A dozen were devoted to "Provincial Life," and the third of this group was *Le Lys dans la vallée*, or *The Lily of the Valley*.

Balzac conceived the novel and began writing it early in 1835, while staying at the Hotel zur Goldenen Birne in Vienna. Though he was visiting his wealthy mistress and future wife, Eveline Hanska, and her husband, he worked steadily on the book. "It is called *Le Lys dans la vallée*," he wrote the Marquise de Castries, an exasperating, aristocratic blonde whom he had failed to seduce. "Perhaps I deceive myself, but I imagine it will draw forth many tears. I have surprised myself in tears whilst writing it."

Balzac penned the first chapter in Vienna, where his preoccupation with Mme Hanska limited his work schedule to twelve-hour days. He mailed the chapter off to F. Buloz for serialization in the *Revue de Paris*, devoted more time to Mme Hanska, and finally hastened back to France and the book. "I worked night and day in Paris, only sleeping two hours in the twenty-four," he told Mlle Zulma Caurraud. "I thus brought in the *Lys*." Swathed in a silk-lined white cashmere robe, Balzac would begin his toils every morning at two o'clock. He wrote on a table illuminated by green-shaded candles, while he consumed coffee by the gallon—it is said he died of "fifty thousand cups of coffee." Previous books he had written hastily, feverishly, but this book was, by his own admission, one of his "most polished stones . . . slowly and laboriously constructed."

The story is in the form of a first-person confession by an idealistic, scholarly, repressed young man, Félix de Vandenesse. He recounts his harsh upbringing under a tyrannical mother. At twenty, still a virgin, Félix is bewitched by an unknown beauty at a ball in Tours. Later, on a hiking-trip through France, he meets his dream lady again through a family friend. She is the long-suffering, lily-white Mme Henrietta de Mortsauf, mother of two frail youngsters and wife of the sickly, domineering Count de Mortsauf. Soon Félix is a regular visitor at the château in Clochegourde. He tries to make love to the Madame, but in three months gets no further than the hand-kissing stage.

Traveling to Paris to pursue a career, Félix rises in the diplomatic service of the King. He acquires maturity, polish—and better penmanship, since he writes Mme de Mortsauf twice weekly for two years. He succeeds in making two visits to her, and during one of these visits he devotes two months to helping the Madame nurse her stricken husband back to health. During this travail he is drawn even more closely to his love. "Did she not come to wake me at the first twitter of the birds, in her morning wrapper, which sometimes allowed me a glimpse of the dazzling treasures which, in my fond hopes, I looked upon as mine? . . . Insensibly we found ourselves domesticated, half married."

Recalled to Paris by the King, Félix meets Lady Arabella Dudley and finds an outlet for his passions. For Lady Dudley is "one of those illustrious ladies who are half sovereigns. Immense riches, descent from a family which from the Conquest had been guiltless of any *mésalliance*, marriage with one of the most distinguished old men of the English peerage, all these advantages were but accessories which enhanced the beauty of her person, her charms, her manners, her intelligence, an indescribable brilliancy which dazzled before fascinating." She cheerfully offers to become his mistress. He makes no move. She appears in his room. He makes a move. Since she is married to an English lord and has two children in London, their affair becomes a scandal.

But carnal love is not enough. "Lady Arabella contents the instincts, the organs, the appetites, the vices and virtues of the subtle matter of which we are made. She was mistress of the body. Mme de Mortsauf was spouse of the soul." When Mme de Mortsauf does not reply to his letters, Félix hurries to Clochegourde. But he does not go alone. Lady Dudley accompanies him, rents a cottage at a discreet distance, and nightly rides her Arabian steed to rendezvous with him.

In Paris again, his affair with Lady Dudley intensified, Félix hears that Mme de Mortsauf is dying of "some secret grief." He rushes to Clochegourde. Wasted and ill, she rises and dresses to receive him. When he enters, she embraces him and pours out her love. "You shall not escape me again! I want to be loved, I will indulge in follies like Lady Dudley." But it is too late. She dies. And at dawn, with her husband and the priests asleep, Félix bends over her reposeful corpse. "Then, I was able, unwitnessed, to kiss her forehead with all the love that she had never allowed me to express."

Dazed, Félix returns to Lady Arabella Dudley. He finds her with her husband and children. She is haughty. "As to our intimacy, that eternal passion, those protestations of dying if I ceased to love her . . . all had vanished like a dream."

By July 1835 Balzac had finished *The Lily of the Valley*. Most of the installments ran in the *Revue de Paris*. But when the periodical fell into a disagreement with Balzac, he refused to give them the last chapters. A lawsuit occurred. Balzac won, published the remainder of his story in another periodical, and "his adversaries put themselves hopelessly in the wrong by reviewing the termination of the book, when it appeared elsewhere, in a strain of virulent but clumsy ridicule."

This fuss, of course, helped to promote the sales of the periodicals in which *The Lily of the Valley* appeared, but it took the edge off the book edition brought out by Werdet in 1836. "Piracy is killing us," Balzac complained to Mme Hanska. "Have the newspapers had any influence on the sale of the *Lys?* I know not, but this I do know, that, out of two thousand copies, Werdet has only sold twelve hundred, whilst the Belgian piracy has already thrown off three thousand copies."

The Lily of the Valley was, for Balzac, a departure from his

previous writing. For, while its prose was full of shrewd observation, of encyclopedic detail, of crude but poetic style, it
avoided the vulgarity, cynical realism, and sensuality of his
other works. Critics disagreed on it then as they continue to
disagree on it to this day. George Saintsbury thought *The Lily*
"of a somewhat sickly sweetness." But Peter Quennell regarded it as "extraordinarily fresh and clear and brilliant" and
praised "its elegant workmanship—so unlike the haphazard
workmanship of his other books."

It is more than possible that in 1836, there were as many
readers who bought *The Lily* for the sensation of guessing the
originals of Balzac's characters as there were those who purchased it for the pleasure of Balzac's style. Balzac was notorious
throughout his life for borrowing from living persons for his
fiction. When he wrote *Beatrix*, he frankly admitted to Mme
Hanska that he employed Marie d'Agoult and George Sand as
his models. Though, almost at the same time, he reassured
George Sand that the characters were entirely imaginary, which
provoked Sand to reply: "Please don't worry yourself over my
susceptibilities. . . . I am too used to writing novels not to
know that the novelist never indulges in portraiture, that, even
if he would, one cannot copy a living model. Heavens! where
would art be if one did not invent, for good or bad, three
quarters of the characters in whom the stupid, inquisitive, public likes to think that it can see originals who are known to it?"

Nevertheless, *The Lily of the Valley* was filled with realistic
portraiture. It was one of three novels in which Balzac revealed his own early years. When Félix found his mother
"pitiless," it was Balzac being autobiographical. Mme de
Mortsauf was drawn closely after Balzac's mistress and help-
mate Mme de Berny, who was twenty-two years his senior,
the wife of a long-ailing husband, and the mother of nine children. When Mme de Berny, who had financed him, and had
once prevented him from suicide, died the year after *The Lily
of the Valley* was published, Balzac declared to a friend: "Madame de Mortsaul in *Le Lys* only faintly shadows forth some of

the slighter qualities of this woman; there is but a very pale reflection of her, for I have a horror of unveiling my private emotions to the public." Finally, there was Lady Arabella Dudley—one of Balzac's most "fascinating" creations, Peter Quennell called her. And she, of course, was Lady Jane Ellenborough.

But in the more than century since *The Lily of the Valley* first appeared, Lady Ellenborough was disassociated from the character of Lady Dudley. There were several reasons for this. Balzac and Lady Ellenborough did not correspond. Balzac, fearing Mme Hanska's wrath, never mentioned Jane by her full name. And, most important, after Lady Ellenborough's death in Damascus her family and friends made vigorous efforts to destroy her papers and secure the skeleton in the closet. All of this conspired to deceive latter-day critics and biographers. In recent years they attributed the inspiration for Lady Arabella Dudley to a wide variety of colorful women—Caroline Lamb, Lady Hester Stanhope, Mme d'Abrantes, Duchesse de Castries, and, most frequently of all, Mme Émile Guidoboni-Visconti.

Like Lady Ellenborough, Mme Guidoboni-Visconti was English. Her maiden name was Frances Sarah Lowell. She had many love affairs, including one with Balzac in Italy during 1836. Though it is known that she once prevented his imprisonment, through a payment of ten thousand francs to the court, a disagreement occurred between them that embittered Balzac. While Balzac admitted portraying her in *Beatrix*, he vehemently denied she was any part of *The Lily of the Valley*. As a matter of fact, he conceived and wrote the character of Lady Dudley almost a year before he met Mme Guidoboni-Visconti.

Much of the confusion over the actual prototype was created by a cryptic reference in a letter Balzac wrote Mme Hanska during October 1836. Mme Hanska had heard gossip about the originals of Balzac's characters. Balzac replied: "Do they not say I have described Madame V, who is neither young nor handsome, and who is moreover an Englishwoman? This is a specimen of the opinions and judgments to which one is ex-

The Real Lady Arabella Dudley

posed! . . . You, who know all about my life, also know that I had the proofs of the *Lys* at Vienna, and you had the goodness to trouble yourself with them whilst I was running about the city and suburbs in my character of an ingenuous tourist. The manuscript of the *Lys* was written at Sache, corrected at La Boulonniere, before I had even seen the lady in question."

Since Balzac did not, in other letters, refer to Mme Visconti by initial only, there can be little doubt that he was referring to Lady Ellenborough, who had returned to Paris in 1835 as Mme Venningen and renewed her acquaintance with the author. As to Balzac's assertion that he had not seen "the lady in question" before he wrote *The Lily of the Valley*, he was obviously trying to reassure a jealous mistress. But though Mme Hanska knew that Mme Venningen had arrived in Paris in 1835, she apparently did not know that Mme V had been in Paris four years earlier as Lady Ellenborough.

Most contemporaries of Balzac identified Lady Dudley with Lady Ellenborough. And as thorough a researcher as Elinor Mary O'Donoghue, who, under the name of E. M. Oddie, wrote about Lady Ellenborough, concluded: "That Lady Arabella Dudley, however exaggerated a figure she cuts in *La Lys dans la vallée*, a novel which idealized a very different type of mistress, was the living human Jane and not the creation of Balzac's fertile brain, is certain. The fabric of the chapters in which she figures are shot with the gold of her personality, and the clues to her identity are many and unmistakable."

If we had no other evidence beyond *The Lily of the Valley* itself, it would still be clear that Balzac had borrowed heavily from Jane Ellenborough's personality and background. In the book, Lady Arabella Dudley abandoned two sons in England for the gay life of Paris; Lady Ellenborough left behind one son, a year and a half old, for her flight to Paris. In the book, Lady Dudley rode an Arabian horse to her nocturnal meetings with her French lover; Lady Ellenborough, when Mme Venningen, galloped on an Arabian steed to secret meetings with her Greek lover. In the book, Lady Dudley's husband was "one

of the most eminent old statesmen of England . . . stiff, full
of conceit, cold, with the sneering air he must have worn in
Parliament"; and Lady Ellenborough's husband was "a vain
man, too masterful and overconfident" and, in the opinion of
Lord Melbourne to Queen Victoria, "an unpopular man . . .
his manners have been considered contemptuous and overbear-
ing."

In the book, Balzac named Lady Dudley after Lady Ellenborough's little boy, Arthur Dudley, who in turn had been
named after Great Britain's Foreign Secretary. The hero-narrator of the story, Félix, was derived from Prince Felix
Schwarzenberg, the Austrian who was Lady Ellenborough's
lover. But the most conclusive evidence of all was in Balzac's
description of his fictional nymphomaniac, a description that
tallied precisely with that of Lady Ellenborough:

"This beautiful lady, so slim, so frail, this milk-white woman,
so languid, so delicate, so gentle, with such a tender face,
crowned with fine, fawn-colored hair, this creature whose brilliancy seems phosphorescent and transient, is an organization
of iron. However fiery it may be, no horse resists her nervous
wrist, this apparently weak but tireless hand. She has the foot
of a roe, a small, hard, muscular foot, under an indescribably
graceful exterior. . . . Her body knows no perspiration, it
inhales the warmth in the atmosphere, and lives in the water
for fear of dying. Her passion, too, is quite African."

The real Lady Arabella Dudley was born in England on
April 3, 1807, and christened Jane Elizabeth Digby. Her father
was Admiral Sir Henry Digby, who gained wealth capturing
Spanish prize ships, and fame fighting under Nelson at Traf-
algar. Her mother was the attractive Jane Coke, daughter of the
renowned Coke of Norfolk. Originally, her mother had married
Viscount Andover. But he died early without heir, and after
six years of widowhood her mother married Admiral Digby,
though she persisted to the end of her days in retaining the title
Lady Andover.

Jane was the first child produced by Lady Andover's second

marriage. There were two brothers by the time she was four, but her striking appearance made her the family favorite. When she was thirteen, a relative observed her studying with her cousins at Holkham, and reported that he had seen "little Miss Digby—oh! so beautiful."

It was this beauty that made her mother push her into an early debut in London. The Digbys took a residence at 78 Harley Street and sponsored Jane's coming-out. She was only sixteen when at her coming-out party she first met thirty-three-year-old Edward Law, Lord Ellenborough.

Lord Ellenborough, son of a Lord Chief Justice, had already attained the distinction of being one of the most disliked men in England. Educated at Eton and Cambridge, he served in Parliament as the Tory member from St. Michaels. His star rose when he married Lady Katherine Octavia Stewart, sister of the powerful and detested Lord Castlereagh. When Lord Castlereagh, oppressor of the English masses, died by his own hand, slashing his throat with a penknife, crowds of impoverished Londoners stoned his coffin as it passed toward Westminster Abbey. Though Lord Ellenborough had broken with his brother-in-law before his suicide, and aligned himself with the Duke of Wellington, the people of England did not forgive him his friendship for Castlereagh. Too, Lord Ellenborough's personality made him countless enemies. He was egotistical, pompous, ambitious, though undeniably a man of political ability.

When he met Jane Digby, he had been a widower four years. Lady Octavia Ellenborough had died in 1819, at the age of twenty-six. Despite his unattractive appearance—Lord Ellenborough was stodgy, flabby, and old for his years—he still had somewhat the reputation of a roué. He was a wealthy man, with estates in Hertfordshire and an income of ten thousand pounds annually. And it was generally felt that he would rise high in government.

He fell in love with Jane Digby at first sight. In his eyes, she was desirable in every way. She came of good family. She was the season's youngest and prettiest debutante. Above all, she might give him an heir. After several months' acquaintance, he proposed marriage. For Jane, he was somewhat less than desirable. She wanted a Byron, and she was getting a businessman. She wanted a gay, young lover, and she was getting a stuffy politician seventeen years her elder. But Jane's parents regarded him as the perfect catch. His station would give her luxury and position. His maturity would curb her childishly romantic impulses.

The couple were married on September 15, 1824, at Admiral Digby's house in London, with Lord Ellenborough's uncle, the Bishop of Bath and Wells, conducting the ceremony. Lord and Lady Ellenborough then went to Brighton for their honeymoon. The honeymoon, as revealed later, was "a flat failure." Whether or not this was attributable to the lord's impatience with his young wife's inexperience is not known. But it is known that in the first days of his marriage he cast an amorous glance elsewhere. Joseph Jekyll, a gossipy friend of the lord's, mentioned seeing "the pastry cook's girl at Brighton, whom Ellenborough preferred to his bride. Very pretty."

Back in London, Lord Ellenborough was soon deeply involved in politics. He had little time for affection or companionship. He left his young bride to her own devices. Confused and dismayed, Jane Ellenborough quickly entered into the whirl of London's international-society set, dominated by the Princess Esterhazy, wife of the Austrian Ambassador. At the weekly balls Jane Ellenborough's breath-taking beauty attracted the flattery and attention of dozens of polished young diplomats. They ridiculed faithfulness to an older, occupied husband. But for over two years Jane did not unbend. And when she finally did, it was not with a foreign diplomat, but with a scholarly English librarian.

In March 1827 a twenty-seven-year-old employee of the British Museum, Sir Frederick Madden, went to Holkham to classify Grandfather Coke's extensive Greek library. Shortly after his arrival, he noted in his diary: "Lady Ellenborough, daughter of Lady Andover, arrived to dinner, and will stay a fortnight. She is not yet twenty, and one of the most lovely women I ever saw, quite fair, blue eyes that would move a saint, and lips that would tempt one to forswear Heaven to touch them." Ten days later Madden forswore heaven. There was a late game of whist, and after it, he noted, "Lady E lingered behind the rest of the party, and at midnight I escorted her to her room. . . . Fool that I was! I will not add what passed. . . . Gracious God, was there ever such a fortune!"

Jane regretted the interlude only briefly. She promptly took up with her young cousin, Colonel George Anson, and their affair became the talk of Mayfair. Meanwhile, Lord Ellenborough had stirred himself sufficiently to hope for an heir. In February 1828 Jane bore him a son, Arthur Dudley, who died two years later when she was in Paris. It was after the birth of the boy that Lord Ellenborough ceased sharing his bed with his wife. But for Jane this was of no consequence. For she had already met Prince Felix Schwarzenberg.

Prince Schwarzenberg was twenty-eight years old when he left his diplomatic mission in Brazil and arrived in Falmouth, England, to serve as special attaché to Prince Esterhazy, Ambassador to Great Britain. Schwarzenberg was a handsome man, tall and thin and stiff, with an angular face, penetrating eyes, long, straight nose, and great black mustache. His court biographer in Vienna insisted that he possessed mystical powers. "The excessive life-force of the Prince is illustrated by the fact that he had a magnetic influence over women—not in the romantic and figurative way, but actually and medically. His sister was supposed to come especially to visit him and touch his hand to acquire more strength."

Magnetic force or no, he was a compelling person. His manner was, his friends insisted, "artless . . . kind and friendly." His interests were broad—he studied anatomy and wrote musical comedies—and he conversed on all subjects with wit. His background was cosmopolitan. He had been a cavalry captain in Vienna when Metternich determined to convert him into a diplomat. He served in St. Petersburg, Rio de Janeiro, Paris, and Madrid before arriving in London. His one weakness as a career diplomat was his easy susceptibility to attractive women.

Shortly after his arrival, attending a British Foreign Office reception, he saw Lady Ellenborough. They met, they danced, and their passion was immediate and mutual. Within short weeks they were lovers. At first Jane was cautious, but soon she didn't care. As Edmond About, the lively French journalist and novelist, reported it: "One fine morning she climbed up on the roofs, and distinctly shouted to the whole United Kingdom, 'I am the mistress of Prince von Schwarzenberg!' All the ladies, who also had lovers, but did not tell it, were horribly shocked."

Schwarzenberg shared rooms with a count from the Embassy, in Harley Street, close by the Digby residence. This gave Jane an excuse to visit Harley Street almost every afternoon when the Count was out and the Prince was in. Usually she dismissed her groom and green carriage at the corner, and walked to Schwarzenberg's rooms. He was always anxiously waiting, his door already open.

What transpired thereafter was explained to the House of Lords, in excruciating detail, by one John Ward, a "gentleman's gentleman," who was employed in lodgings directly across the street. Mr. Ward became curious about the lady who appeared almost daily at the Prince's doorway.

"Do you recollect," Mr. Ward was asked, "seeing the lady in the drawing-room on the first floor in the company of Prince Schwarzenberg?"

"Frequently."

"And do you recollect seeing anything particular occur between them?"

"Yes."

"What was that?"

"I once saw Prince Schwarzenberg lacing her stays."

But, as it developed, Mr. Ward's constant watchfulness was soon rewarded by an even greater sensation. Once the lovers, in their passion, did not bother to draw the bedroom blinds, and Mr. Ward clearly saw them in bed together.

Soon, afternoons were not enough. Jane and Schwarzenberg began to meet evenings, though it was more dangerous. On one occasion both arrived separately, unescorted, at a house-party in Wimbledon. When the evening was over, they left a few minutes apart, in different carriages. At Putney Heath her carriage drew abreast of his, and she left her vehicle to enter his and ride off. When this evidence was presented to the House of Commons, one member, Mr. Hume, saw nothing wrong in Jane's action. "Would anybody believe," he asked, "that a lady dressed to go out to dinner could be guilty of anything improper?" This question, according to the official record, was "met with a laugh, as if the Members were astonished at Mr. Hume's simplicity."

All through 1828 Jane continued to arrive at parties and balls unescorted, followed shortly by Prince Schwarzenberg. The frankness of the affair became a whispered scandal. When the English Derby was run and a horse named Cadland defeated a horse named The Colonel, Joseph Jekyll hurriedly wrote his sister: "Torrents of scandal afloat. They call Schwarzenberg 'Cadland' as he has beat The Colonel (Anson) out of Lady E's good graces. It is added that she talks publicly of her loves."

When rumors of the liaison sifted down to Margaret Steele, Jane's onetime governess, she begged her mistress to desist. Jane ignored her. Then Miss Steele, all moral indignation and anger, went to Lord Ellenborough. She tried to warn him, she later told the House of Commons, that his young wife was "associating with bad companions . . . persons of rank." When Miss Steele was asked why she objected to her mistress associating with persons of rank, she snapped: "Because I knew them by repute to be gay and profligate men." She was then asked: "What did Lord Ellenborough do when you warned him?" Miss Steele replied: "He laughed. . . . I was shocked."

Lord Ellenborough laughed because he did not believe the innuendoes of a foolish spinster. On February 6, 1829, when his wife asked permission to take their son to Brighton for some fresh sea air, Lord Ellenborough saw no reason to object. He was busier than ever. Under the sponsorship of the new Prime Minister, the Duke of Wellington, he had been appointed Lord of the Privy Seal. His political diary informs us that on the day his wife, son, and two nurses traveled to Brighton, Lord Ellenborough was occupied with a debate in the House of Commons and with a meeting involving the Premier.

In Brighton, Jane took a suite in the exclusive Norfolk Hotel, where she had previously vacationed with Lord Ellenborough. Shortly after she had packed her son off to bed, Prince Schwarzenberg arrived at the hotel in a yellow carriage. His carpetbag, plainly initialed F.S. and topped by the imperial crown, was delivered to his suite. He summoned a waiter, William Walton, and inquired if there were many new guests in the hotel. The waiter replied that only one other, a Lady Ellenborough, had arrived that day. Prince Schwarzenberg thought he knew her, and sent his card. As Mr. Walton delivered the card, he tried to read it. But it was in a foreign language.

At midnight, when the hotel was still, the Prince emerged from his suite, moved softly toward Lady Ellenborough's rooms, and entered. Unfortunately, he was seen. A night porter, Robert Hepple, who had remained awake to admit a family that had gone to the theater, observed the furtive entry of the "foreign gentleman." Mr. Hepple, concerned only with the high moral tone of the hotel, as he later explained, approached Lady Ellenborough's door and put his eye to the keyhole. It was blocked by a key. Undiscouraged, he then placed his ear to the keyhole. "What did you hear?" he was asked in the House of Lords. "Kissing," he replied. Anything else? "The creaking of a bed," he replied. By three o'clock Prince Schwarzenberg left for his own quarters, and Mr. Hepple salvaged some sleep.

Three months later Lady Ellenborough was in an advanced

stage of pregnancy. Since her husband had not slept with her in more than a year, her condition provided a temporary embarrassment. She had to speak to someone, and so she spoke to Miss Steele, her companion. "God knows what will become of me," she said. "The child to which I shall soon give birth is Prince Schwarzenberg's." 74469

But the scandal had already spread so far that it had reached the ears of Lord Ellenborough's uncle, the Bishop of Bath and Wells. Like Miss Steele before him, the Bishop tried to warn Lord Ellenborough. Whether or not his warning had any effect, we shall never know. For Jane Ellenborough decided herself to unburden her heart to her husband. On the evening of May 22, 1829, she revealed to Lord Ellenborough her love for the Prince. The shock of revelation, however, was not sufficient to keep Ellenborough from his duties that same evening. "Dined at Lord Hill's," his diary notes. "A party chiefly military." But it is significant that for the following day there is no entry in Lord Ellenborough's diary.

During the weeks after, the three participants were in a state of perpetual emotion. Schwarzenberg, at the instigation of his mentor, Prince Esterhazy, was hustled across the Channel, in an effort to avoid the embarrassment of a duel or lawsuit. Jane, in retreat at her mother's, busied herself with packing and preparing a farewell note to her husband. "Though my family naturally wish that all should be again as it once was between us, those feelings of honour which I still retain towards you make me still acquiesce in your decision. God bless you, dearest Edward. Janet." Dearest Edward's decision was, of course, divorce.

While Jane left for Paris to meet Schwarzenberg, Lord Ellenborough remained in London to face the notoriety of debate over his private life in Parliament. Somehow he survived the scandal. From the day the divorce was granted over shouts of "Not Content," he never mentioned Jane's name again, but built a memorial to his first wife and remained unmarried and unpopular until his death in 1871, by which time he had gained

great honors as Queen Victoria's Governor General of India
and as First Lord of the Admiralty.

For Jane, the reunion with Prince Schwarzenberg in Paris
was an unhappy one. She gave birth to their illegitimate daughter, but the love-child became a symbol of folly. When the
Prince left her, he was permitted to take and raise their child.
It was more than twenty years before she saw Schwarzenberg
and her daughter again. She was then the wife of a Greek, with
a son she adored. Schwarzenberg was a major general in the
Austrian Army, still a bachelor, assigned to the court of the
King of Naples. He arrived in Naples, from Turin, with Jane's
grown daughter and with his sister. Jane arrived in Naples with
her boy. She met Schwarzenberg. What transpired between
them is not known. Isabel Burton, wife of the translator of
The Arabian Nights, insisted long after that Jane had loved
Schwarzenberg to the day of her death. "It was easy to see that
Schwarzenberg had been the love of her life," Mrs. Burton
wrote, "for her eyes would light up with a glory when she
mentioned him and she whispered his name with bated breath."
From all evidence, Mrs. Burton was romanticizing. For a half-
century after he left her, Jane, in her letters, plainly regretted
her affair with Schwarzenberg and displayed no affection for
him.

After breaking with Jane in Paris, Prince Schwarzenberg
went on to spend six years in Germany and ten years in Italy,
before becoming Premier of Austria. As for Jane, though
stranded in Paris, she was comfortable. She had three thousand
pounds annually, for life, from Lord Ellenborough, as well as
other income. She had her brief affair with Balzac and immortality in the pages of *La Comédie humaine*. But life lay ahead,
and she was bored. So in 1831 she went to Munich, that lively,
Teutonic Athens ruled over by the eccentric, versifying æs-
thete, forty-five-year-old King Ludwig of Bavaria.

King Ludwig was a remarkable man. At an early age he had
fallen in love with the antiquity of Greece and Italy, and had
decided to superimpose that antiquity on Munich, much to the

confusion of the good burghers of Bavaria. Though parsimonious in his personal affairs—he wore frayed suits, made his children eat black bread to save money, denied his servants onions because they were expensive, and gave his mistresses nothing more than poems—he lavished a fortune on palaces, churches, museums, Hellenic temples, and the excavations of ancient Greece and Rome. His mania was beauty—in architecture and in women. Though married to Theresa of Saxe-Hildburghausen, an attractive *"Hausfrau* who was to give him seven children and never a moment of anxiety," he changed mistresses more frequently than his wardrobe. It was, in fact, a beautiful woman who caused his downfall.

When Ludwig was sixty years old, he received a petition from a newly arrived dancer who wished to perform in the royal theater. When he wouldn't receive her, she forced her way into his study, tore open her bodice, exposing her breasts to his gaze. The King not only permitted her to appear in the royal theater, but he took her for his mistress. She was the twenty-eight-year-old Lola Montez, born Marie Gilbert in Ireland, who had acquired a few Spanish dance steps, a mantilla, and castenets to help promote her international career. Her atheistic sentiments, and intrusion into Bavarian politics, irritated the Jesuits, who incited riots against the King and Lola Montez. Once when a mob of students gathered outside her dwelling to heckle her, Lola appeared on the second-story balcony and poured champagne on their heads. In the end, Lola was forced to flee Munich for Switzerland, and the King was forced to abdicate. He died in Nice, and Lola Montez died in Brooklyn, both shorn of power.

But fifteen years before Lola Montez, it was Jane Ellenborough who shared the King's bed and his favor. When Ludwig heard of Lady Ellenborough's beauty, he asked to meet her. The moment she was presented, King Ludwig commanded his court painter, Carl Stieler, to preserve her classical features in the Schonheits-Galerie—the Gallery of Beauty—located in the Residenz. In this gallery there hung portraits of all the beautiful women King Ludwig had loved or merely admired. Jane was painted as all the others had been—ringlets, big eyes, ivory complexion, well-exposed bosom. Several times a week the King wandered through his gallery, studying the beauties, seeking inspiration for what one biographer has called his "execrable verse."

The affair between Jane and King Ludwig progressed pleasantly. He was clever, learned, kindly, and naïve. He called her Ianthe and she called him Basily, both Greek names. From Ludwig she gained a renewed self-confidence, a brief sense of peace, and a permanent interest in painting and in ancient history. The affair eventually became quite public and quite respectable.

A little over a year after she had become the King's mistress, Lady Ellenborough suddenly married a tall, redheaded official in the Munich court, Baron Carl Venningen, whom she had met earlier while out horseback-riding. Since she gave birth to a son just six weeks after her marriage, it was generally thought that the child was King Ludwig's and that he had forced her to wed to avoid scandal.

Though Baron Venningen's Catholic family tried to prevent the union, he married Jane in Italy during November of 1832. It is more than likely that Jane was still carrying on her affair with King Ludwig, who was also in Italy at the time. But soon enough Ludwig was left to contemplate his Gallery of Beauty. For Jane, now the Baroness Venningen, found Carl Venningen the "most admirable man" in what was to be a long lifetime of men.

Jane remained faithful to Venningen for almost three years. They divided their time between the Baron's estates in Munich and Baden, and took occasional trips to Sicily. There was one constant source of disagreement. Venningen wanted his wife to become a German-type *Hausfrau*. She had given him two children, but he hoped for more. The prospect of being constantly pregnant, as well as anchored to the Baron's estates and his small Bavarian circle, appalled Jane. She dreamed of new faces, new adventures, new sites. The idea of playing *Hausfrau*, even on a regal scale, was a source of irritation. Still, Jane had great affection for Venningen, and the marriage might have lasted many more years if Count Spyridon Theotoky had not appeared on the scene.

Indirectly, it was King Ludwig who was responsible for the entrance of Count Theotoky into Munich society and into Jane's life. Ludwig, while importing Greek culture, had exported, in 1832, his seventeen-year-old son, Otto, to Athens. There the Teutonic boy reigned as modern Greece's first King. This move encouraged many old Greek families to send their sons to Munich for education in the ways of their new ruler. Among the first of these Greeks, arriving to study German military affairs, was Count Spyridon Theotoky. He was tall and slender, with a mop of black hair, curling mustaches, finely chiseled features. What he lacked in money, he made up in manners, charm, gaiety.

They met at a royal ball given by King Ludwig for the monarch of Prussia. Before the evening was over, Jane was calling him Spyro, and when the evening was over, they left the ball together. Their love for each other was spontaneous. She was utterly entranced, not only by Theotoky's physical charms, but by his romantic references to his home in Corfu and his father's residence on the Ægean island of Tenos. Theotoky begged her to run off with him. She could obtain an easy divorce in Greece and then marry him.

When she accompanied Venningen on a trip to Baden, she was torn with indecision. Count Theotoky followed, romantically, recklessly, taking quarters at Heidelberg. In Baden, Jane took great risks. While the Baron slept, she would slip out late at night, lead her Arabian horse from the stables, and ride to a rendezvous with the Count. One evening while her husband was away on a short business trip, Jane went to a dance Theotoky was attending. They left in a carriage together. Baron Venningen, returning home earlier than expected, saw them. He had heard rumors about his wife and the Greek, but had tried to discount them. Now, seeing them together, his suspicions were confirmed. He wheeled about and gave chase. Jane and Theotoky, realizing they had been discovered, fled for the French frontier. But at the frontier they were delayed, and there Venningen caught them.

Quite naturally enraged, Venningen insisted upon immediate satisfaction. An impromptu duel, with pistols, was arranged in a wooded area off the highway. The coachmen acted as seconds. The Baron and the Count paced off, pivoted, and the more experienced Venningen fired first. The bullet imbedded itself above Theotoky's heart. He sagged to the grass and lay dying in his own blood. Hysterically, Jane threw herself upon him. A frontier physician, hastily summoned, saw little hope. "He had but a few hours to live," reported Count Apponyi. "He then declared to the husband that he was innocent and the victim of the most infamous calumny. He insisted that between him and the Baroness there had never been anything beyond a deep and sincere friendship. Then he clasped the hand of his friend, and, with a deep sigh, shut his eyes. Fortunately for him, he did not shut them forever."

Returned to the Burg Venningen to die in bed, Count Theotoky became an immobile embarrassment by persisting in remaining alive. In several weeks he was well, and the disposition of Jane had to be met again. While all Bavaria buzzed with the story of the three of them—husband, wife, and lover under one roof—Jane asked Venningen for her freedom. Graciously, he gave it. He packed Jane and Count Theotoky off for Paris, and retained for life Jane's gratitude and her two children. Baron Venningen, until he died of a heart attack while horseback-riding in Munich forty years later, corresponded regularly and affectionately with Jane. Mostly he wrote her of their son, Heribert, who grew up to marry a girl half English (who gave Jane three grandchildren), and their daughter, Bertha, who became insane and died in an asylum.

It was five years before Jane saw Theotoky's Greece or his wedding ring. Her marriage was delayed until she could obtain her divorce from Venningen and her admission into the Greek Orthodox Church. Jane was thirty-four when, after being baptized in a bathtub, she became the Countess Theotoky in Paris during 1841. Immediately after, she set out to visit her father-in-law, Count Joannes Theotoky, who was Governor of the treeless, perpendicular isle of Tenos.

Eventually she moved to Dukades, Theotoky's estate on Corfu. She busied herself making the new home attractive. She gave her husband an English library and herself a French drawing-room, and on the spacious, unattended grounds she made a garden and planted a cypress tree, which may still be seen. There were constant parties, nights of eating, drinking, singing, and Jane was happy. Then, suddenly, Count Spyridon Theotoky was promoted to a colonelcy in the Greek Army, appointed aide-de-camp to King Otto, and ordered to Athens. And the marriage fell apart.

In Athens, which young King Otto had made the new capital of Greece to replace Nauplia, Jane built a house and stables and entertained lavishly. She gave birth to a son named Leonidas. Of the six children she had in her life, by husbands and lovers, Leonidas, a blond, gentle child who resembled her, was her favorite. She adored the boy, and took him, dressed in gold lace, on a vacation to Italy. One day while she was chatting with Italian friends in her villa near the Lucca Baths, little Leonidas tried to slide down the second-story banister. He slipped, plunged to the marble floor below, and was instantly killed.

Shortly after, Jane divorced Theotoky. Apparently the child had been their last link. With the boy gone, they had little to hold them together. They had been together fifteen years, five years as lovers, ten years as husband and wife, but had gradually grown apart. Theotoky became increasingly extravagant with Jane's income and increasingly attentive to other women. After the divorce, he went on to marry three more times before his death in Russia. As for Jane, months before her marriage was officially severed, she had turned to another lover. Years earlier, in Munich, she had been the mistress of King Ludwig.

Now, in Athens, she became the mistress of his son, King Otto.

King Otto was his father's son in one respect: he was a classicist. But when England, France, and Russia compromised to put him on the throne of Greece, he was an unlikely choice. The trouble was basic. King Otto was interested in Greece's past; the Greek people were interested in their present. Athens, a crude village of twenty thousand, was impoverished. The wealthiest families subsisted on vegetables, the poorest on salted fish. "If you stop a workman on the promenade," said Edmond About, "and ask him if he would sell his shoes for a reasonable price, you can bet ten to one he'll walk home barefooted."

Besides his disinterest in the national economy, King Otto invited antagonism for other reasons. He was a Catholic, which the Greeks resented. He was a Bavarian, loading his court and army with Germans imported from Munich, which the Greeks resented even more. Above all, he was a weakling. Though not without charm, his manner was unfortunate. "It is practically impossible not to laugh before His Majesty of Greece," confessed Edouard Thouvenal, a French diplomat. "Instead of speaking, he swallows his saliva with infinite difficulty for five minutes before giving birth to a sentence." Actually, King Otto's domineering wife did most of his speaking, writing, and thinking for him. She had been the Princess Amalie of Oldenburg. The royal marriage, prearranged, was barren of children or love. The joke around Athens at the time was that the King read everything without signing it and the Queen signed anything without reading it.

Queen Amalie disliked Jane for her beauty, conversation, dancing ability, and horsemanship. And she despised Jane for taking away her husband. Jane reciprocated this hostility. When in 1862, a year after a student tried to assassinate the Queen, the royal couple fled Athens on a British warship, Jane heard the news in Syria and exclaimed with pleasure: "So then my wish is granted and my rival the Queen is annihilated."

Though Jane was forty-five and King Otto only thirty at

the time of their affair, Jane's beauty was well preserved. Edmond About met her in Athens in 1852, when the affair was still in progress, and he found her striking. "Ianthe is a wonderful example of health and physical beauty. She is tall and slender without being thin. If her waistline were a bit lower, it would be impossible to find a woman with a better figure. . . . Her complexion has preserved that milky whiteness that blooms best under English fogs. But at the lightest emotion she blushes. You might say that this fine transparent skin is little more than a net which imprisons her passions. You can see her passions, agitating, coloring, as they move about their jail."

Once when she was having tea with the youthful Edmond About, Jane referred indirectly to her affairs with King Ludwig and King Otto. She asked About: "Do you believe in fortune-telling by cards? Long ago, I consulted Mademoiselle Lenormant and she told me I would turn many men's heads—"

About interrupted gallantly. "It would require no sorceress to predict that."

"—particularly three crowned heads."

"Have you found them?"

"I looked thoroughly, but to date I found only two."

"That is because the third one is yet to come."

This conversation took place at the Pentelikon residence of a remarkable, eccentric, expatriate Frenchwoman, who had brought Jane and About together. The Frenchwoman was the wealthy Sophie de Barbe-Marbois, the Duchess de Plaisance. She had been born in Philadelphia, married one of Napoleon's generals, become a lady-in-waiting to the Empress Marie Louise, and finally retired to Athens to found a new religion. She resided in a home she would not finish building—"through the superstitious fear of dying when she had completed anything," About thought. The Duchess dwelt in isolation, a tiny, crusty, white-haired old lady, protected by six fierce Irish wolfhounds. One of her few friends, perhaps her oldest friend, was Jane Ellenborough.

Jane needed the Duchess desperately. For after taking up

with King Otto and subsequently with one of his generals, she was ostracized by the Athens court and Greek society at the instigation of Queen Amalie. Only the Duchess de Plaisance defended Jane's affairs, calling each a "free union."

But the companionship of the Duchess was not enough. Without a real man's love, Jane was unhappy and alone in hostile Athens. Already weary of King Otto, she determined to travel in search of she knew not what. She went to Turkey, Italy, Switzerland. Her mysterious months in those countries were to become the least known of her entire life. She left behind her, especially in Italy, a trail of gossip and rumor that confounded biographers for decades. Many writers, more interested in sensation than in fact, preferred to believe she cavorted about Rome like a modern Messalina. A Vienna correspondent in the Near East reported to his paper: "She went to Italy where, as she told me herself, she was married six times in succession." Others echoed this report and credited Jane with five Italian husbands and one Spanish one. More conservative writers thought she had taken many lovers in Italy, but only two husbands.

However, the two Italian husbands, either by Jane's word or the record, remain undocumented. The lovers were another thing. It is probable that Jane had a number of indiscriminate affairs in this period. One story that persists involves her simultaneously with three Italian suitors.

But the over-emotionalism of the Latins, the chaos of her social life in Rome, did little to soothe her. She returned to Athens, took up briefly with King Otto again, and then, one day, she met General Xristodolous Hadji-Petros and forgot all about the King.

Jane had gone on a tour of northern Greece. There the men of the mountains, thin, nervous, silent men, were called Palikars —"the brave ones." Half patriots, half bandits, these Palikars had fought valiantly in helping Greece win its independence. The leader of these mountain men was seventy-year-old General Hadji-Petros. He was tall for his race, and young for his years, and he reigned as an absolute brigand sovereign over his people. Actually, for his service to the cause of liberation, he had been appointed Governor of the Province of Lamia.

Jane saw him first in the village of Lamia. He wore a red cap, gold jacket, pleated white skirt, and sat gracefully astride a horse harnessed in silver. Though he was twenty-five years older than she, Jane was entranced. She managed an introduction, then accompanied him into the hills with his troops. She became his mistress at once, slept with him before bonfires under the stars, drank red wine from gourds, and ate bread from goatskin containers.

She learned that he was a widower, with an attractive son named Eirini, who died a few years later. She enjoyed being treated as a bandit queen. "She imagined she was born a Palikar," Edmond About reported. "She ruled over Lamia. The whole city was at her feet. When she went out for her walk, the drums beat out a greeting."

The drums were heard in Athens, too. Queen Amalie saw a chance to revenge herself upon Jane. She signed an order reproving General Hadji-Petros for immorality, and temporarily suspending him from the Governorship of Lamia and his command of the Palikars.

The General was distressed. He promptly protested to the Queen with a most unfortunate bit of prose. "Your Majesty has dismissed me," he wrote, "undoubtedly because I am living with the Countess Theotoky. But whatever my enemies may have told you, I can assure you on my word of honor as a soldier that if I am this woman's lover, it is not for love's sake, but purely for self-interest. She is rich and I am poor. I have a position to maintain and children to educate."

To humiliate Jane, Queen Amalie made the letter public. Curiously, Jane did not seem to mind. She was convinced that the General wrote the letter merely to gain reinstatement. She suggested that they return to Athens together. The General agreed. Jane rented two bungalows, connected by a garden, in the suburbs. In one she lived with her young French maid,

Eugénie, whom she had brought from Paris when she married Theotoky; in the other she established the General and his retinue of faithful Palikars. But the bungalows were too small and uncomfortable. She was as out of place in the little house, About remarked, "as a portrait by Lawrence hanging in a kitchen."

She contracted to have a huge mansion built for the General and herself at Piræus, a small, primitive village four miles from Athens. Her bedroom was built like a throne room. The General had his private suite. His Palikars had a barracks among the almond trees in the rear. And, of course, Jane had her stables. It was idyllic.

The idyll soon wore thin. The General was increasingly crotchety and uncommunicative. He smelled of garlic and took to cuffing Jane about. All of this she endured, as long as she felt that Hadji-Petros loved her. But when she learned that he was sleeping with her maid, Eugénie, her disillusionment was complete.

Sick at heart, she cast about for direction. And then she remembered the ruins of ancient Palmyra, deep in the Syrian desert between Baghdad and the Mediterranean. She had heard about Palmyra first from King Ludwig. And then, again, from Theotoky and King Otto. Suddenly it seemed a haven. She left Athens without notice or preparation. She said only that she was going to buy Arabian mares in the East.

Actually, it was the turning-point in her life. Without realizing it, though perhaps she sensed it, she was moving closer to that which she had always sought. Few of those who knew her, even those close to her, really understood what Jane Ellenborough was after. Many dismissed her as a nymphomaniac, a frenzied female who constantly demanded new bed companions in her search for sexual gratification. That she possessed a consuming and persistent need for sexual love, there can be little doubt. But her essential need was deeper. Her search—like that of all humanity—was for peace of mind. She felt that she would find this peace if she found the right mate in the right place. In

Syria she found the place. And there also she found the mate. And her long journey came to an end. But it did not happen immediately.

First there was Saleh. And this was pure sex and little else. She met him in May 1853 while riding along the Jordan, en route to Jerusalem and Palmyra, with a contrite Eugénie and an Arab escort. She saw a thoroughbred mare and asked who owned it. She was told that the mare was owned by a Bedouin shiek who lived near by. He was a young, handsome Arab named Saleh.

As Jane repeated the story of the meeting to the Duchess in Athens later, and as the Duchess repeated it to Edmond About, Jane tried to buy the mare and Saleh refused to sell. "Unfortunately, this horse cannot be tamed," he said. "But even if she could be tamed, I would not set a price on her. I value her more than anything in the world, even more than my three wives."

"A fine horse is a treasure," Jane admitted, "but so are three wives, if they are beautiful. Bring your horse to me, and let us see if she can be tamed."

Saleh signaled two Arabs, who brought forth the rearing animal. The mare was quickly saddled. Jane mounted her, stayed with her, calmed and broke her. Saleh's gaze was not on the horse, but on Jane. When she dismounted, he went to her. "Woman often succeeds where man fails, because she knows when to yield. The mare is priceless, now that you have tamed her. If you still want her, you may buy her—but not with money."

We are told that Jane studied Saleh's handsome face and physique for a moment, before agreeing upon payment. "I will pay for your horse the price you expect," she said. "I did not come all this way to bargain. But one thing you must know— in my country, women are too proud to share a man's heart. They enter his tent on the condition that they reign in it alone. I will pay the price you wish for your horse, but only if you send away your harem."

Saleh quickly replied: "The men of my country have as many

women as they can afford. I should look like a twelve-hundred-franc employee if I sent away my harem and lived with one woman. Too, I must obey my religion, set an example for my followers, and follow the custom of the Turks. To us, polygamy is necessary."

The disagreement continued for some time. But Saleh's passion soon overcame his scruples. By late afternoon he had sent away his harem, and by evening Jane had entered his black tent.

The affair continued with great intensity for several months. Jane was sufficiently satisfied with Saleh's virility to wish it to continue indefinitely. Toward this end, she decided to return briefly to Athens and settle her affairs. But first she must see Palmyra. She left Saleh with difficulty and pushed on to Jerusalem and Damascus.

Damascus, capital of Syria, was a complete surprise. Jane was stimulated and excited by the Moslem religious center. As she rode up the crooked Street Called Straight, she did not notice the piles of refuse, the hawkish desert Arabs, the chanting merchants. She saw only what Kinglake had seen earlier: "This 'Holy' Damascus, this 'earthly paradise' of the Prophet, so fair to the eye that he dared not trust himself to tarry in her blissful shades—she is a city of hidden palaces, of copses, and gardens and fountains, and bubbling streams." It was with difficulty that she roused herself to leave its domes and minarets for Palmyra.

When the English Consul heard of her plan to visit Palmyra, he was horrified. He warned her that it was a dangerous ten-day trek by horse across hot sands, through bandit-infested country. Jane ignored his warning. She was determined to mount a caravan at once.

Jane made inquiries. She learned that two Arab tribes, the Shammar and the Anazeh, each with twenty-eight thousand tents, controlled the Syrian desert beyond. One of the most trustworthy branches of the Anazeh was the small Mezrab tribe, with a hundred tents. They could be depended upon to guide her, find the waterholes, fight off raiders. Jane asked the Mezrabs to send a representative to discuss price.

The Real Lady Arabella Dudley

And thus she met Medjuel. She could not know that it was the most important meeting in her entire life. Her mind was on Saleh. And Medjuel's appearance was not such as to make her forget her Bedouin lover. Medjuel was a short, leathery, bearded man. Isabel Burton called him "that dirty little black . . . much darker than an Arab generally is." Lady Anne Blunt, Lord Byron's granddaughter, described him more accurately: "In appearance he shows all the characteristics of good Bedouin blood. He is short and slight in stature, with exceedingly small hands and feet, a dark olive complexion, beard originally black but now turning grey, and dark eyes and eyebrows."

Medjuel's real attraction, however, was not in his appearance. He was an erudite and cultured man, with a knowledge of desert lore and several languages, though English was not one of them. Lady Blunt thought him "well bred and agreeable." And Isabel Burton grudgingly admitted that, despite his color, he was "very intelligent and charming."

His background was as aristocratic as Jane's. His family was one of the first four noble families of the desert. He had been the second of nine sons, and was in line to succeed his childless brother, Sheik Mohammed, as head of the tribe. It was his linguistic knowledge that secured him the nomination to bargain with the wealthy Englishwoman.

If Jane did not notice him, Medjuel certainly noticed her. He was struck dumb by her beauty. He agreed to the first price she offered—eight thousand francs—for escort and caravan to Palmyra. When he returned, somewhat dazed, to his tribe, he expected to be chastized for the poor bargain he had made. But his brother wasn't interested. For his brother had made a better bargain with the Gomussa, an allied tribe. The bargain was that the Mezrabs would lead Jane into a mock Gomussa ambush. She would be kidnapped and held for ransom, or robbed and abandoned. The money would then be divided.

When Medjuel objected, he was ridiculed into silence. The tribe was poor. The golden opportunity must not be lost. The caravan, with Medjuel in charge, was quickly prepared, and soon was on its way to Palmyra. Since Jane spoke no Arabic, the only person she could communicate with was Medjuel, who knew French. She asked him about Palmyra. He told her stories of the walled city's heyday in A.D. 250, under the rule of the half Greek, half Arabic eighteen-year-old Queen Zenobia. He told her of Queen Zenobia, astride a camel, challenging the might of the Roman Empire, and of the siege that forced her to flee, and of her eventual capture and death in chains. Jane was fascinated, not only with the history, but with Medjuel's recital of it. She confided her past to him, and her present affair with Saleh. He told her of his wife and two sons. He did not tell her that he was madly in love with her.

Medjuel was riding beside her when they moved into the ambush. Suddenly, from every direction, Gomussa raiders, lances high, shrieking and screaming, charged in. Medjuel's instructions were to pretend a halfhearted defense and then abandon Jane. But he could not bring himself to do it. Rallying his followers, he plunged, flaying, into the mass of startled at- tackers. After a short, sharp struggle, during which Medjuel would not give ground, his allies and fellow conspirators turned tail and fled into the dunes.

Jane was impressed and grateful. The caravan continued to Palmyra and there camped among the two thousand broken marble columns. Medjuel led Jane around the remains of the seven-mile wall that had once protected the oasis, showed her the sites of the ancient palaces and temples.

On the way back to Damascus, just outside the gates, Med- juel summoned up the courage to propose marriage. He told Jane that he was in love with her. He told Jane that he would divorce his wife for her. Jane would not have it. She liked Med- juel, liked his dignity, manners, humor. But she would not have him leave his wife. Besides, though she did not have to tell him again, her mind was on Saleh. Medjuel did not press his suit. He left her without once holding her hand or attempting to kiss her.

It was late in 1853 when she returned to Athens. She stayed

only long enough to rearrange her financial affairs and pack her effects. She was anxious to return to Saleh. The Duchess tried to dissuade her from leaving. When the Duchess saw she couldn't, she quarreled with Jane, so as to be sure that she would not miss her. Jane returned to Saleh. But so had his three wives. The bargain was broken.

Angrily, Jane left for Baghdad. As her guide, she hired Sheik El Barrak, a hot-tempered, brutal, animal man. He had heard that she had been Saleh's mistress, and he had taken the job only to seduce her. The moment they were on the road, he began making advances. She disliked him and rejected him. But eventually, because of utter weariness and his insensitive persistence, she gave in and slept with him.

By the time they reached Mezrab territory, they weren't speaking. She had fed a starving camel from their supplies, and he had ranted at the waste. She despised him. Then, aware that she was among the Mezrabs, she remembered Medjuel, she remembered his kindness and sweetness. She began to inquire after him. And suddenly, one afternoon, he appeared. He had heard of her arrival. He brought her as a gift a young Arabian mare. She was overwhelmed by the gift and by the sight of him. She knew at last that she was in love.

Jane dismissed El Barrak, and happily rode to Damascus with Medjuel. He told her that he had divorced his wife, returned her to her family with the dowry, but had kept his sons, Japhet and Schebibb. Now, once again, he asked Jane to marry him. This time, filled with excitement, she accepted.

There were immediate obstacles. Medjuel's entire family opposed the marriage. Her blood was not as blue as his, her faith was not Mohammedan, her background was not the background of the desert. Jane met similar opposition from the British Consul in Damascus. He could not believe his ears when he heard that she wanted to marry a Bedouin. He reminded her that she was a Digby, an Ellenborough, an English subject who would by this marriage become a Turkish national. He told her that it was sheer madness, that he would declare her a lunatic before co-operating. But in the end he co-operated, as did Medjuel's family. Medjuel owned a small house in Homs. There, in 1855, Lady Ellenborough became Jane Digby el Mezrab. She was forty-eight and he was forty-five. The marriage, as it turned out, was her last, her longest, and her best.

A compromise about their mode of living was effected at once. Six months of each year would be spent, Western style, in her Damascus villa, and the other six months would be spent, Bedouin style, in his desert tent. The compromise lasted the entire twenty-six years of their marriage and was completely satisfactory to both of them.

Except for brief forays into the desert, when Medjuel joined his fellow tribesmen in fighting the Shammars, they were never separated but once. A year after their marriage Jane decided to return to England for a visit. She had not seen her homeland for a quarter of a century, not since the day in 1829 when she fled her noble lord and her family to join Schwarzenberg in Paris.

The decision to bridge the broken years and the wreckage and scandal of her past was a difficult one to make. Her father had died and there were family matters to be settled. Yet there may have been more at stake. She had taken up a life so different from any she had ever known, a relationship considered insane and bizarre by family and friends, that she may have wanted to test her own feelings. Perhaps there would never be peace in the desert until she had laid the ghost of English respectability. And so, for the first and last time, she went home.

Surely there is the perfect subject for a drama in Jane Digby el Mezrab's return. She walked down the gangplank at Folkestone, dressed at the height of Paris fashion, on December 19, 1856. Jane Steele, the sister of her childhood governess, was waiting for her. They embraced, wept a little, and then drove to Tunbridge Wells.

Jane's mother, Lady Andover, a corpulent eighty, was waiting, full of warmth, as was Jane's old governess, Margaret Steele. Her brother Edward came to visit for three days. But when she tried to show him her water colors of Palmyra, restraint set in. The family did not wish to hear of her marriage to an Arab, and Margaret Steele persisted in referring to her as Mme Theotoky. For a brief moment she was depressed. "My family ties burst asunder; no children; no English home!" she noted. "I am not gay as I gaze around and think of what might have been and what is." But then her beloved younger brother, Reverend Kenelm Digby, appeared, full of questions about Medjuel and the desert, and suddenly Jane was happy and she knew what was right. The East was her home and Medjuel was her husband, and she wrote him, quite incredulously: "*I* in England!"

There was a secret visit to London to see old friends. It has been claimed that Jane's entire visit to England was made furtively because it had been a condition of Ellenborough's alimony arrangement that she never return. More likely, Jane kept her visit quiet for fear of embarrassing her family. For England had changed. Fornication was not in fashion. Victoria was on the throne.

After a fiftieth birthday party and four months with her family, she departed England forever. In Paris she bought a piano and painting-equipment, and a month later she was in Damascus. "With beating heart I arrived," she said. "Then he arrived, Medjuel, the dear, the adored one, and in that moment of happiness I forgot all else."

For the most, her life in Syria was serene. Her sprawling villa outside the Damascus gates was furnished in the comfortable Arabic manner, except for her private rooms, which were decorated with French furniture, English books received regularly from London, and her own water colors of Palmyra and Greece. The grounds were large, with a lily pond, a garden in which Jane planted seeds imported from England, and a stable for her Arabian horses. Her pets roamed everywhere, among them a gazelle, a turkey, a pelican, and at least a hundred Persian cats. Here, according to Isabel Burton, "she led a semi-

European life. She blackened her eyes with kohl, and lived in a curiously untidy manner. But otherwise she was not in the least extraordinary."

But when Jane accompanied Medjuel into the desert, she was quite extraordinary, as even Mrs. Burton had to admit. "When she was in the desert," wrote Mrs. Burton, "she used to milk the camels, serve her husband, prepare his food, wash his hands, face and feet, and stood and waited on him while he ate, like any Arab woman, and gloried in so doing." She loved the desert and played Bedouin to the hilt. Because her blond hair was considered bad luck by the tribesmen, she dyed it black and wore it in braids. Dressed in a light-blue cotton gown and often barefoot, she worked and she rode. The Mezrabs adored her, called her Mother of Milk because of her creamy complexion, and White Devil because of her courage. When the tribes moved south to graze their camels, courage was needed. There were constant battles over grazing-areas. Once when a band of Shammars swooped down on the Mezrab tents, many of Medjuel's tribesmen fled. Jane snatched up a rifle, and with her first shot killed the approaching sheik. The attackers broke and retreated.

Occasionally through the long years of her marriage Jane's happiness was sorely tried. In the beginning, religion had been no issue. While Medjuel was devout and daily turned his face toward Mecca, Jane was disinterested in any orthodox faith. Her attitude was changed by the infamous July massacres of 1860. Mobs stormed through Damascus, burning the European quarter, killing the Dutch Consul, wounding the American Consul; Christian corpses littered the streets. While Jane took in refugees, Medjuel stood guard over her with a gun. But no Arabs entered her villa. All regarded her as one of their own. When the massacres were done, Jane did not forget their horror. Defiantly, she returned to her Protestant faith, even to attending church twice every Sunday.

The greatest problem in her marriage, however, was not one that revolved about being an infidel, but rather one that concerned infidelity. When she had married Medjuel, she had made a rash agreement with him. Moslem men, she knew, were permitted to possess more than one wife. Jane had told Medjuel that if ever, in the years to come, he felt he required another woman, he might take one, as long as he kept her presence a secret. With the years, this promise haunted her. Twice, when he rode off into the desert to fight or to look after his herds, she heard rumors that he was visiting another wife whom he kept in hiding. In each case, tortured with jealousy, she accused Medjuel of unfaithfulness, and each time he proved to her that he had not seen another woman, that he had no other woman, that he wished none.

Jane's fears were renewed when one of Medjuel's sons died and the boy's widow was brought into the house to live with them. The widow was a gorgeous young Bedouin girl named Ouadjid. For many years Jane feared that Medjuel had secretly married the girl or was keeping her as a mistress. Jane ached with the realization that Ouadjid was young and she was old. A single thought oppressed her: if only she had her youth again, if only Medjuel had known her as Schwarzenberg and Balzac and King Ludwig had known her, if only she had met Medjuel long before. It was the only time she hated age. And even after her suspected rival died in 1880, Jane confessed: "I am jealous of her memory."

On the other hand, she was still beautiful enough, and rich enough, to attract men, and the proposals made to her were a constant source of anger to Medjuel. When she was fifty-one, Sheik Fares ibn Meziad tried to marry her, but failed. When she was seventy-one, her young dragoman, Anton, tried to sleep with her, but was rejected. During her entire life in Damascus, her legendary past made her a target for romantic adventurers, foreigners who wished to build reputations as lovers by reporting that they had seduced Lady Ellenborough. Typical among these was a Bavarian-born English citizen, Carl Haag, who was one of Queen Victoria's favorite court painters. He hired Jane and Medjuel to show him about the desert, and when he returned to London he hinted that he had been her lover—all this in an effort to publicize his works. Despite the gossip, it is probably untrue that Jane was ever unfaithful to Medjuel. She loved him too much, and she never tired of him. In her seventy-third year, when her husband was himself seventy, she complained: "It is now a month and twenty days since Medjuel last slept with me! What can be the reason?"

The constancy of Jane's devotion for Medjuel, as well as the fullest picture of her last years, may be found in the writings of the many travelers she received and entertained in Damascus. One of the most vivid of these accounts was set down by Lord Redesdale after visiting Jane in 1871:

"I found Lady Ellenborough—Mrs. Digby as she now called herself—living in a European house, furnished, so far at any rate as the rooms in which we were received were concerned, like those of an English lady; in the desert with the tribe she would be altogether Arab. Her tables were covered with the miniatures, knick knacks and ornaments, indigenous to Mayfair—quite out of tune with Damascus. The owner was, like her belongings, a little old-fashioned, and very nice to look upon, as she had the remains of great good looks, and the most gracious and beautiful old world manners.

"She was very much interested in hearing about England, and asked many questions about friends she had known in the old days. She seemed to think that the world had stood still since she left it, for she spoke of people who, if not dead, were quite old folk, as if they were in the hey day of blooming youth. She asked after the old Lord Chantallam—grandfather of the present Earl. How was he? 'Wonderful,' I said, 'cutting us all out skating at Highclere two or three months ago.' Lady Ellenborough looked puzzled. 'But why should he not?' she asked. 'Well,' I answered, 'you must remember that he is past seventy years of age.' 'Dear me, is that possible, that handsome young man?' Her old friends remained in her mind just as she had known them—Lady Palmerston, Lady Jersey, Lady Londonderry, still reigning beauties, still queens of Almacks.

The Real Lady Arabella Dudley

"It was strange to hear a delicately nurtured English lady talking of her life in the desert with 'her' tribe. She told us how, the summer before, a hostile tribe had raided them and stole some of their mares, and how, this next summer, they must ride out to avenge the outrage, and get back the lost treasures. There would be fierce fighting, she said, and she must be there to nurse the chief should anything happen to him. 'In fact,' she added, 'we have our foot in the stirrup, for we must start for the desert tomorrow morning.'"

Six years later, when Jane was sixty-seven, Sir Edwin Pears, who represented the London *Daily News* in Constantinople, managed to meet her through her banker. Sir Edwin saw her four times in all, and eventually took the liberty of asking her personal questions. He inquired as to her relationship with her husband's tribe. She told him that it was excellent, and related several anecdotes to prove it. Sir Edwin recorded one of the best:

"On one occasion, by mistake, the whole of her husband's tribe flocked into Damascus and took possession of her home, sleeping on the stairs, the landings, and anywhere they could lie down. She was the only woman in the house, and could not get into communication with her husband. I made some remark, which I forget, intimating that she must have been alarmed with the crowd of these wild fellows. She immediately retorted that she was greatly alarmed, but not, as I appeared to think, at anything which her husband's tribe would do. Her fear was that some of the many Turkish soldiers near her house would make some remark derogatory to her, in which case, she said, not a Turk in the neighborhood would have been left alive."

Of all the visitors Jane entertained during her twenty-six years as Medjuel's wife, the most fabulous, by far, was Sir Richard Burton, the quite incredible Burton of Arabia. He was Captain Burton when he arrived, fresh from four years in Brazil, to serve as the new English Consul in Damascus. He was a tall, powerful, bearded man, handsome and athletic. He was a great scholar, explorer, writer, and lover. He was a rebel, an iconoclast, a smasher of ikons. If Jane knew nine tongues, he knew more, including Jataki, an Afghan dialect about which he had penned a grammar.

The new English Consul, as Jane soon learned, had led an adventurous life. After being ejected from Oxford, he had served with the British Army in India. There he was nick-named White Nigger for his practice of disguising himself as a native and wandering about the bazaars. In 1853 he determined to visit the birthplace of the Prophet. After dying his skin, studying the intricate Mohammedan ritual, and having himself painfully circumcised, he became the first Englishman to survive the pilgrimage to Mecca. In Africa, though once badly wounded in the Somaliland, he went on to discover Lake Tanganyika and the sources of the Nile. In 1860 he took a covered wagon from Missouri to Utah to observe American polygamy at first hand. When he asked Brigham Young if he might become a member of the church, the old Mormon replied: "No, Captain, I think you have done that sort of thing before."

He was in constant revolt against authority. When English Intelligence asked for a report on life in Karachi, Burton sup-plied them with a detailed account of Indian sex perversion. When Queen Victoria ordered him to talk the African King of Dahomey out of the practice of human sacrifice, Burton in-formed her that he thought the customs of Dahomey no more revolting than those of England. When his wife begged him to write a nice book, Burton told her that he was preparing *The Scented Garden*, which dealt with "female circumcision" and "the Fellahs copulating with crocodiles."

Jane was intrigued with Burton. Night after night Jane and Medjuel entertained him in the villa, and Burton thought her quite "the cleverest woman" he had ever met. Since he was obsessed with sex, most of his questions dealt with the love life of Arabian women. He was, at the time, writing his classic translation of *The Arabian Nights*. In his Terminal Essay to the book, in which he discussed the erotic habits of all nationalities, an essay which was later expurgated, he used a considerable amount of material that Jane had given him. Such was their admiration for each other that one of Burton's biographers remarked that, had Jane "been thirty years younger, there might have been much between her and Richard Burton."

Three months after Burton's arrival in Damascus, his plump wife appeared on the scene with her English maid, her Saint Bernard, and her aggressive Catholicism. Isabel Burton was a snob. She was impressed by titles, and Jane had a title. Isabel took to Jane at once. Medjuel was another matter. Where her husband appreciated Medjuel for what he was, Isabel was repelled by his skin. When she saw Jane and Medjuel together, she shuddered.

"What was incomprehensible to me," wrote Isabel, "was how she could have given up all she had in England to live with that dirty little black—or nearly so—husband. I went to see her one day and when he opened the door to me I thought at first he was a native servant. I could understand her leaving a coarse, cruel husband, much older than herself, whom she never loved (every woman has not the strength of mind and the pride to stand by what she has done); I could understand her running away with Schwarzenberg; but the contact with that black skin I could not understand. Her sheik was dark—darker than a Persian—much darker than an Arab generally is."

It was partially through Isabel's intolerance that Burton lasted less than two years as English Consul in Damascus and that Jane was unhappily deprived of his friendship. Burton's appointment to Damascus was resented from the outset because of his desecration of Mecca. Isabel simply compounded the resentment. She, who had seen tears on her plaster Madonna, was determined to convert all of Damascus to Catholicism. An energetic and overwhelming woman, she pounced upon the Moslem poor and tried to bribe them into Catholicism with gifts of food. She nursed dying Arab children, then baptized them for Rome over the protests of their mothers. Once, showing titled English visitors through a mosque, she ordered a praying Moslem to move aside, since he was blocking the view of a tomb. When he refused, she hit him across the face with her riding-whip.

Meanwhile, Burton, attempting to halt corruption in Damascus, cracked down on influential financiers, involved himself in a Greek riot, and tried to purchase land for a colony of his wife's converts. Protests poured into the British Foreign Office in London, and overnight Burton was dismissed. He left Damascus at once. Shortly after, Isabel followed him.

If this was the last Jane was to see of Isabel Burton, it was not the last she was to hear of her. The following year—the Burtons, after a vacation in Iceland, had taken over the English Consulate at Trieste—Jane returned from a war in the Syrian desert to find herself declared dead.

She read her obituaries with amazement. The most sensational one, raking up the scandals of Jane's past, appeared in *La Revue Britannique*, published in Paris during March 1873, and was reprinted throughout Europe. "A noble lady, who had made a great use—or abuse—of marriage, has died recently," the obituary began. "Lady Ellenborough, some thirty years ago, left her first husband to run off with Count von Schwarzenberg. She retired to Italy where she married six consecutive times." The obituary went on to report that Jane had died a widow, since her husband, "a camel driver named Sheik Abdul," had preceded her to the grave.

With growing astonishment, Jane read on. The very next issue of *La Revue Britannique* carried a long letter from Trieste, a defense and eulogy written by Isabel Burton.

"I lived for two years as an intimate friend of Lady Ellenborough in Damascus, where my husband, Captain Burton, was Consul. Since she knew that, after her death, all sorts of falsehoods, painful to her family, would appear in the papers, she asked me to write her biography, and for an hour a day she dictated the good and the bad with equal frankness. I was pledged not to publish this until after her death and that of certain near relatives."

Then, after some inaccuracies of her own about Jane's marriage to Medjuel, Isabel Burton concluded:

The Real Lady Arabella Dudley

"*Bon sang ne peut mentir*—True blood will always tell. I never met a nobler heart, nor one more charitable to the poor. She fulfilled all the duties of a good Christian lady and an Englishwoman. All those who knew her in her last days will weep for her. She had but one fault in Europe (and who knows whether it was really her fault) but she made up for it in the East through fifteen years of virtue and repentance. She is departed. Be the world kind to her."

With more annoyance than anger, Jane wrote the press that she was very much alive and in the best of health. She firmly denied ever having dictated a single word, for any projected biography, to Isabel Burton. It was true, of course, that many people had wanted her to publish her story. When Sir Valentine Chirol had asked why she didn't set down her memoirs, she had replied: "I just couldn't. The list of my husbands and lovers would read like a naughty edition of the Almanach de Gotha." What had happened, most probably, in the case of Isabel Burton was that she had wanted to do a book about Jane. Since she knew Jane wouldn't co-operate, she made detailed notes after evenings spent conversing with her. The moment she thought Jane was dead, she attempted to establish her exclusive rights to the potential best-seller by announcing to the world that the facts had been dictated to her. Jane's resurrection intimidated Isabel into silence forever after.

Jane Digby el Mezrab survived her obituaries by eight full years. She became more and more a recluse, spending her time only with Medjuel and close friends, until at last she succumbed to dysentery in her Damascus bedroom during August of 1881. Medjuel watched her burial, in the Protestant plot of the Jewish Cemetery, from the saddle of her favorite white mare. The cross on her grave bore only two words in English: *Madame Digby*. And beneath, carved in Medjuel's own hand, a quotation from the Koran.

In the pages of Balzac, Lady Arabella Dudley continued her tumultous existence without rest. But Mme Digby had at last found peace.

V

The Real Dr. Jekyll and
Mr. Hyde

*"The day for them, the night for me; the grimy cynical
night that makes all cats grey, and all honesties of one
complexion. Shall a man not have half a life of his own?"*
W. E. HENLEY AND R. L. STEVENSON

On a dark winter night in 1885, in the bedroom of his house
at Bournemouth, Scotland, the feverish, ailing Robert
Louis Stevenson suddenly began to shout and scream in his
sleep. His wife, startled awake by what she called his "cries of
horror," hastily shook him from his nightmare.

Though in a cold sweat, Stevenson angrily reproved her.
"Why did you wake me? I was dreaming a fine bogey tale."

The bogey tale was *The Strange Case of Dr. Jekyll and Mr.
Hyde*.

For two days before, though bedridden, Stevenson, in a
desperate effort to supply his insistent publishers with a popular
shilling shocker or, as he called it, "crawler," had racked his
brain for the right story. The horrible dream provided the
story. "I dreamed," he recollected later, "the scene at the
window, and a scene afterwards split in two, in which Hyde,
pursued for some crime, took the powder and underwent the
change in the presence of his pursuers." He had been roused
from his nightmare, he told his wife, at the exact moment of
conceiving "the first transformation scene."

The dream was indeed a grotesque calculated to make one
scream in one's sleep. Mr. Hyde, wanted for murder, had just

obtained the mysterious drug from Dr. Lanyon. Then, as the "abnormal and misbegotten" Hyde mixed the powders in a glass, Dr. Lanyon witnessed the first transformation.

"He put the glass to his lips and drank at one gulp. A cry followed; he reeled, staggered, clutched at the table and held on, staring with injected eyes, gasping with open mouth; and as I looked there came, I thought, a change—he seemed to swell —his face became suddenly black and the features seemed to melt and alter—and the next moment I had sprung to my feet and leaped back against the wall, my arm raised to shield me from that prodigy, my mind submerged in terror.

" 'O God!' I screamed, and 'O God!' again and again; for there before my eyes—pale and shaken, and half fainting, and groping before him with his hands, like a man restored from death—there stood Henry Jekyll!"

Stevenson slept little that night. By daybreak he was propped up in his bed, thermometer in mouth, pencil in hand, furiously writing the first abortive draft of *The Strange Case of Dr. Jekyll and Mr. Hyde*. He was interrupted only once, by his doctor, to whom he cheerfully remarked: "I've got my shilling shocker!"

But, as he readily admitted, he had not dreamed it all. The basis for the story—the duality of man's nature—had long been in his mind. For more than twenty years he had sought the right means of telling the tale. "I had long been trying . . . to find a body, a vehicle, for that strong sense of man's double being which must at times come in upon and overwhelm the mind of every thinking creature." As he admitted, simply, to Andrew Lang: "I want to write about a fellow who was two fellows."

He had known all his life a fellow who was two fellows, and that was where the notion really took root. For the real Dr. Jekyll and Mr. Hyde had dwelt in Edinburgh only ninety-seven years before, and the memory of his presence and of his incredible double life had long haunted Stevenson. His name was William Brodie, and his activity between maturity and death exemplified for Stevenson the good and evil in every man. By day Brodie had been a prosperous businessman and respected city official; by night, a gambler and cheat who kept two mistresses and was the masked leader of a notorious gang.

Since childhood, Stevenson had been obsessed by Brodie. In his nursery stood a handmade chest of drawers that "creaked eerily in the night" and had been fashioned by the old two-faced gent who was once "a considerable House-Carpenter and Burgess of the City of Edinburgh." Stevenson's nanny, Alison Cunningham, that rigid Calvinistic daughter of a fisherman, had imbued him with a fear of the devil, hell, and sin—and had fascinated him with legends of Brodie and the double life. When Cummy took him walking through the Old Town, he could still see the narrow, alley-like sidestreet that was Brodie's Close, and the court and mansion, with its elaborate oaken door, where Brodie and his sister had entertained Scottish gentry. And more than once the young Stevenson peered in awed silence, in the museum of the Society of Antiquaries, at the dark lantern and twenty-five massive false keys used by Brodie during the depredations committed in his secret second life.

When Stevenson was fourteen, he showed a friend named Baildon a crude play he had written on the life of William Brodie. Not until he was twenty-five did Stevenson show the play to another person. In 1875 he was introduced to that energetic cripple, W. E. Henley, in the Old Infirmary of Edinburgh. Henley thought playwrighting might be the means to financial security. Four years later Stevenson gave Henley the early draft of his drama on Brodie, and their collaboration began.

The five-act play they created, *Deacon Brodie; or The Double Life*, after first being rejected by Henry Irving, was privately printed in 1880 and tried out in Bradford in 1882. Thereafter, it was produced in Aberdeen in 1883, in London in 1884, in Montreal and New York in 1887. Except for an inexplicable success in Chicago, it was a flat failure everywhere. When George Bernard Shaw saw it in London, he thought it childish and unbelievable, filled with "pasteboard scenes and characters," yet agreed that Brodie would be remembered long after other hit plays of the same period were forgotten.

The Real Dr. Jekyll and Mr. Hyde

In the play, Stevenson and Henley took little license with Deacon Brodie's life. Many scenes were based, with scant dramatization, on events that had happened. One in particular, when Brodie tries to rob his sister's fiancé just after entertaining him, was based on a similar occurrence in the life of the real Brodie. Stevenson, persisting in his determination to capture Brodie on paper, outlined the actual incident in an essay:

"Many stories are told of this redoubtable Edinburgh burglar, but the one I have in mind most vividly gives the key of all the rest. A friend of Brodie's . . . had told him of a projected visit to the country, and afterwards, detained by some affairs, put it off and stayed the night in town. The good man had lain some time awake; it was far on in the small hours by the Tron bell; when suddenly there came a creak, a jar, a faint light. Softly he clambered out of bed and up to a false window which looked upon another room, and there, by the glimmer of a thieves' lantern, was his good friend the Deacon in a mask.

"It is characteristic of the town and the town's manners that this little episode should have been quietly tided over. . . . But still, by the mind's eye, he may be seen, a man harassed below a mountain of duplicity, slinking from a magistrate's supper-room to a thieves' ken, and pickeering among the closes by the flicker of a dark lamp."

For Stevenson, this little factual essay was not enough. Nor was the play with Henley enough. In the play he had re-created the outer Brodie, but failed utterly to capture the dual nature of the inner man.

The essence of Brodie's inner struggle continued to fascinate Stevenson because he sensed, long before the appearance of Sigmund Freud and the publication of the word *schizophrenia*, that this conflict was deep in all men and universal. He knew because he found it in himself.

Stevenson had been raised in a restricted, religious Edinburgh household, dominated by a stern, though kindly father. His father, Thomas Stevenson, was a successful civil engineer who specialized in constructing lighthouses. He expected his son to follow in his footsteps. When the imaginative, consumptive boy refused, insisting that he wanted to be a writer, his father was appalled. A compromise on profession was reached. Young Stevenson agreed to study for the bar. But he was in constant revolt. He longed, in a lesser way, to emulate Deacon Brodie. He knew that within him were stirring desires that had nothing to do with the society in which he lived and the man he was supposed to become. He wanted to satisfy these desires, and to some extent he did.

He took to frequenting the disreputable Old Town of Edinburgh at night, just as Brodie had done. In rebellion against restriction, in an effort to free the repressions of his sinful and evil side, he regularly visited low taverns and brothels, consorted with rough seamen, thieves, and whores. He was, a friend remarked, "a man beset with fleshly frailties." He himself confessed: "I am by nature what they call a very bad person and very greedy of sensation." The street women, who nicknamed him Velvet Coat, regarded him as somewhat of a lovable oddity. "The women were most kind and gentle to me," he said. He had an affair with a blacksmith's daughter, and it was thought that this adventure produced an illegitimate child.

After this phase he felt that Mr. Hyde had been safely imprisoned. But now the revolt took another form. There was a terrible scene with his father when he abandoned law for full-time authorship. In France he fell in love with a dumpy, imaginative American woman, Fanny Osbourne, who was married, had two children, and was ten years his senior. By steerage he followed her to San Francisco, where she obtained a divorce. He married her and returned to Edinburgh to face it out with his parents.

But they liked Fanny, and gave Stevenson the house on the sea at Bournemouth and five hundred pounds toward furniture. Stevenson had won, and now he better understood the nature of the enemy inside. He was more determined than ever to exorcise Mr. Hyde.

For three years, coughing and hemorrhaging constantly, he

suffered the life of "a beastly householder" at Skerryvore in Bournemouth. Even as he wrote *Travels with a Donkey* and *Treasure Island*, neither of which was an immediate financial success, he brooded over Brodie.

In France, some years before, he had turned from fact to fiction in an effort to develop his thoughts on the double life. He had written a short story called "The Travelling Companion" about a dual personality. The editor he sent it to rejected it, "on the plea," said Stevenson, "that it was a work of genius and indecent, and which I burned the other day on the ground that it was not a work of genius." Now, in Scotland, he tackled the theme again in a short story called "Markheim." This was more successful, but still not satisfactory.

Meanwhile, the pressures of daily existence mounted. He was dunned for nonpayment of bills. He was anxious to remain independent of his father. He was worried about the support and good opinion of his wife and stepson. And he was more and more often ill. He was a frail man, five feet ten and slender. He smoked incessantly in order to work, and took opium in order to sleep. And he was bitterly discouraged.

"I had written little books and little essays and short stories, and had got patted on the back and paid for them—though not enough to live upon. I had quite a reputation. I was the successful man. I passed my days in toil, the futility of which would sometimes make my cheek to burn, that I should spend a man's energy upon this business, and yet could not earn a livelihood."

His publishers, Longmans, suggested that he try a potboiler, an easy, popular horror story, to rescue himself from financial difficulty. "For two days I went about racking my brains for a plot of any sort," he said, "and on the second night I dreamed . . ."

He had never worked so hard before, and never would again. The story poured out in one great, fantastic cascade of words, and yet would be, as his friend Henry James noted, "a masterpiece of concision." He wrote it fast because he had it all. He had William Brodie and the double life. And the dream had given him the horrifying mechanics by which he might convert the theme and character into literature.

In three days the feverish task was done. Stevenson had completed thirty thousand words of *Dr. Jekyll and Mr. Hyde.* He came downstairs with the manuscript and told his wife and his stepson, Lloyd Osbourne, that he was ready to read it aloud to them. While they sat listening, Stevenson, full of animation and gestures, read the tale in his deep, resonant voice. Lloyd recalled that he listened "spellbound." Fanny sat in phlegmatic silence. Presently the reading was done. Stevenson turned to his wife, waited for praise. There was none.

Gently, but firmly, Fanny told Stevenson what she thought. She thought he had missed the entire point. He had omitted the allegory, and instead of a masterpiece he had achieved only a superficial "crawler." As in his play on Deacon Brodie, he had sacrificed depth and insight for "magnificent sensationalism." She insisted that he had lost the allegory "probably from haste and the compelling influence of the dream."

His stepson, Lloyd, never forgot what happened next. Stevenson, his sensitivity outraged, shook with anger as he upbraided his wife. There followed, we are told, a "painful scene." Stevenson stormed out of the room. A short time later he returned, considerably calmed. He still had the manuscript in hand. He went to his wife. "You are right," he said. "I have absolutely missed the allegory, which, after all, is the whole point of it—the very essence of it." And then, without another word, he walked to the fireplace and threw the manuscript into the blaze. Fanny leaped to her feet, begging him to rescue the story before he wasted much that might be salvaged. But he refused. "It was all wrong," he said. "In trying to save some of it, I should have got hopelessly off the track. The only way was to put temptation beyond my reach."

He returned to his bed—but with pencil and fresh paper. His right lung was worse, and his fever rose. He admitted no one, unless he rang his copper bell. He wrote for three days more, almost without sleep, and in the end he had a completely new thirty-thousand-word version of *The Strange Case of Dr. Jekyll and Mr. Hyde*. "The amount of work this involved was appalling," Fanny recalled. "That an invalid in my husband's condition of health should have been able to perform the manual labor alone of putting sixty thousand words on paper in six days seems incredible."

This time Stevenson knew that the story was right. And Fanny agreed. After a few minor revisions, he shipped it off to Longmans in London. His fever went down; his good spirits revived. He had captured the image of Deacon William Brodie at last.

Stevenson's fictionization of the double life is told through the person of Mr. Utterson, friend and attorney to the kindly Dr. Henry Jekyll. Utterson is mystified by Dr. Jekyll's will, which provides that, in case of death, his fortune be left to an Edward Hyde. Utterson is disturbed because he has heard that Hyde is a loathsome person who once trampled down a small child. He is even more disturbed when he meets the pale, dwarfish, hissing Hyde and finds him a man with "Satan's signature" upon his face. Utterson is certain that Dr. Jekyll is being blackmailed by Mr. Hyde.

When Mr. Hyde wantonly murders a member of Parliament, Utterson and the police go to Dr. Jekyll at once. Jekyll shows them a note from Hyde, in which Hyde explains that he has escaped. Later, when Dr. Jekyll locks himself in his laboratory for a week, communicating with his servants only through notes that request a special drug, Utterson becomes convinced that the man locked in the laboratory is not Dr. Jekyll but the much-sought Mr. Hyde. The laboratory is broken into. And there, indeed, is Mr. Hyde—dead by suicide.

Utterson finds no trace of Dr. Jekyll, but finds two letters. In one, the late Dr. Lanyon, a friend of Jekyll's, reveals how Mr. Hyde came to him one night to claim a drug for Dr. Jekyll

—and then, in Lanyon's presence, mixing a white powder into a red liquid, transformed himself into Dr. Jekyll. The other letter, from Dr. Jekyll, explains the entire mystery.

Dr. Jekyll relates that he had long been troubled and curious about two sides to his nature—one industrious and honorable, the other desiring gaiety and the pleasures of the flesh. Dr. Jekyll reasoned that if he possessed two personalities, he might also possess two physical beings that represented those personalities. Eventually he concocted a chemical mixture which transformed him at will into his evil being, whom he named Edward Hyde. The first time he saw Hyde in the mirror, he confesses, "When I looked upon that ugly idol in the glass, I was conscious of no repugnance, rather of a leap of welcome. This, too, was myself."

Thus, as he wished, Dr. Jekyll lived two lives and satisfied both sides of his personality. Then, one morning Dr. Jekyll woke to a shock of horror—"My eye fell upon my hand. . . . It was the hand of Edward Hyde." Frightened by the involuntary change, Dr. Jekyll determined to repress forever the "secret pleasures" of Hyde for the life of "the elderly and discontented doctor." But the desire to again be Hyde would not so easily be stilled. As Mr. Hyde once more, Dr. Jekyll committed the senseless murder. He was able to change back to Dr. Jekyll before Utterson and the police arrived.

One day, sunning himself on a bench in Regent's Park, Dr. Jekyll was horrified to find himself involuntarily going through the convulsions that turned him into the physical Mr. Hyde. He knew he could not reach his laboratory, since Hyde was wanted for murder. He obtained the powders through Dr. Lanyon and reached his room as Dr. Jekyll only moments before he became Mr. Hyde again. He knew then that the evil in him had taken over. When he had used up his drug, he could not leave his room. And before Utterson and the police entered, he killed himself.

The Strange Case of Dr. Jekyll and Mr. Hyde, a slender 149-page book, was published by Longmans in January of 1886 at

The Real Dr. Jekyll and Mr. Hyde

one shilling. It created no stir until *The Times* of London praised it. Then, overnight, it became a best-seller. Where *Treasure Island* had sold only 5,600 copies, *Dr. Jekyll and Mr. Hyde* sold 40,000 copies in six months.

Reviewers leaped on the bandwagon. "It is many years," wrote *The Academy*, "since English fiction has been enriched by any work at once so weirdly imaginative in conception and so faultlessly ingenious in construction." When a clergyman in St. Paul's used the book for his Sunday sermon, half the Church of England followed suit.

What made the story popular then, and has kept it alive in the many years since, was the "allegory" that Fanny Stevenson insisted be written into the book. "Stevenson said something eternally true that had never been said in fiction quite so explicitly or quite so nearly convincingly before," Moray McLaren has stated. "In one short novel of the thriller kind he anticipated a large part of the basis of modern psychology." G. K. Chesterton felt that "the real stab of the story is not in the discovery that the one man is two men, but in the discovery that the two men are one man."

For this immortality, Deacon William Brodie never received direct acknowledgment from Stevenson. The author always credited the inspiration for Jekyll and Hyde to his Brownies, the little people who came to him in his sleep. He even blamed the Brownies for those things in the story that the reviewers didn't like. "For, the business of the powders," he wrote, "which so many have censured, is, I am relieved to say, not mine at all, but the Brownies'." But William Roughead, the great Scottish crime authority, firmly held that Stevenson "was more indebted to a Brodie than to a Brownie."

The entire locale of the story, as G. K. Chesterton has pointed out, while labeled London, is plainly Deacon Brodie's Edinburgh, just as the characters are Scotchmen not Englishmen. Where Mr. Hyde went upon his depraved errands attired in plain black, Brodie always changed from white coat and breeches into old-fashioned black before his raids. Where Mr.

Hyde was once discovered in his laboratory disguised by a mask, Brodie often employed crepe masks in his double life. Where, after the murder, "Hyde had a song upon his lips as he compounded the draught," Brodie had a song upon his lips on the eve of his greatest crime. Where Dr. Jekyll and Mr. Hyde maintained a house in London and an apartment in Soho, Deacon Brodie maintained three separate dwellings for his two selves.

The similarities of detail between the fictional Dr. Jekyll and Mr. Hyde and the actual William Brodie are many, but of minor import beside the one major parallel. Dr. Jekyll discovered "that man is not truly one, but truly two," and he discovered it, for the most, from Deacon Brodie.

"It was Deacon Brodie who fathered Dr. Jekyll," John Hampden has stated in an introduction to the novel. Many of Stevenson's personal friends said as much in print, earlier. One old friend, Mrs. E. Blantyre Simpson, was positive that "Deacon Brodie . . . suggested to Tusitala [Stevenson's Samoan name] the two-sidedness of human character 'commingled out of good and evil,' the smug front to the world, the villain behind the mask." William Roughead concurred that "there can be little doubt that Stevenson's subconscious was influenced by his old acquaintance with Deacon Brodie . . . that admirable double dealer, whose character supplies so striking an example of the individuality of man's nature and the alternation of good and evil."

The original Dr. Jekyll and Mr. Hyde was the first of eleven children born, according to the Edinburgh records, to "Francis Brodie, wright, burgess, and Cecil Grant, his spouse." The date was September 28, 1741—just two years after Hume wrote his *Treatise on Human Nature*—and the infant boy was named William Brodie.

Of the eleven children produced by the Brodies, William was one of three who survived to maturity. His father was a man of substance. He was perhaps the most prosperous cabinetmaker and wright or carpenter in all Edinburgh. He was twice elected to the Town Council. His home was "a handsome and commodious dwelling" in the Lawnmarket. It was two-storied, well furnished, and the living-room ceiling was decorated with a mural of the Three Wise Men. Francis Brodie was sufficiently successful to have the sidestreet on which his house and court were located named after him: it was called Brodie's Close.

We know little of William Brodie's early years. It would appear that he was well educated, for he wrote English in a fair hand, though he was a poor speller, and had considerable knowledge of French. Too, he seems to have had background in music and literature. Before his majority, he went to work in his father's cabinet shops as an apprentice, and eventually became his father's partner. From his handiwork that has survived, it is evident that he was a talented wright and cabinetmaker.

William Brodie rose rapidly. By the time he was twenty-two he had become a Burgess, or freeman, of Edinburgh, as well as a Guild Brother. By 1781, when he was forty, he was Deacon of the Incorporation of Wrights. The title Deacon had no religious significance, but was awarded him as head of his trade union. As Deacon William Brodie, he was elected to the Town Council, the governing-body of Edinburgh, to succeed his father. With the exception of one year, he served on the Council until his death seven years later.

Because of his standing in Edinburgh, Brodie was admitted, at the age of thirty-four, to the town's leading social organization. This was the very exclusive Cape Club, which met regularly in a reputable coffeehouse called James Mann's Tavern. Each new member was assigned, amid general hilarity, a fictitious title. Brodie became Sir Lluyd. Among Brodie's companions in the Club was a fellow Scot, Sir Henry Raeburn, a goldsmith turned portrait-painter, who married wealth in the third year of Brodie's membership and then went to Italy to work at his canvases. Through his contacts in the Club, Brodie may very well have met Dr. Samuel Johnson, who, attired in gray wig and brown suit, arrived in Edinburgh during 1773 for a four-day visit with James Boswell. Dr. Johnson, unhappily, found Deacon Brodie's Edinburgh "very mean" and somewhat resembling "the old part of Birmingham."

Among Deacon Brodie's more notable friends and good companions was certainly Robert Burns, the plowboy poet, who had been brought to Edinburgh in the summer of 1786 to bask in the popularity of his first book of verse. The author of "Auld Lang Syne," lionized but still poor, shared quarters with a lawyer's apprentice in the Lawnmarket, just across from Brodie.

In those years of outward prosperity Deacon William Brodie cut quite a figure as a Scotch gentleman. He was a short man—five feet four—but a natty dresser, usually affecting spotless white coat, vest, and breeches. His hair was dark, his sideburns fashionably long, his brow high and noble, his brown eyes bright and amused, and his manner of speech deliberate and droll. A man of rare humor, much charm and wit, he was beloved throughout the community. His habits were above reproach.

When the shops of the town closed at eight o'clock, most tradesmen joined the gentry in the respectable convivialities of the better taverns in the Old Town. But, except for less and less frequent excursions with fellow members of the aristocratic Cape Club, Deacon Brodie rarely joined his brethren over the flowing bowl. It was his custom, upon completion of the day's labors, to repair to his home and there partake of a sober supper with his elderly father and his unmarried sister, Jean. At meal's end, as far as his customers, his gentlemen friends, his colleagues on the Town Council, and his family knew, the Deacon called it a day.

They did not know, of course, that only one Deacon had called it a day. The other Deacon Brodie lived by night. "There's something in hypocrisy after all," Henley and Stevenson made their Deacon muse as he prepared to embark through a bedroom window upon his second and secret life. "If we were as good as we seem, what would the world be? The city has its vizard on, and we—at night we are our naked selves. Trysts are keeping, bottles cracking, knives are stripping; and here is Deacon Brodie flaming forth the man of men he is! . . . The day for them, the night for me; the grimy cynical night that makes all cats grey, and all honesties of one complexion. Shall a man not have *half* a life of his own?—not eight hours out of twenty-four? . . . Only the stars to see me! I'm a man once more till morning."

For twenty years before his death Deacon William Brodie led a precarious double life. The model of gentility in the daytime, the Deacon became transformed into gambler, drunkard, and thief with the coming of night. For two decades he led two separate lives, and they never crossed and were never exposed until the very end. Though his mistresses and colleagues in dissipation and crime knew his real identity and true station, his relatives, friends, and business associates remained entirely innocent of his second self.

Edinburgh society knew William Brodie for a determined bachelor. He had no wife, wished none; he had no sweethearts and ruffled no petticoats. But in the low taverns of the town, where no gentleman ever entered, Brodie was known for quite a ladies' man. The fact is—he secretly kept two mistresses, in two households, and they bore him five children in thirteen years. And not until his private life was made public did one mistress know that the other existed.

Unfortunately, we know little of these women, and few details of the Deacon's relationship with them. Their names were Anne Grant and Jean Watt, and of the two, Brodie met Anne Grant first and loved her most. She was the only woman to whom he wrote after he fled to Europe, and it was this letter that helped cost him his life. He met Anne when he was in his early thirties. He set her up in an apartment in Cant's Close. He had three children by her, two girls and a boy. When he was in trouble, it was Anne and these children he was most concerned about. His eldest daughter by Anne was his favorite, and the only one of his brood to visit him before his death. "My eldest daughter Cecill," he wrote from abroad, "should be put apprentice to the milliner or mantua-making business; but I wish she could learn a little writing and arithmetic first. I wish to God some of my friends would take some charge of Cecill; she is a fine, sensible girl, considering the little opportunity she has had for improvement."

Jean Watt was a later acquisition. Brodie obtained upstairs rooms for her in Libberton's Wynd, a short walk from his own home. She gave him two boys. One, who was seven at the time of Brodie's death, the Deacon named Francis Brodie after his father. We have some evidence that mistress Jean was a hellion. "What has become of Jean Watt?" Brodie inquired from Amsterdam. "She is a devil." But, devil or no, it was Jean who came forward during Brodie's time of trial to commit perjury in an effort to save his neck.

Had these mistresses been the extent of Deacon Brodie's second life, he would surely have lived to a fine old age. But they were mere diversions. The Deacon's real nightly addictions were gambling and sport. With regularity he indulged his passion for cards and dice in a low pub owned by James Clark in that happily named thoroughfare, the Fleshmarket Close. Here, consorting with sharpers, ex-convicts, tough laborers, the well-mannered Deacon lost vast sums of money. He drank heavily, he brawled, and he eventually sank so low as to employ loaded dice in desperate efforts to recoup his losses.

Another favored pastime of the Deacon's also cost him dearly in cash. He was fascinated by the old Roman sport of cockfighting. A century before, cockfighting had been a noble amusement, often patronized by members of the royal house. Hens who bred winners were treated as bluebloods; champion roosters were as renowned as Derby favorites. But the honorable sport had, by Brodie's time, fallen upon evil days. Roosters were no longer sent into the pits to fight naturally, with their own spurs, until one fell wounded or exhausted. Cockfights in Edinburgh and London were now an accommodation for sadists and gamblers. The beaks of the roosters were filed razor-sharp, and artificial steel spurs were fastened to the fowl.

However, it is evident that Brodie looked upon the "art of

cocking" as something more than a mere opportunity to wager. He purchased the best-bred gamecocks, kept them in a pen of his wood yard, and carefully trained them. He blunted their spurs with "hots"—padded rolls of leather—when they worked out, and lovingly stowed them in straw baskets when they were exhausted. He trained them for six weeks each, and then fasted them three days before throwing them into the combat pit at Michael Henderson's.

Henderson was a stabler in the Grassmarket who owned the most popular cockpit in Edinburgh. He was undoubtedly of shady character, yet apparently a decent sort and a family man, and Brodie trusted him completely. Even in his darkest hour, when he was in flight from the law, Brodie found time to write Henderson the query of the real *aficionado:* "Write me how the main went; how you came on in it; if my black cock fought and gained, etc., etc." Plainly, Brodie was a regular spectator at Henderson's cockpits, and we know that in his wagering he was a consistent loser.

Eventually, it is thought, his secret losses became so great, and the burden of supporting three households—his father's and his two mistresses'—so difficult, that he turned his attentions to another spare-time source of revenue. Certainly at an early period he decided to become a thief. This was not an occupation to enter into lightly. Robbery was in those days a crime punishable by death. Yet the Deacon felt himself sufficiently equipped for the new profession. His second life was unknown to the city at large. His official position on the Town Council and his reputation for honesty and integrity would keep him beyond the slightest suspicion. As part of his daytime profession, he entered the best shops to repair them, and could thus study their layouts. He fixed locks and bolts—took them apart and put them together.

Best of all, he was in a position to make skeleton keys. Edinburgh was a trusting city, with little crime, and only a Sheriff and creaking police force of 120 Town Guardsmen to maintain order. The good merchants of the city, in keeping with time-honored custom, hung the keys to their shops on the inside of their entrance doors or in the hallways, removing them at closing-time. On his business visits, Brodie realized, it would be a simple matter to take a hasty impression of these keys when the proprietors were otherwise occupied. And this is exactly what Brodie proceeded to do, employing a small black box filled with putty for his purposes.

But the question—one that has bothered the Deacon's adherents in the almost two centuries since his real criminal career began—still remains: was money his sole motive?

He had gambled away a fortune. But though his coffers were drained, they were never emptied. He had, before his arrest, the complete ownership of his house, his considerable business, and eighteen hundred pounds in cash assets. "He was far above the reach of want," the public prosecutor later observed. "He had a lawful employment, which might have enabled him to hold his station in society, with respectability and credit; he has been more than once officially at the head of his profession, and was a member of the City Council." Money may have been a consideration, but it was not the main one.

The court blamed his fall on "bad company." More likely, though, it was his dominant second nature, bored by conservatism and respectability, that admired and wished to emulate the excitement of those who lived by their wits. "His crimes appear to be rather the result of infatuation than depravity," the *Edinburgh Evening Courant* stated after his death. "He seemed to be more attracted by the dexterity of thieving than the profit arising from it. To excel in the performance of some paltry legerdemain or sleight-of-hand tricks, to be able to converse in the cant or flash language of thieves, or to chant with spirit a song from *The Beggar's Opera* was to him the highest ambition."

Brodie had many times attended the performances of John Gay's *The Beggar's Opera* at the Old Theatre Royal. He knew the songs by heart. He never failed to delight in the comic satire of the dashing highwayman, Captain Macheath, who owned a gang of thieves and mistresses, and was twice jailed, yet released through the clamor of the masses who adored him. Brodie constantly saw himself as the heroic highwayman—with two loves, as Macheath had, and a gang of thieves in a tavern, as Macheath had, and a life spiced with adventure, as Macheath had.

But perhaps even Macheath isn't explanation enough. Perhaps it was Stevenson who best understood Brodie's descent into crime by understanding "the thorough and primitive duality of man":

"At that time my virtue slumbered; my evil, kept awake by ambition, was alert and swift to seize the occasion; and the thing that was projected was Edward Hyde. . . . Men have before hired braves to transact their crimes, while their own person and reputation sat under shelter. I was the first that ever did so for his pleasures. I was the first that could thus plod in the public eye with a load of genial respectability, and in a moment, like a schoolboy, strip off these lendings and spring headlong into the sea of liberty. But for me, in my impenetrable mantle, the safety was complete. Think of it—I did not even exist! Let me but escape into my laboratory door, give me but a second or two to mix and swallow the draught that I had always standing ready; and whatever he had done, Edward Hyde would pass away like the stain of breath upon a mirror; and there in his stead, quietly at home . . . would be Henry Jekyll."

One day in August of 1768—people were talking about the Redcoats in the distant colonial city of Boston—Deacon William Brodie, master carpenter, was summoned to make a repair in the banking-house of Johnston and Smith. For the first time the black putty case was opened and impressed against the key in the hallway. Several nights later, changing from his white business suit to an all-black suit, and with a black crepe mask in one pocket and a false key in the other, Brodie returned to the banking-house. Swiftly he emptied the drawers of eight hundred pounds sterling and escaped.

It was an auspicious beginning. And thus he worked alone, at nights, whenever the mood was upon him, for eighteen years. We have no clear record of how many shops he rifled and how many private homes he broke into. The Deacon was a poor historian. It was not until he worked with accomplices that better memories served us.

There were bad moments, of course. There was the occasion, mentioned by Stevenson, when Brodie attempted to violate the home of a magistrate friend whom he mistakenly thought to be out of town. Brodie was masked, but, nevertheless, the friend recognized him. The friend could not believe his eyes. And this saved Brodie's neck.

On another occasion, a similar inability of a victim to believe her sight and senses protected Brodie from being exposed. On a Sunday, when he was certain she would be in church, Brodie entered the dwelling of an elderly lady acquaintance in order to relieve her of the burdens of excessive wealth. Fully masked, he slipped into her bedroom—only to find himself face to face with her. The old lady, having felt somewhat indisposed, had decided to forgo the kirk for the pleasures of her rocker and the Good Book. Now she stared up at the disguised intruder with disbelief and momentary paralysis. Brodie decided to brazen it out. He strode to the table beside her, calmly picked up the keys to her bureau, opened the drawer, removed a considerable number of pound notes, closed and locked the drawer, returned the key to the table, bowed gallantly, and retired. The moment he was gone, the old lady found her voice. "Surely that was Deacon Brodie!" she gasped. The idea was too improbable to repeat. And so she kept her silence; and the Deacon kept her cash.

However, such close calls, while they gave a degree of piquancy to his excursions, also gave the Deacon pause. He realized the need for a partner. Or partners. Collaboration offered the possibilities of more protection, as well as opportunities for expansion. We don't know the exact date when this thought entered Brodie's head. We know only that it occurred some time after his father had died.

Francis Brodie, secure in the knowledge that his name and estate were in good hands, blissfully unaware that his male heir was not one person but two, had gone to his reward on June 1 of 1782. According to the record, he "died of the Palsy at his own house in Edinburgh, at 5 o'clock afternoon, in the 74th year of his age." His death made William Brodie independently wealthy. There were two sisters, of course. One, Jean, the spinster, continued to live in the great house and attend its affairs. The other, Jacobina, had married a local upholsterer named Matthew Sheriff. Since both women were undemanding, and trusted their brother's integrity completely, Brodie was fairly well in control of his inheritance. This included the house, the cabinet business, four apartment buildings, a great deal of land property, and ten thousand pounds in cash.

Though Brodie, rolling dice at Clark's and betting on the cocks at Henderson's, made severe inroads on these holdings, his business prospered and his situation was secure. Nevertheless, he continued to dream of a gang of cutthroats under his command. But it was not until he met, over the grog pots and dicing-tables at Michael Henderson's, the persons of George Smith, Andrew Ainslie, and John Brown, that the Deacon's dream began to take on the look of reality.

The three were ruffians of varied shade, though all black. George Smith, a mild man with a concave face and a deep religious streak, was a wandering peddler. He had once been a locksmith and possessed no criminal record, but was not above earning a dishonest pound. He arrived in Edinburgh during the summer of 1786 with a horse-drawn cart. He put up at Henderson's inn and set out to hawk his wares. Suddenly he fell ill, sent for his wife to care for him, and was forced to dispose of his possessions to pay his board.

While recuperating, Smith played at dice and cards, for small stakes, with Andrew Ainslie and John Brown. Ainslie was a stolid, not too bright ex-shoemaker, who gambled for his livelihood. John Brown, with whom he roomed, was more promising. He was tough, hot-tempered, and shrewd. Two years before, he had been tried at Old Bailey for stealing twenty guineas and had been sentenced to seven years' exile in Australia. He had escaped to Edinburgh and was momentarily between jobs.

A mutual friend named Graham introduced Deacon Brodie to George Smith, the convalescent. Later, through Smith, the Deacon's social circle was enriched by the acquaintance of Ainslie and Brown. But it was Smith whom the Deacon cultivated first. The peddler had all the qualifications for partnership—an even disposition, a complete lack of cash, and, foremost, a good deal of practical experience with locks. As Smith remembered it later, "Brodie, in the course of conversation, suggested to the declarant that several things could be done in this place, if prudently managed, to great advantage, and proposed to the declarant that they should lay their heads together for that purpose."

That they laid their heads together, and in full accord, was soon evident. In October 1786 Brodie and Smith entered the shop of James Wemyss, Goldsmith, and removed twenty-six gold rings, forty-six silver knee buckles, and a variety of earrings and crosses. A month later the partners visited Davidson M'Kain Hardware shop. Smith used a false key and iron crow to open the door, while Brodie stood watch outside. After a half-hour Smith emerged with a collection of gold watches, rings, pins, and purses. Two weeks after, the collaborators returned to the same hardware store, but fled when they found it occupied. Early in December they forced their way into the business place of John Law, Tobacconist, located a can containing money, and departed twelve pounds the richer.

As the Christmas holiday approached, Brodie began to feel more expansive. He had recently repaired the door of a jewelry shop in Bridge Street. "It'll make a very proper shop for breaking into," he told Smith. On the night set for the robbery

Brodie, winning heavily at cards in Clark's tavern, was loath to leave. Irked, Smith went himself to pay a Yuletide call on John and Andrew Bruce, Jewelers. He stuffed an assortment of watches and trinkets into two stockings, and refused to divide the loot with Brodie. Though the take was worth 350 pounds, Smith was forced to dispose of it for 105 pounds to a fence in Chesterfield, one John Tasker, who had been banished from Scotland for his activities. Smith asked the good Deacon to keep the money for him, and the Deacon kept most of it permanently. For, sad to report, Smith was an abominable card-player, and Brodie "gained a great part of it at play."

By now Edinburgh was in an uproar of fear and discontent over the series of mysterious night robberies. Brodie thought it would be wise if Smith, a transient, gave some show of permanency in the community and also established some explanation for his income. Toward this end, Smith and his wife leased a house in Cowgate and opened a small grocery shop as a cover. Then, at Brodie's suggestion, the pair decided to lie low for eight months until the fretting community fell calm.

In August of 1787 the partners were back in circulation, but with an addition. Andrew Ainslie was added to the combine. Inspired by Smith's recently acquired knowledge of the grocer's trade, Brodie cast a covetous glance at the shop of John Carnegie, Grocer. While Brodie stood lookout, Smith and Ainslie filled two sacks with 350 pounds of black tea, an expensive item, but were forced to abandon one heavy sack in their flight.

Two months later the gang was at full strength. The Deacon had his Judas, the surly, experienced John Brown. Encouraged, Brodie suggested a theft that had style. Once, in pursuit of learning, he had visited the University of Edinburgh and been impressed by the historic silver mace in the college library. "We must have it," he told his colleagues. Ainslie was sent to scout it, and found the mace still in the library. On October 29, 1787, the four of them, according to Smith's later recollection, "went to the College of Edinburgh about one o'clock in the morning. Having got access at the under gate, they opened the under door leading to the Library with a false key, which broke in the lock, and thereafter they broke open the door of the Library with an iron crow, and carried away the College mace."

Public reaction to this outrage—and certainly none was more indignant than the good Deacon—was loud and long. A small reward was offered, but to no avail. The mace was in the hands of the distant fence, John Tasker, and it was never recovered.

Another Christmas was approaching, and the Deacon determined to celebrate it by obtaining gifts for his men and himself. A shoemaker's store was visited and ten pairs of boots and twenty pairs of men's shoes were removed. Then, the day before Christmas, Brown was sent to have a drink with one John Tapp, who dispensed general merchandise. While Brown and Tapp bent their elbows in the shop below, the Deacon, Smith, and Ainslie, using a key fashioned after a putty impression, entered Tapp's residence above. They hastily removed "eighteen guinea notes, and a twenty shilling one, a silver watch, some rings, and a miniature picture of a gentleman belonging to Tapp's wife." Curiously, Mrs. Tapp made no public mention of missing the "picture of a gentleman." The gang forthwith shipped their loot to Chesterfield, and a merry Christmas was had by all except Mr. Tapp.

To begin the New Year right, Brodie suggested bigger game. All hands agreed. Brodie selected, for the next target, Inglis, Horner and Company, Silk Merchants, since "the goods there was very rich and valuable, and a small bulk of them carried off would amount to a large sum." With little difficulty, the quartet broke into the silk shop and made off with—according to the enraged proprietors—"a considerable quantity of black lutestrings, black armozeens, black florentines, and rasdimore silks. All of the silks were rolled on pins." Except for some white satin and ten yards of lead-colored silk which John Brown held out and "gave to a girl, an acquaintance of his of the name of Johnston," the rest of the take, estimated at five hundred pounds' value, was packed into two trunks to await shipment to Mr. Tasker.

Until this raid the community had been vocal and vigilant, but had made no serious financial effort toward stopping the thefts. But Inglis and Horner refused to take the robbery lying down. They petitioned Whitehall in London for help, and Whitehall co-operated. The Crown immediately advertised that a reward of a hundred pounds and "his Majesty's most gracious pardon is hereby offered to an accomplice, if there was more than one concerned, who shall, within six months from this date, give such information to William Scott, procurator-fiscal for the shire of Edinburgh, as shall be the means of apprehending and securing all or any of the persons guilty of or accessory to the said crime."

This offer was published regularly during the next months, and, as we shall see, it contributed greatly to ending William Brodie's double life. A week after the Inglis, Horner and Company robbery, however, another event occurred to threaten Brodie's double life. He was, as usual, indulging in his favorite after-dinner indoor sport at Clark's when a master chimney-sweep named John Hamilton asked to join the dice game. In short order Brodie and company had separated Mr. Hamilton from six guineas, whereupon Mr. Hamilton snatched up the dice and discovered that they were, in his own words, "loaded, or false dice, filled at one end or corner with lead."

Mr. Hamilton lodged immediate charges against Brodie with the Sheriff. Brodie replied that the dice belonged to the house, and that, had they been loaded, Hamilton would not have played at all, since Hamilton "was a noted adept in the science of gambling, and it was not very credible that he would have allowed himself to be imposed upon in the manner he had alleged."

This was a bad moment for Brodie, but short-lived. The Sheriff had the choice of a chimneysweep's word or the word of an honored member of the Town Council. The case was thrown out—and not too soon, it would seem. For on February 4, 1788, Brodie was summoned to jury duty, and was able to sit in the Justiciary Court with his reputation unblemished. The case Brodie was called upon to help judge involved the murder of a ferryman by an Excise officer and a soldier. The ferryman, caught loading illegal stills, had resisted, and been ordered shot by the Excise man. Brodie and his fellow jurors voted to acquit the Excise man and the soldier.

The trial, beyond giving Brodie a much needed rest, had another beneficial effect. Watching the Excise man in court, listening to the constant talk of tax-collections and tax funds, helped turn Brodie's reveries to the biggest prize of all.

In the Henley and Stevenson drama, it was Brown who was made to suggest the robbing of the General Excise Office for Scotland, and it was Brodie who objected, saying: " 'Tis too big and too dangerous. I shirk King George; he has a fat pocket, but he has a long arm." But in fact it was Brodie who really conceived the big Excise Office raid, who planned it down to the last detail, and who helped direct it to its miserable conclusion.

The General Excise Office for Scotland was an old mansion converted into a government building, fenced in by a low wall and steel railing. The building looked out on Chessel's Court, a large yard entered by an arch from High Street. Daily, to the counting-rooms of the General Excise were brought hundreds of pounds collected in taxes throughout Scotland.

Deacon Brodie gave four weeks to preparing for the assault. Several times in years past he had visited the Excise Office with a friend named Corbett, who lived outside Edinburgh. Now, accompanied by George Smith and the ever present putty box, Brodie visited the Excise on the pretext of inquiring for his friend Corbett. While Brodie engaged the cashier in conversation, Smith quickly applied the putty to the large key hanging behind the outer entrance door.

Returning to Smith's quarters, Brodie drew a careful map of the Excise Office interior, which was memorized by all hands.

Smith, working from his putty impression, filed down a false key. Shortly after, during an early evening Smith and Brown risked putting the key to test. It easily opened the outer Excise door, but an inner door to the cashier's cubicle was found closed. It was decided that when the moment came this second door would have to be forced. Smith suggested that a colter or cutter of a plow might do the job. Brown and Ainslie promptly obliged by borrowing a colter and two iron wedges from an inattentive farmer in Duddingston.

Next, Brodie sent Ainslie to spy by night on the habits of the employees of the Excise Office. Ainslie's report was heartening. The last revenue clerk left at eight o'clock. He locked the outer door, deposited the key with the housekeeper who dwelt in the court, then departed. After that, the Excise Office remained unattended until ten o'clock when one of the two night porters came on to guard it. In short, there were two full hours when the Excise was wide open to entry.

On Tuesday evening, March 4, 1788, the clan gathered at Mr. and Mrs. Smith's house in Cowgate for their last briefing. It had been decided to stage the robbery the following night when an elderly, ineffectual watchman named William Mac-Kay was on duty. As Smith recalled the plan, "Ainslie was to keep on the outside of the office, hanging over the palisadoes in the entry with a whistle of ivory, which was purchased by Brodie the night before, with which, if the man belonging to the Excise Office came, he was to give one whistle, and if any serious alarm was perceived he was to give three whistles, and then make the best of his way to the Excise gardens in the Canongate in order to assist the declarant, Brodie, and Brown to get out at the back window of the hall, it being determined in case of surprise to bolt the outer door on the inside and make the best of their way by the window."

Every contingency was considered. Or so Brodie thought. If Ainslie whistled three times, they would escape through the rear window and down a rope ladder Smith had prepared. If only one whistle was sounded, they would hold fast, overwhelm the night porter, gag and bind him, and pretend they were smugglers from another city who were merely trying to recover their confiscated goods. When the robbery was completed, they would drop a spur in the rear garden. This, Brodie insisted, would deceive their pursuers and "make it believed it had been done by some person on horseback."

The next day, the critical day of March 5, Deacon Brodie was unusually busy. He worked at his trade all morning, yet found time at two o'clock in the afternoon to leave the ivory whistle, decoy spur, and false key at Smith's residence. By three o'clock, in high good humor, he had returned to Brodie's Close to host a dinner for five guests. According to one of his guests, his brother-in-law: "There was present at dinner in company a stranger gentleman whose name I do not know, the prisoner's two sisters, and an old lady, his aunt. We drank together from dinner to tea, which I think was brought in about six o'clock. . . . Before I came away, Mr. Brodie pressed me to stay supper with him, but I declined his invitation."

Night fell early. It was a blustering winter's evening, and the thin layer of snow outdoors had frozen hard. With his last guest gone and his supper finished, Brodie retired to his room. Though he had promised to rendezvous with the gang at seven, it was almost eight when he had completed his change of attire from fashionable white to the old-fashioned black suit. Taking up his cocked hat, great coat, two pistols, and dark lantern, he departed Brodie's Close.

At Smith's house, the others, having finished a supper of herring, beer, and gin, were tensely waiting. Brodie, slightly intoxicated, sauntered in waving a pistol and bellowing a verse from *The Beggar's Opera*:

> *Let us take the road;*
> *Hark! I hear the sound of coaches!*
> *The hour of attack approaches;*
> *To your arms, brave boys, and load.*

The others were in no mood for Macheath. Hastily the four

armed themselves. Ainslie took a heavy stick, while Brodie, Smith, and Brown took two pistols apiece, loading each with powder and double ball. "We were determined not to be taken," said Smith, "whatever should be the consequence." Smith, Brown, and Ainslie had black crepe masks, and Brodie had one of his father's old wigs, which he turned over to Smith.

They left singly, a few minutes apart, Ainslie going first, then Brown, Smith, and finally Brodie. Ainslie arrived at the General Excise Office alone. Except for a few street lamps swinging in the wind, the court was dark and deserted. Ainslie slipped behind the ancient iron railing and stretched himself flat along the parapet wall, watching the outer door. In a moment an Excise employee emerged, locked the door, walked across the court to leave the key with the housekeeper. When the employee left, Brown, who was approaching, saw him and decided to shadow him. Brown followed the man all the way home. "My reason for so doing was to see that he had not gone on an errand and to return."

Meanwhile, at the Excise, Smith had arrived. Receiving an all-clear nod from Ainslie, he moved to the outer door, inserted the false key, opened it, and quickly disappeared inside. Several minutes later Brodie appeared. When he heard that Brown was not inside with Smith, he seemed annoyed. He turned to look for Brown, but saw him entering the court. Brown reached through the railing, took the plow colter, which he had nicknamed Great Samuel, from Ainslie, then hurriedly followed Brodie inside.

Ainslie remained on watch at the court railing. Brodie hid in the hallway behind the outer door, to prevent sudden entry and to block off a surprise attack. Brown joined Smith at the first entrance to the cashier's room. Expertly, Smith picked this door open with a pair of curling-irons. Beyond it was another door. Smith and Brown together cracked it open with the colter and iron crowbar. Inside the Excise revenue rooms at last, they began search for the estimated sixteen hundred pounds they expected to find.

"After we got in," Brown stated, "Smith, who had a dark lanthorn with him, opened every press and desk in the room where he suspected there was any money; some by violence and others with keys which we found in the room. We continued there about a half-an-hour, and found about sixteen pounds of money in a desk in the cashier's room, which we carried away with us."

As they continued their desperate half-hour's search, ransacking the room for the wealth they knew must be in it (as a matter of fact, six hundred pounds was hidden from them in a secret drawer), an unforeseen event took place outside. It was a contingency that could not be accounted for—had not been accounted for, in fact—and it turned the Excise raid into a bitter fiasco. For at eight thirty James Bonar, Deputy-Solicitor for the General Excise, returned unexpectedly to pick up some papers he had forgotten in his upstairs office.

Bonar was not surprised to find the door unlocked. He assumed that some Excise clerks were working late. Noisily he opened the door and started inside. "Just as I entered," he remembered, "a man, who appeared to be dressed in a black coat and cocked hat, stepped out. He seemed to be in a hurry, and I stepped aside to give way to him. He was a square-built man and rather taller than me. I took no suspicion, thinking it was some of the people belonging to the office, detained later than usual. I went upstairs to the solicitor's office, and into the room in which I usually write. I remained there about ten minutes, came down again, and then went away."

Bonar did not know what havoc he had wrought in his brief visit. His sudden appearance had startled Ainslie into complete immobility. His entry into the building had frightened Deacon Brodie witless. Forgetting about his companions, Brodie leaped past the official, rushed across the court, and fled. Completely befuddled, first by Bonar's entry, then by Brodie's exit, then by Bonar's final departure, Andrew Ainslie took to his ivory whistle. He blasted three times, then raced to the rear to help his colleagues escape down the rope ladder. There was no rope ladder in sight, and there were no colleagues.

For, deep in the cashier's room, Smith and Brown were unable to hear Ainslie's whistle. But they heard other off stage noises. "We heard some person come upstairs," said Brown. They did not worry, because, according to Smith, they were "trusting to Brodie's being at the door and staunch."

Then, just as they started to leave the cashier's room to continue their hunt in another office, Smith recalled, they heard "a person coming hastily down the stairs, which made them stop or they must have met him." Shocked at the narrow escape, both fell back into the shadows, where Brown whispered angrily to Smith: "Here must be treachery. Get out your pistols and cock them." They watched as Bonar slammed out the front door. Then, pistols ready, they cautiously approached the door. "Brodie and Ainslie were both gone," Brown said flatly.

Leaving colter, crowbar, and spur in the hallway, and the outer door unlocked, Smith and Brown fled the scene of their "most dangerous and heinous" crime.

At ten o'clock the night porter, William MacKay, came on duty. Examining the Excise Office, he noticed the front door open. He hurried to the housekeeper in the court and there learned that it had been properly locked at eight fifteen. Troubled, MacKay returned to the Excise Office, and inside he found the colter, crowbar, and spur in the hall and saw that the desks in the cashier's office had been opened. At once he sent the alarm to the officials of His Majesty's Excise—and the word was out.

Meanwhile, Smith, Brown, and Ainslie had returned to Smith's house in Cowgate. And the good Deacon was snug in bed with his "devil"—Jean Watt. After his shameful flight, he had made his way to Brodie's Close, discarded his black suit for his respectable white one, then hurried to nearby Libberton's Wynd to sleep with his mistress.

The following morning, well rested, Brodie took his leave of

Jean. He went directly to Smith, who received him coldly. Brodie then walked to Burnet's Close, where Ainslie and Brown were rooming. "He came in laughing," said Ainslie, "and said that he had been with Smith, who had accused him of running away the previous evening. I told him that I also thought he had run off; but he said that he had stood true." Confident that he had regained the trust of his companions, Brodie returned to his cabinet shop.

Early the next evening, Friday, March 7, 1788, the gang met again at Smith's to divide their pitiful loot. "When I called at Smith's house," said Ainslie, "in the room above the stairs I found Smith and Brodie, and saw the money lying on a chair. I got a fourth share of it in small notes, and at the same time I got some gold from Mr. Brodie in payment of money he owed me."

With the financial business of the partnership settled, the members separated. Smith and Ainslie went to buy stagecoach tickets for Mrs. Smith, who was to leave for Chesterfield to deliver the trunks of Inglis and Horner silks to Tasker. Deacon Brodie returned to his decorous mansion to join his sister at supper. As for John Brown—he went to the police.

If there is such a thing as honor among thieves, then Brown was a rogue among rogues. Many factors conspired to make him inform on his associates. He was angry with Brodie, of course, but that was the least of it. He needed money. He had expected, for his share of the Excise raid, 400 pounds, and had got only four. The Inglis and Horner reward promised to enrich him with 150 pounds. It also promised him full pardon. The last was as appealing as cash, since Brown was still under sentence of transport to Australia.

It was late evening when Brown walked into the Sheriff-Clerk's office of Edinburgh and announced that he had information to reveal on the General Excise robbery, the Inglis, Horner and Company robbery, and a half-dozen other crimes. Immediately he was taken to the Procurator-Fiscal, where he made a full confession. He blamed Ainslie and Smith for everything, but shrewdly made no mention of Brodie. Plainly, he was saving the good Deacon for blackmail.

The next morning, when Brodie awakened, he learned that all Edinburgh was in a furor of excitement. The members of the gang who had broken into the Excise and committed countless robberies in the eighteen months past were under arrest. Brodie was thunderstruck. But he did not panic at once. Since he had not been arrested, he realized that the others had not yet implicated him. Hearing that Brown was in Chesterfield, helping the authorities recover the trunks of silk, and Ainslie and Smith were in prison, Brodie realized that he must buy their silence at any price.

In his role of Town Councillor, Deacon Brodie audaciously appeared at the Tolbooth and congratulated the guards on their remarkable catch. Then, pretending curiosity, he asked if he might have a look at the two prisoners. He was told that no one could see them. He pressed the point no further and retired.

We may be sure the Deacon slept few hours that night. He was faced with a critical decision. To remain and depend upon the precarious silence of his colleagues? Or to flee at once? By daybreak he had made his decision. By four o'clock Sunday afternoon he was on a coach bound for Newcastle. There he transferred to a faster coach for London. Once in London, he left the conveyance before it reached the stage offices, taking his leave at the foot of Old Street, Moorfields.

Meanwhile, back in Edinburgh, George Smith, languishing in the Tolbooth, heard by some means that Brodie had left the city. Angered by this cowardice, he sent for the Sheriff and announced that "he wished to have an opportunity of making a clean breast, and telling the truth." We can be sure that the authorities listened in stupefied silence as they heard the name of the respected Deacon William Brodie exposed as the chief of an armed gang and the brains behind the robberies. To support his assertions, Smith led the police to Brodie's house, where false keys, pistols, picklocks, and putty case were found.

When Brown and Ainslie promptly corroborated Smith's

confession, the Deacon's double life was public. The disbelief that swept Edinburgh was echoed in the *Evening Courant:* "With what amazement must it strike every friend to virtue and honesty to find that a person is charged with a crime who very lately held a distinguished rank among his fellow-citizens?"

The Sheriff-Clerk's office immediately circulated an advertisement:

"Whereas William Brodie, a considerable House-Carpenter, and Burgess of the City of Edinburgh, has been charged with being concerned in breaking into the General Excise Office for Scotland, and stealing from the Cashier's office there a sum of money—and as the said William Brodie has either made his escape from Edinburgh, or is still concealed about that place— a Reward of One Hundred and Fifty Pounds Sterling is hereby offered to any person who will produce him alive."

A detailed description of Brodie accompanied the offer of reward. It read in part: "William Brodie is about five feet four inches—is about forty-eight years of age—broad at the shoulders, and very small over the loins—has dark brown full eyes— under the right eye there is the scar of a cut—a particular motion with his mouth and lips when he speaks, which he does full and slow, his mouth being commonly open at the time, and his tongue doubling up, as it were, shows itself towards the roof of his mouth—usually wears a stick under hand, and moves in a proud swaggering sort of style." Brodie found this description, which he read in London, most irritating. He blamed it on "that designing villain Brown. . . . I can see some strokes of his pencil in my portrait. May God forgive him for all his crimes and falsehoods."

Even as the description was being published throughout Great Britain, George Williamson, portly King's Messenger for Scotland, was assigned to hunt the fugitive down. He quickly traced Brodie to London, but then lost the trail completely. With the help of Bow Street runners, he combed London for his quarry. He visited low taverns, and he visited cockpits, and he even went as far afield as Dover. But Brodie had disappeared, and after eighteen days Williamson gave up the chase. He didn't realize, of course, how very close he had come to success.

For Brodie had twice barely avoided Williamson in the streets of London. "Were I to write you all that has happened to me," Brodie wrote Michael Henderson, "and the hairbreadth escapes I made from a well-scented pack of bloodhounds, it would make a small volume. I arrived in London on Wednesday, 12th March, where I remained snug and safe in the house of an old female friend until Sunday, 23rd March (whose care for me I shall never forget, and only wish I may ever have it in my power to reward her sufficiently), within five hundred yards of Bow Street.

"I did not keep the house all this time, but so altered, excepting the scar under my eye, I think you could not have swore to me. I saw Mr. Williamson twice; but although countrymen commonly shake hands when they meet from home, yet I did not choose to make so free with him notwithstanding he brought a letter to me. He is a clever man, and I give him credit for his conduct."

Two weeks from the day of his flight from Edinburgh, Deacon Brodie, through the help of a criminal lawyer in London, secured passage on a small sailing-vessel, the *Endeavour*, bound for Leith, Scotland. Assuming the name of John Dixon, he boarded the boat at Blackwell. The only two other passengers on ship, John Geddes, a Mid-Calder tobacconist, and his wife, who were returning home after a vacation in London, watched Mr. Dixon come on at midnight. "He was dressed in a blue great coat," said Geddes, "with a red collar, round wig, black vest, breeches and boots. He was allotted a bed in the stateroom, near the fire, as he was sick."

No sooner had the sloop weighed anchor than it ran aground in the fog. It was high and dry for ten days. Brodie displayed no apprehension. He went ashore twice—once for a bottle of milk, and again to join the Geddes couple and the Captain for dinner in a near-by village. The moment the ship was freed and pointed toward Scotland, Brodie handed the Captain a sealed order signed by the boat's owners. It directed the Captain to change his course for Holland, and to leave Mr. Dixon at Ostend before continuing to Scotland. The Captain obliged. But due to rough seas, the *Endeavour* was forced to disembark Brodie at Flushing instead.

Before leaving the boat, Brodie asked his fellow passenger, Geddes, a favor. He had written three letters to friends in Edinburgh. One was addressed to Anne Grant, another to Michael Henderson, and the third to Matthew Sheriff. Would Mr. Geddes be kind enough to deliver them the next time he was in Edinburgh? Geddes said he would be pleased to do so.

From Flushing, Brodie hired a skiff for Ostend. Then he proceeded to Amsterdam, took an upstairs room in a tavern near the wharves, and awaited passage on a vessel that was soon to leave for Charleston, South Carolina. Since he expected to visit New York, he begged his friends, in the letters sent with Geddes, to write him there in the name of John Dixon, and in the care of the Reverend Dr. Mason.

But no correspondence ever reached the Reverend Dr. Mason. For Brodie had put too much trust in the vacationing tobacconist. Geddes, upon his arrival in Leith, heard about the notorious Deacon and wondered if the Deacon and Dixon might be one and the same. Three weeks later he read a description of Brodie and was sure. He promptly ripped open the three letters entrusted to his care, read them, and hurried off to deliver them to the Sheriff of Edinburgh.

The authorities were jubilant over the letters. For, in them, Brodie not only gave away his location and his plans, but obliquely indicated his guilt. He incriminated himself seriously with two written remarks. Commenting on Smith, Ainslie, and Brown, he wrote: "Whatever these men may say, I had no hand in any of their depredations, excepting the last, which I shall ever repent." And again: "I shall ever repent keeping such company, and whatever they may allege, I had no direct concern in any of their depredations, excepting the last fatal one."

His Majesty's couriers moved swiftly. Sir James Harris, British Consul in Amsterdam, was notified. He hired an Irishman, John Daly, to search for the fugitive. Daly made his way to the wharves and questioned dockhands who usually helped passengers disembark. Two persons remembered a man of Brodie's description. They directed Daly to an alehouse owned by one John Bacon. Daly inquired for Mr. Dixon and was sent upstairs.

Daly knocked on the door. There was no reply. He opened the door and went inside. The room was empty. He searched it thoroughly without result. Then his gaze fell upon a large cupboard. He went to it, wrenched it open, and there, crouched inside, was the Deacon.

Daly was courteous but firm. "How do you do, Captain John Dixon, alias William Brodie? Come along with me."

There was no use resisting. Daly was a robust man, the Deacon an ill and dispirited one. The Deacon, after the long exodus, submitted meekly.

Though Brodie refused to acknowledge his true identity or to make any confession, he was extradited soon enough to England. In London he was turned over at last to the hands of the clever Mr. Williamson, King's Messenger for Scotland. During the two-day journey back to Edinburgh, Brodie regaled his companion with stories of life abroad. According to William Creech, Brodie cheerfully related how "he met with a Scots woman at Amsterdam, who asked him if he had been long from Scotland. She said that there was one Brodie, a citizen of Edinburgh, accused of robbing the Excise Office, and a great reward was offered for apprehending him. She little knew who she was speaking to, said Mr. Brodie."

Upon his return to Edinburgh, Brodie, secreted from public view, was questioned. He was vague and evasive. He was deposited in the Tolbooth jail, under constant guard, to await the judgment of his peers. He learned that only he and George Smith were to be tried. Ainslie had joined Brown in turning

State's evidence, and both had been granted pardons in order that they might be legally qualified to testify for the prosecution. The charge against Brodie and Smith was, not robberies, but a single robbery—the act of felony in breaking into the Excise Office.

In the five weeks before trial, Brodie hired for his defense, and consulted with, the foremost attorney in all Scotland. This was the tall, distinguished, seventy-one-year-old Henry Erskine, respected Dean of the Faculty of Advocates. George Smith, without funds and without a case, might have been less fortunate but for a stroke of luck. He accepted the services of a thirty-one-year-old newcomer named John Clerk, who was to dominate the legal forensics of the trial. Clerk was a fearless, candid, crippled bachelor with a roaring temper. And though he had been admitted to the bar only three years before, the solemnity of the court cowed him not at all. Once when he was limping down High Street, Clerk heard a lady point him out to a friend. "There goes Johnny Clerk, the lame lawyer," she said. Clerk turned around. "Madam," he called out, "I may be a lame man, but I'm not a lame lawyer."

At nine o'clock Wednesday morning, August 27, 1788, the trial of Deacon William Brodie and George Smith began. Brodie, dressed in cocked hat, dark-blue coat, and black satin breeches, and Smith, "poorly clothed," were carried into the Justiciary Court in chairs. They then rose and took their places behind a railing, facing Lord Braxfield and his four fellow judges across the room.

Lord Braxfield dominated the bench as if he had been born on it. He was called variously "the Jeffreys of Scotland" and "the Hanging Judge." He looked, said Lord Cockburn, "like a formidable blacksmith." He was a man of low humor and great sarcasm, and the possessor of a thick gravel voice. He spared no one, not even his own family. When a servant once gave notice because he could no longer bear the scoldings of Braxfield's wife, the old magistrate grunted: "Good Lord, you've got little to complain about—be thankful you're not married to her!" Braxfield attained some measure of literary immortality by serving as the model for Robert Louis Stevenson's *Weir of Hermiston*, which Stevenson was still writing on the day of his death in Samoa during 1894. Stevenson's stern Lord Justice-Clerk Weir, who was to eventually condemn to death his own son in the unfinished novel, was regarded by the author as by "far my best character."

And now, by an accident of history, the inspirations for two of Stevenson's strangest characters, the Weir of Hermiston, and Dr. Jekyll and Mr. Hyde, stood face to face on an early morning in Edinburgh.

Besides the five wigged judges, there was present a jury of fifteen substantial Edinburgh males, including five bankers, four merchants, and the publisher Creech, who later became the historian of the trial. The amphitheater and its balcony were jammed to the rafters with an extremely vocal audience that had paid as high as five shillings each for the privilege of attendance.

Sir Ilay Campbell, the Lord Advocate or prosecutor, a wooden workhorse of a man with a monotonous voice, read the opening charge. "You, the said William Brodie, and George Smith, ought to be punished with the pains of law, to deter others from committing the like crimes in all time coming." Then Lord Braxfield addressed the Deacon. "William Brodie, you have heard the indictment raised against you by His Majesty's Advocate—are you guilty of the crime therein charged, or not guilty?" Brodie replied firmly: "My Lord, I am not guilty." The battle was joined.

The prosecution paraded twenty-seven witnesses. Only two were of any importance. For it was on the evidence of Andrew Ainslie and John Brown that the prosecution hoped to hang Brodie and Smith. And it was by destroying the integrity of these witnesses that the defense largely based its case.

Lord Erskine, on the Deacon's behalf, contended that Ainslie could not be trusted in testimony. He pointed out that in Ainslie's first confession to the Sheriff "he positively affirmed that Mr. Brodie had no sort of accession to the crime of which he is now accused." Next, Lord Erskine argued vigorously that Brown's evidence should be discarded because, pardon or no pardon, he was still a corrupt and lying criminal. "My Lords, I have heard it said that the King could make a peer, but that he could not make a gentleman; I am sure that he cannot make a rogue an honest man."

When the judges insisted upon admitting Brown's testimony, Lord Erskine vainly tried to trap Brown in cross-examination. After one series of questions, the surly Brown lost his temper. "Do not think to trap me. You may make something of me by fair means, but not by foul. I do not understand the meaning of being thus teased by impertinent questions." To this, Lord Erskine replied: "The more violent the gentleman is, so much the better for my client. The jury will take notice of the manner in which he gives his evidence." When Lord Braxfield warned Brown to hold his tongue, Brown turned to him. "My Lord, in giving my evidence, I have said nothing but the truth, and I have rather softened the matter than otherwise, with regard to Mr. Brodie."

For the defense, seven witnesses were summoned. Through Brodie's mistress, Jean Watt, Lord Erskine tried to provide an alibi for his client. He wanted to prove that while Smith, Ainslie, and Brown were raiding the Excise, the good Deacon was in bed with his woman. Jean Watt told the court: "I am well acquainted with the prisoner, William Brodie. I remember that on Wednesday, the 5th of March last, Mr. Brodie came to my house just at the time the eight o'clock bell was ringing, and he remained in it all night, and was not out from the time he came in until a little before nine o'clock the next morning. We went early to bed, about ten o'clock, as Mr. Brodie complained that night of being much indisposed with a sore throat. It was the last night Mr. Brodie slept in my house. He slept with me that night. I have a family of children to him."

It was after midnight in the courtroom when Campbell rose to sum up the prosecution's case. He hammered at Brodie's alibi, arguing that Jean Watt was "a woman of an abandoned character" and that her relationship with the defendant was such as to permit her to commit perjury. He referred to the accusations of Brodie by his two recently cleansed colleagues, and he insisted that Brodie had, in effect, confessed to participation in the Excise robbery in his letters from Amsterdam. He concluded: "Gentlemen, I shall only further add that if the prisoner William Brodie . . . has been guilty of the crime laid to his charge, and is allowed to escape punishment, the consequences to the inhabitants of this populous city may be of the most serious nature."

Now the rambunctious John Clerk rose to make the best of a bad thing for George Smith. He announced that the evidence against Smith was utterly unreliable. He called Smith's accusers, Ainslie and Brown, "two corbies or infernal scoundrels." He stated: "I think a great deal of the most improper evidence has been received for the Crown." When Lord Braxfield and the other judges thought this a reflection on the court, Clerk heatedly overrode them and shouted against Brown: "I say to you that no convicted felon ought, by the good and glorious law of Scotland, to be received as a witness in this or any other case in the British dominions." While the spectators wildly applauded, Clerk and Braxfield engaged in a running verbal dogfight. Clerk was warned to speak no further against Ainslie and Brown. He insisted upon the right to speak as he wished. "I have met with no politeness from the Court," he snapped. "You have interrupted me, you have snubbed me rather too often, my Lord."

Angrily, Lord Braxfield turned to Lord Erskine and told him to proceed for Brodie. This Erskine refused to do. Braxfield then announced that the trial was over and that he would charge the jury. As Braxfield faced the jury, John Clerk leaped to his feet, shook his fist at Braxfield, and roared: "Hang my client if you daur, my Lord, without hearing me in his defence!" The sensation created by this outburst was beyond belief. As Roughhead has reported: "The Bench was paralyzed, the Bar aghast; the jury trembled, the audience was dumbfounded." For the first time Lord Braxfield backed down, and Clerk finished his defense.

It was three o'clock in the morning when Lord Erskine rose to exonerate the double life. Calmly he defended Deacon Brodie's gambling as a common affliction, and defended his flight to Holland as a reasonable bit of panic, since he feared being implicated with men with whom he had played cards and dice. Lord Erskine strongly reiterated the soundness of the Deacon's alibi. He argued that Miss Watt's word was to be preferred to John Brown's. Of Brown he commented: "A more hardened and determined villain can hardly be figured." After one hour of brilliant oratory, he closed with: "In the hands of an upright and intelligent jury I leave this unfortunate gentleman."

At four o'clock Lord Braxfield addressed his charge to the fifteen jurors. "Taking all the circumstances of this case together, gentlemen," he said, "I can have no doubt in my own mind that Mr. Brodie was present at the breaking into the Excise Office." It was dawn when the jury was sent off to deliberate and the court was adjourned. Brodie and Smith had stood at the bar, and the court had been in session, for twenty-one consecutive hours—one of the longest marathons of its kind in all legal history.

At one o'clock Thursday afternoon the court reconvened. Brodie waited quietly, and Smith nervously, as Lord Braxfield took the written verdict, sealed with black wax, from the chancellor or foreman of the jury. The verdict was opened and passed among the judges, who read it in silence, and then Braxfield addressed himself to the defendants. "They all, in one voice, find the pannels [prisoners] William Brodie and George Smith guilty of the crime charged against them in the said indictment."

Hurriedly, then, Lord Braxfield announced the sentence. The convicted were to suffer their punishment in the Tolbooth prison yard on October 1. "There, betwixt the hours of two and four o'clock afternoon to be hanged by the necks, by the hands of the Common Executioner, upon a Gibbet, until they be dead."

At once Deacon Brodie tried to make a speech. But Lord Erskine begged him to be silent. Brodie then bowed to the judges, looked at Smith, and, according to an eyewitness, "accused his companion of pusillanimity, and even kicked him as they were leaving the court."

The penalty of hanging for a mere felony may seem, in these slightly more enlightened days, a barbaric injustice. But the old Scots were righteous, unbending folk, and they regarded armed robbery as dangerously criminal and deserving of harsh punishment, as we today regard murder, kidnapping, and rape. Nevertheless, there was much sympathy generated in Edinburgh for the good Deacon, and many efforts were made to commute his sentence to transportation, and even to lighten his lot in prison.

Brodie and Smith were confined, with two other prisoners sentenced to death for burglary, to what was known as the Iron Room of the Tolbooth. Each was chained by one leg to a long iron bar. When Brodie was offered a private cell, he declined the honor, but did accept a longer chain which enabled him to make use of a writing-table near by.

Daily, he composed letters to an assortment of friends, Councilors, peers, asking them to intercede on his behalf. To the Duchess of Buccleuch he wrote: "Lett me beseech your Ladyship to pardon My Boldness in making the present address. The wretched can only fly to the Humane and the powerful for Relief. . . . I feel the Natural horror at Death, and particularly a violent Ignominious Death, and would willingly avoid it even on the condition of spending my Future years at Bottony Bay."

As he waited for replies to his appeals, Brodie played draughts on a board he had carved on the cell floor, often playing with his left hand against his right. When the other two inmates of the Iron Room were granted a six-week delay,

Brodie remarked to Smith: "George, what would you and I give for six weeks longer? Six weeks would be an age to us!" But there was no six weeks longer and no reprieve. The sentence stood, and October 1 drew closer.

Six days before his execution, Brodie received his only visit from a member of his family. His oldest daughter, and his favorite, Cecill Grant, appeared. He embraced her and broke into tears. After she was gone, his good humor returned, and he sat down to write his will. He stated that since the government was confiscating all his worldly goods, he had "nothing else to dispose of but my good and bad qualifications." To a close friend, John Grieve, he bequeathed "all my political knowledge in securing magistrates and packing corporations"; to his landlord, William Little, he willed "my whole stock of economy, pride and self conceit"; to Hamilton, the accusing chimneysweep, he left "my dexterity in cards and dice"; and "To my good friends and old companions, Brown and Ainslie, I freely give and bequeath all my bad qualities, not doubting, however, but there own will secure them a rope at last."

The Deacon was prophetic on the futures of Brown and Ainslie. Brown was eventually hung in England for another crime, and Ainslie's activities finally provoked a sentence of transportation to Botany Bay.

The day before his execution, Brodie received several old friends. One remarked sadly that the Deacon's trouble came of associating "with bad women." The Deacon refused to take this analysis seriously, and lustily broke into the verse from *The Beggar's Opera* which began: " 'Tis woman that seduces all mankind!"

His last evening was disturbed by the sounds of hammering in the prison yard. He glanced at Smith. "George, do you know what noise that is?"

George didn't.

Brodie smiled. "I'll tell you. It is the drawing out of the fatal beam on which you and I must suffer tomorrow. I know it well." He listened again. He thought the workmen sounded like shipbuilders. "For the short voyage I'm going to make, so much preparation is unnecessary." He reflected upon death. "A leap in the dark," he thought. And at eleven o'clock he lay down on his mattress and went to sleep.

He was awake at four, but did not rise until eight. His chain was removed. He powdered his hair, and attired himself in a black suit. He was impatient with a visiting clergyman, but lingered over his last dinner of beefsteak and port. At two o'clock he followed Smith out of the cell.

The crowd of spectators in the prison yard was, according to the *Caledonian Mercury*, "the greatest ever know." Over forty thousand persons were pressed together "in one compact and immoveable column." When Brodie saw the crowd, he frowned. "This is awful!"

At the scaffold he bowed graciously to the magistrates of the court. A friend edged closer to say he was sorry to see the Deacon in this situation. Brodie shrugged. "What would you have? It is *fortune de la guerre.*" Before ascending the scaffold, he briefly knelt and improvised a prayer. "O Lord, I acknowledge Thee as the Great Ruler of the world, although I lament much that I know so little of Thee." Rising, he nudged the trembling Smith. "Go up, George, you are first in hand."

On the scaffolding, Brodie coolly examined the rope. He thought it was too short and should be adjusted. While the executioner adjusted it, Brodie stepped down among his friends and apologized for the delay. "It's a new construction and wants nothing but practice to make it complete." He went up to the rope again, still found it at the wrong length, and descended to join his friends once more. "The executioner is a bungling fellow," he said, "and ought to be punished for his stupidity." The third time the rope was right.

Brodie untied his cravat and accepted the noose around his neck. He shook hands with Smith. He called down to a friend, reminding him to tell the world "he died like a man." He then pulled the white cap of execution over his face, folded his arms, and waited. The trap was sprung, and he dropped into space— and the two lives of Deacon Brodie were ended.

Yet, he had hoped for a third life. The day before, he had requested the Lord Provost to let his corpse be delivered promptly to friends for interment. There was a reason for this request. In prison he had received a French physician, Dr. Peter Degravers, who promised to bring him to life after the hanging.

Before the execution, Dr. Degravers had appeared in Brodie's cell and drawn pencil marks on his temples and arms, in order to save time in operating after the hanging. The doctor also left a small silver tube, which Brodie slid into his throat an hour before the hanging. This was to prevent strangulation. Brodie also wired himself, beneath his clothes, from shoulders to ankles, to prevent jerking when he fell through the drop. Finally, friends had bribed the executioner to keep the rope short. This, of course, explained Brodie's precaution that the rope be just right.

"After he was cut down," an eyewitness to the incident reported, "his body was immediately given to two of his own workmen, who, by order of the guard, placed it in a cart and drove at a furious rate round the back of the Castle. The object of this order was probably an idea that the jolting motion of the cart might be the means of resuscitation, as had once actually happened in the case of the celebrated 'half-hangit Maggie Dickson.' The body was afterwards conveyed to one of Brodie's own workshops in the Lawnmarket, where Degravers was in attendance. He attempted bleeding, etc., but all would not do. Brodie was fairly gone."

He had died, it appeared, of a broken neck.

Nevertheless, when the story of Dr. Degravers's attempt got out, it convinced many citizens of Edinburgh that Brodie had somehow survived the execution. The story was told and re-told through the years. And there is a legend in Scotland today that after his resurrection he fled the country and was recognized strolling in Paris years later. But his grave may still be seen behind St. Cuthbert's Chapel of Ease in Edinburgh, and in the Museum of Antiquaries still stand his dark lantern and his set of false keys.

No, Deacon William Brodie was not revived—until Robert Louis Stevenson was awakened from a nightmare.

VI

The Real Marie Roget

"People begin to see that something more goes to the composition of a fine murder than two blockheads to kill and be killed—a knife—a purse—and a dark lane."

THOMAS DE QUINCEY

For eighteen months during 1837 and 1838, Edgar Allan Poe, after being fired as editor of a Richmond literary magazine for excessive drinking, was a resident of New York City. He dwelt, with his pale, somewhat retarded child-bride, Virginia, and his matronly, possessive aunt and mother-in-law, Maria Clemm, in a cheap apartment on Sixth Avenue.

Poe, trying unsuccessfully to free-lance for magazines, often restless with despair, became a familiar figure on Broadway. Few persons who saw him forgot him. In his neat, shabby, black flare-tail coat and mended military cape, striding nervously, briskly along, he had the look of a neurotic peacock. His head, set large on a slender frame, seemed always in the clouds. His hair and scrub mustache were dark brown, his eyes sad and gray, and it was remarked that he had "hands like bird claws."

His destination in many of these walks, as a few would remember after his death, was John Anderson's tobacco shop at 319 Broadway, near Thomas Street. This small store was a popular hangout for famous authors like James Fenimore Cooper, as well as for magazine editors, newspaper reporters, and gamblers employed in the vicinity. And here Poe came for gossip and stimulation, and certainly for contacts.

The Real Marie Roget

When he had money, which was not often, Poe bought cigars or plugs of tobacco from the beautiful salesgirl behind the counter. She was employed, largely because of her vivacity and comeliness, as a full-time clerk, and her name was Mary Cecilia Rogers. It may be assumed that Poe, through the frequency of his visits and small purchases, knew her fairly well. He could not know, however, how soon Miss Rogers would serve him in another capacity.

By early 1839 the strange, eloquent, self-styled "magazinist" was no longer a regular customer at John Anderson, Tobacconist. Poe was established at $800 a year salary—the greatest sum he would ever earn in his life, and considerably more than his total income from the ten books he would write—as managing editor of a periodical in near-by Philadelphia. The periodical was owned by a reformed comedian named William Burton, who eventually sold it to George Graham, a cabinet-maker turned publisher.

Poe was retained as editor of *Graham's Magazine*, and he worked doggedly in a third-floor cubicle shared with a Swedish assistant, reading and purchasing manuscripts, laying out new issues, and writing criticism and fiction. In short months his industry and ability helped boom the circulation of *Graham's* from 5,000 to 37,000. Occasionally, as his duties demanded it, he made the uncomfortable six-hour train trip to New York City. It may be assumed that on these short visits he looked in on John Anderson's tobacco shop and renewed his acquaintance with Mary Rogers, the attractive clerk behind the counter.

We do not know the date when Edgar Allan Poe last laid eyes on Mary Rogers. But we do know, approximately, the date when he first saw her name in the public prints. Poe was a habitual reader of the sensational penny papers. Some of his finest fiction was culled from seemingly insignificant news items. Only months before, having read of an escaped orangutan, he had conceived the world's first detective story and published it in *Graham's* as "The Murders in the Rue Morgue." Thus it was, in early August of 1841, that Poe consulted his latest batch of New York newspapers and stumbled upon the familiar name of Mary Rogers.

He came across the bald news item on the second page of the *New York Sunday Mercury* for August 1. Since it was often filled with errors, he consulted the other papers. James Gordon Bennett's gaudy *New York Herald* for August 5 fully substantiated the *Mercury*'s story. We can believe that what Poe read grieved him deeply. For what he read told him that the pretty girl who had so often sold him tobacco in the shop on Broadway had been brutally murdered. According to both accounts, Mary Cecilia Rogers was found floating in the Hudson River off Hoboken on Wednesday, July 28, 1841. She had been beaten and strangled, and was quite dead when fished out of the water.

Poe's reaction to the crime was no different from that of most decent New Yorkers. True, they were used to murder. Only five years before, at a time when most newspapers thought crime an improper subject to report, James Gorden Bennett, that brash and colorful cross-eyed Scot, had given the *New York Herald* a circulation of 50,000 with his reporting of the Ellen Jewett case. Miss Jewett, an attractive prostitute, had been bloodily dispatched in a house of ill fame, and Mr. Bennett broke a tradition of journalistic silence on such matters by having a look at the corpse and reporting to all and gentry: "The body looked as white, as full, as polished as the purest Parian marble. The perfect figure, the exquisite limbs, the fine face, the full arms, the beautiful bust, all, all surpassed in every respect the Venus de Medici." This story broke the ice, and thereafter the constant reader had gore delivered daily at his breakfast.

Yet, despite this saturation of homicide, the murder of young Mary Rogers affected the citizenry with a shock of dismay. Miss Rogers was not just another anonymous victim. She had been, the woodcuts and columns made plain, a Grecian beauty endowed with every virtue—and virginity besides. She had worked honestly for a living. She had been adored and respected by customers of consequence. She had been the kind of woman one married, or had for sister or daughter. She had been a girl with whom half of New York could identify. And now she was dead—killed with ferocity, in secret—and now no one was safe.

We have, fortunately, the typical reaction of a New Yorker of the period. Philip Hone, a cultured, wealthy citizen who dabbled in politics and kept voluminous diaries, read the accounts of Miss Rogers's slaying at about the same time Poe did, and recorded his feelings:

"Friday, Aug. 6—Shocking Murder. The body of a young female named Mary Cecilia Rogers was found on Thursday last in the river near Hoboken, with horrid marks of violation and violence on her person. She was a beautiful girl, an attendant in the cigar shop of John Anderson in Broadway. She left home for a walk on the Sunday previous and was seen near Barclay Street in company with a young man, as if on an excursion to Hoboken; since which no trace of her was found, until the dreadful discovery on Thursday.

"She is said to have been a girl of exceeding good character and behavior, engaged to be married, and has no doubt fallen victim to the brutal lust of some of the gang of banditti that walk unscathed and violate the laws with impunity in this moral and religious city. No discoveries have yet been made."

The mystery of Mary Rogers was a nine-week wonder. The leading Manhattan journals, the *Herald*, the *Commercial Advertiser*, the *Courier and Enquirer*, the *Tribune*, inspired by the possibilities of record circulation, and the underpaid metropolitan police, inspired by offers of rewards amounting to the unheard-of figure of $1,195, kept the case boiling. Dozens of suspects, including two of Mary's suitors, a sailor, two abortionists, a wood-engraver, and several Bowery gangs, were closely questioned. Every suspect and every clue led to dead end. By mid-October another murder, equally savage, had taken over the headlines and the attention of the law, and the hunt for the killer of Mary Rogers was actually, if not technically, abandoned.

But if Mary Rogers was forgotten in New York, she was not forgotten in Philadelphia. From that first day when he had read of Mary's death, Poe followed every new development in the case. He read as many papers as he could find, but principally a periodical called *Brother Jonathan*, which gave the case the most complete coverage and often condensed the accounts of rival sheets. Poe's later knowledge of the details of the crime makes it quite apparent that he filed away every clipping relating to Mary's death and also made copious notes on the theories prevailing.

The murder fascinated Poe for reasons other than his personal knowledge of the victim. Undoubtedly the crime had particular appeal to Poe because it remained unsolved. This untidy fact made it a puzzle. Quite plainly, the pieces were all there. But they had not been properly put together. Poe was, as we know, a fanatic about puzzles. He enjoyed nothing more than to match his mentality against the most difficult cryptograms, codes, riddles, enigmas. Mary Rogers was such a challenge to his intellect.

He toyed with the idea of a story based on Mary Rogers, but he did not write it for fully six months after news of the crime had died down. When he finally did convert it into his second detective tale, it was created less out of an inner compulsion than out of an outer need for additional finances. Indirectly, it was Virginia Poe who was responsible for Mary Rogers's being put to paper.

The weeks when Poe had been following the crime were, relatively, the most peaceful and secure of his entire life. In all the years before, he had never known normality. Orphaned by his actor parents at the age of two, he had spent five years in England with his guardian, a Scotch merchant. Entering the University of Virginia, he caroused and ran up gambling debts amounting to $2,500, and was withdrawn after less than a year's attendance. Poe enlisted in the army as a private, was bought out by his guardian, then sent to West Point, where he was promptly court-martialed for neglecting roll calls and disobeying his superiors. On a visit to Baltimore, he met his father's youngest sister, Maria Clemm, and his cousin, a frail child named Virginia, and thereafter he was never apart from them.

When Poe was twenty-four, he married Virginia, who was thirteen. It is thought that their marriage of twelve years was never consummated. We know that Maria Clemm encouraged the marriage. Whether it was because she wanted a provider, as some critics have insisted, or because she wanted a son, we shall never be certain. Of Poe's union with Virginia, Montagu Slater has observed: "He married Virginia and lived under Maria Clemm's apron because for some reason he dare not live with a normal woman, he was afraid of sex and afraid of life. Why? Oscar Wilde included him in a list of celebrated homosexuals."

Poe's sex life, or rather his lack of it, as well as his excessive drinking, made him a cadaver upon which psychiatric amateurs, and professionals as well, have fed since the advent of Freud. Since no analyst ever met or treated him, there is no means by which the accuracy of their guesses may be estimated. One analyst, Marie Bonaparte, who put the known facts of Poe's life on the literary couch some years ago, thought he drank "to fly from the dire and unconscious temptations evoked in him by the dying Virginia." Other psychiatrists have concluded that he loved Virginia and hated her, that he wanted her dead and feared she would die. Whatever his real torments and fears about facing reality, his admirer Baudelaire sensed that his greatest torture was that he had to make money—in a world for which he was unequipped.

But by 1842, in Philadelphia, Poe was briefly making his way for the first time. He was not drinking, and he was less moody than ever. To supplement his meager earnings on *Graham's*, he often wrote stories at night in the downstairs front parlor of the three-story brick house he had rented on the Schuylkill River. Life was difficult but well knit when suddenly, during an evening in January 1842, the whole thing unraveled—forever.

On that fateful evening Virginia was playing the harp and singing. Suddenly she "ruptured a blood-vessel." From that moment until her death five years later, she was an invalid, consumptive and hemorrhaging. And Poe came apart. He drank and he took opium and he destroyed every small opportunity. In four months he was through as editor of *Graham's*.

Soon his financial situation became desperate. He tried to obtain a federal job in Washington, but ruined the chance when he made his appearance drunk and wearing his clothes inside out. In Philadelphia every new day was a threat. Maria Clemm, though she pawned Poe's books, had only molasses and bread to serve for meals. The ailing Virginia kept warm in bed by encouraging her pet cat, Catarina, to curl upon her bosom. In desperation, Poe turned his torn brain back to the subject of free-lance fiction. And at once he remembered Mary Cecilia Rogers.

He wrote her story in May of 1842, seated before the cold fireplace of his Philadelphia parlor, scribbling steadily "on rolls of blue paper meticulously pasted together." He employed, for reference, the clippings he had saved on the actual crime, and his thinly fictionized novelette quoted many of the Mary Rogers news stories word for word. " 'The Mystery of Marie Roget' was composed at a distance from the scene of the atrocity," he explained later, "and with no other means of investigation than the newspapers afforded. Thus much escaped the writer of which he could have availed himself had he been upon the spot and visited the localities." The manuscript, completed, ran to over twenty thousand words in length.

On June 4, 1842, Poe wrote an inquiry to George Roberts, editor of the popular *Boston Times* and *Notion Magazine*:

My Dear Sir.

It is just possible that you may have seen a tale of mine entitled 'The Murders in the Rue Morgue' and published, originally, in 'Graham's Magazine' for April, 1841. Its *theme* was the exercise of ingenuity in the detection of a murderer. I have just completed a similar article, which I shall entitle 'The Mystery

The Real Marie Roget

of Marie Roget—a Sequel to the Murders in the Rue Morgue.'

The story is based upon the assassination of Mary Cecilia Rogers, which created so vast an excitement, some months ago, in New-York. I have, however, handled my design in a manner altogether *novel* in literature. I have imagined a series of nearly exact *coincidences* occurring in Paris. A young grisette, one Marie Roget, had been murdered under precisely similar circumstances with Mary Rogers. Thus, under pretence of showing how Dupin (the hero of The Rue Morgue) unravelled the mystery of Marie's assassination, I, in reality, enter into a very long and rigorous analysis of the New-York tragedy. No point is omitted. I examine, each by each, the opinions and arguments of the press upon the subject, and show that this subject has been, hitherto, *unapproached*. In fact, I believe not only that I have demonstrated the fallacy of the general idea—that the girl was the victim of a gang of ruffians—but have *indicated the assassin* in a manner which will give renewed impetus to investigation.

My main object, nevertheless, as you will readily understand, is an analysis of the true principles which should direct inquiry in similar cases. From the nature of the subject, I feel convinced that the article will excite attention, and it has occurred to me that you would be willing to purchase it for the forthcoming Mammoth Notion. It will make 25 pages of Graham's Magazine; and, at the usual price, would be worth to me $100. For reasons, however, which I need not specify, I am desirous of having this tale printed in Boston, and, if you like it, I will say $50. Will you please write me upon this point?—by return mail, if possible.

Yours very truly,
Edgar A. Poe

Having completed this letter, Poe wrote two more, with similar content, to other editors. One was to a friend, Dr. Joseph Evans Snodgrass, of the *Baltimore Sunday Visitor*. In this letter Poe said: "I am desirous of publishing it *in Baltimore*. . . . Of course I could not afford to make you an absolute present of it—but if you are willing to take it, I will say $40."

(179)

The third letter was to T. W. White, editor of the *Southern Literary Messenger* in Richmond.

All three editors turned down the suggested story. Poe then sold it to the most unlikely market of all—*Snowden's Ladies' Companion* of New York, a periodical which the author contemptuously regarded as "the ne plus ultra of ill-taste, impudence and vulgar humbuggery." *Snowden's* ran "The Mystery of Marie Roget" as a three-part serial in their issues of November and December 1842 and February 1843.

In the very opening paragraphs Poe gives full credit to Mary Rogers for inspiring the creation of Marie Roget. Then, for the second time in his fiction, Poe introduces the world's first imaginary detective, the eccentric Chevalier C. Auguste Dupin, who dwells in the Faubourg Saint-Germain with his friend, companion, and sounding-board, the unnamed narrator of the story. Ever since his solution of the killing of a mother and daughter at the hands of an ape in a sealed room in the Rue Morgue, Dupin has "relapsed into his old habits of moody revery." In fact, he is so deeply "engaged in researches" that he has not left his shuttered rooms for a month, and is therefore unaware of a murder that is creating great agitation throughout Paris.

The body of Marie Roget has been found floating in the Seine. Though the Sûreté has offered a reward of thirty thousand francs, there has been no break in the case. At last, in desperation, Prefect G of the Sûreté calls upon Dupin and offers him a proposition (presumably a sum of cash) if he will undertake the case and save the Prefect's reputation. Dupin agrees to investigate.

After obtaining the Sûreté evidence and back copies of the Paris newspapers, Dupin expounds on all the theories extant. Some sources believe Marie Roget is still alive; others, that she was killed by one of her suitors, Jacques St. Eustache or Beauvais, or by a gang. Dupin rejects all these theories, demolishing each with logic. He feels that the real murderer can be found by a closer study of "the public prints." After a week he has six newspaper "extracts" that indicate the killer. These reveal that, three and a half years before, Marie Roget mysteriously left her job at Le Blanc's perfumery and was thought to have eloped with a young naval officer "much noted for his debaucheries." Dupin reasons that this naval officer returned, made love to Marie, and when she became pregnant he murdered her or saw her die under an abortionist's instrument. He then disposed of her body in the Seine.

Dupin points to the clues that will expose the killer. Letters to the press, trying to throw suspicion on others, must be compared to those written by the naval officer. The abortionist, Mme Deluc, and others, must be questioned. The boat which the officer used to dispose of Marie's body must be found. "This boat shall guide us," says Dupin, "with a rapidity which will surprise even ourselves, to him who employed it in the midnight of the fatal Sabbath. Corroboration will rise upon corroboration, and the murderer will be traced."

But in concluding his story Poe neglects to show Dupin catching and exposing the murderer. Instead, Poe concludes abruptly, using the trick of an inserted editorial note which announces: "We feel it advisable only to state, in brief, that the result desired was brought to pass; and that the Prefect fulfilled punctually, although with reluctance, the terms of his compact with the Chevalier."

There was no immediate discernible reaction to the magazine publication of "The Mystery of Marie Roget." It was not until almost four years later, when the story appeared again as part of a collection of Poe's fiction, that it made any impression at all. In July 1845 the publishing firm of Wiley and Putnam selected "Marie Roget" and eleven others of Poe's narratives, out of the seventy-two he had written, for reprinting in book form. Before publication, however, Poe took great care to revise this story, as well as several others.

In a series of factual footnotes Poe explained that "the lapse of several years since the tragedy upon which the tale is based" made the notes and revisions necessary. "A young girl, Mary

Cecilia Rogers, was murdered in the vicinity of New York,"
he explained, "and although her death occasioned an intense and
long-enduring excitement, the mystery attending it had remained unsolved at the period when the present paper was
written and published (November, 1842). Herein, under pretence of relating the fate of a Parisian grisette, the author has
followed, in minute detail, the essential, while merely paral-
leling the inessential facts of the real murder of Mary Rogers.
Thus all argument founded upon the fiction is applicable to
the truth: and the investigation of the truth was the object.
. . . The confessions of two persons (one of them the Madame
Deluc of the narrative) made, at different periods, long subsequent to the publication, confirmed, in full, not only the general conclusion, but absolutely all the chief hypothetical details
by which that conclusion was attained."

Wiley and Putnam's 228-page pamphlet *Tales by Edgar A.
Poe* appeared as Number XI of the firm's Library of American
Books, priced at fifty cents a copy, of which eight cents went
in royalties to the impoverished author. Upon its appearance
in the bookshops, it was heavily outsold by two competing
imports from abroad: *The Count of Monte Cristo*, by Alexandre
Dumas, and *The Wandering Jew*, by Eugène Sue. Nevertheless,
it did attain a moderate sale.

The real success of the *Tales*, on the heels of "The Raven,"
which had been published six months earlier, was not financial
but critical. The *Boston Courier* pronounced it "thrilling" and
the *New York Post* recommended it as "a rare treat." In London,
the *Literary Gazette* considered its author a genius, and in Paris,
Baudelaire was honored to translate it into French. Of the
twelve tales, "Marie Roget" created the greatest divergence of
opinion. And, in the century since, the novelette has continued
to divide its readers. Edmund Pearson thought it "rather tedious" and Howard Haycraft felt that it had "no life-blood."
Russel Crouse disagreed. "It is a brilliant study in the repudi-
ation of false clues," he said, "a fascinating document in the
field of pseudo-criminology."

The Real Marie Roget

Whatever its actual literary merit, "The Mystery of Marie Roget" attained early immortality as one of the three tales—preceded by "The Rue Morgue" in 1841 and followed by "The Purloined Letter" in 1844—responsible for the founding of the modern detective story. Scholars have variously credited Herodotus, the Bible, and the *Arabian Nights* with this honor. Their erudition must be rejected as utter nonsense. As George Bates has remarked: "The cause of Chaucer's silence on the subject of airplanes was because he had never seen one. You cannot write about policemen before policemen exist to be written of."

Organized crime-detection was in its infancy when Edgar Allan Poe created the character of Dupin. The mystery story was an unheard-of art form when Poe became, in the words of Willard Huntington Wright, "the authentic father of the detective novel as we know it today." In "Marie Roget," and in his two other crime stories, Poe prepared the mold for the first eccentric amateur sleuth and his thick-witted foil, a mold which a thousand authors have used in the years since. In these stories, too, Poe introduced the first of a legion of stupid police officers, red herrings, perfect crimes, and psychological deductions.

After Poe, of course, came the deluge. But in his lifetime he had no idea of what he had wrought. His detective tales, as startling innovations, profited him little. With Virginia's death, he buried Dupin. He dwelt in an alcoholic daze. He became engaged to several wealthy women, but married none. In Baltimore, bleary with drink, drugs, and insanity, he stumbled into the chaos of a Congressional election and was led by hoodlums from poll to poll to vote over and over again as a repeater. Left in a gutter without his clothes or his senses, he was taken to the Washington College Hospital, where he groaned: "I wish to God somebody would blow my damned brains out." It was on a Sunday's dawn that he died murmuring: "God help my poor soul."

But seven years before, when he first wrote "Marie Roget," he saw himself as something better. The character of C. Auguste Dupin was Poe's idealization of himself, "a cool, infallible thinking machine that brought the power of reason to bear on all of life's problems." The name Dupin he had found in an article on the French Sûreté in *Burton's Magazine*. This was probably André Dupin, a French politician who wrote on criminal procedures and died in 1865.

The character of the blundering Prefect G was undoubtedly drawn from the very real, if quite improbable, François Vidocq, a French baker's son who was sent to the galleys for thievery, and who later served as head of the Sûreté for eighteen years. Poe read Vidocq's fanciful four-volume *Mémoires*, which contained the detective's boast that he had placed twenty thousand criminals in jail. Poe was not impressed. He thought Vidocq "a good guesser" and a man who "erred continually by the very intensity of his investigations. He impaired his vision by holding the object too close."

But the most important character in "The Mystery of Marie Roget" was the unhappy victim. And she, as Poe has told us, was Mary Cecilia Rogers.

Despite her subsequent notoriety, Mary Rogers's beginnings remain as enigmatic as her sudden end. For all the columns of copy published in the days following her death, Mary Rogers continues a shadowy, forever tantalizing figure of a young woman. She was born in New York City during 1820. There was, apparently, an older brother, who went to sea in his youth and engaged in a variety of speculative enterprises abroad. We know nothing of Mary's father, except what Poe wrote of her fictional counterpart, Marie Roget: "The father had died during the child's infancy, and from the period of his death . . . the mother and daughter had dwelt together." As Mary grew up, her widowed mother, ill, nervous, harried by debt, sought some means of making a livelihood. This problem was solved by Mary's seafaring brother, who returned from South America with profits gained from an obscure business venture. He presented a portion of these profits to mother and sister, then signed on a ship and sailed out of our story.

The Real Marie Roget

Mrs. Rogers wisely invested her windfall in a boardinghouse located at 126 Nassau Street in New York City. While the house gave Mary and her mother a roof over their heads, it gave them little else. At no time did it entertain more than two or three male boarders, and these were usually struggling clerks or laborers.

To supplement the meager income of the boarding house, Mary Rogers decided to seek outside employment. This was in 1837, when she was seventeen. All accounts agree that she was beautiful. Crude contemporary prints depict her as a dark-eyed brunette, who wore her hair fashionably bunned. She had a complexion without blemish and an aquiline nose, and was much admired for her "dark smile." She was favored, too, with a full, firm bosom, a slender figure, and a manner of great vivacity. She did not have to look far for employment. Her beauty came to the attention to one John Anderson, a snuff-manufacturer who ran a tobacco shop at 319 Broadway, near Thomas Street. Aware that "her good looks and vivacity" would be an asset to a business which catered to male trade, Anderson installed Mary behind his counter. The store was already a popular hangout for gamblers, sporty bachelors, newspaper reporters, and magazine editors. With the appearance of Mary Rogers, the clientele grew and improved.

We know that during 1837 and 1838 Edgar Allan Poe frequented the tobacconist's and was impressed with Mary Rogers. But there were other author customers, more prosperous and better known, who were equally impressed. Fitz-Greene Halleck, the somewhat forbidding, partially deaf, middle-aged poet, who had once served as secretary to John Jacob Astor, often appeared carrying his familiar green cotton umbrella. He was, it is said, sufficiently enchanted by Mary to write a poem rhapsodizing her beauty.

James Fenimore Cooper, on his frequent trips to New York from Cooperstown, was another regular at John Anderson's. He was a breezy, frank, pugnacious man, who had already published *The Spy* and spent a fortune instigating libel suits against reviewers who called his writings "garbage." Cooper was uninhibited in his opinions, and highly vocal, and there can be little doubt that he often sounded off to Mary on the money-madness of America and the provincialism of New York.

The most famous customer, however, was fifty-four-year-old Washington Irving. He dwelt alone in a small stone Dutch cottage on the Hudson, and was known everywhere for his creation of Ichabod Crane and Rip Van Winkle. A stout, genial, unaffected man, Irving must have entranced Mary Rogers with anecdotes of his youth. As a lawyer he had helped defend Aaron Burr. And he counted among his friends Dolly Madison, John Howard Payne, and Mary Godwin Shelley.

Few of the customers attended Mary Rogers after shop hours. At her mother's insistence, the proprietor, when he could, escorted her home at dusk. For New York was shot through with rowdyism. At nightfall the gangs, the Bowery Boys and the Dead Rabbits, rose out of the slums to molest, to maim, and to murder with butcher knives. It was estimated that in the waterfront area alone over fifteen thousand sailors were robbed of two million dollars in a single year.

Though there was much that was unlovely in New York—Dickens disliked the spittoons as much as the slums, and Cooper objected to the pigs in the red-brick streets—there was also much that held attraction for a young lady. There were beer gardens that seated a thousand persons, and behind the wrought-iron fences of the great homes couples danced the polka and the waltz, and to the north of the city were vast green picnic grounds and glistening ponds for boating. There is every reason to believe that Mary Rogers enjoyed these pleasures.

While she may not have dated her customers, there is evidence that Mary Rogers was a gay girl. After her death, much was made of her chastity. Dr. Richard Cook, of Hoboken, who performed the autopsy, announced that Mary had been "a good girl." He reaffirmed to the *New York Herald* "that previous to this shocking outrage, she had evidently been a person of chastity and correct habits." Surely the good doctor's diagnosis was more sentimental than scientific. From the number and variety of the young men who were interrogated after her death and who seemed to know her intimately, it is unlikely that Mary Rogers was a virgin.

Especially she seemed to have great affection for numerous of her mother's boardinghouse guests. William Keekuck, a young sailor who had boarded with Mrs. Rogers in 1840, had occasionally dated Mary, as had his older brother before him. Alfred Crommelin, for whom she left a rose on the last day of her life, was a handsome boarder characterized by the press as her "former suitor." Daniel Payne, a cork-cutter and an alcoholic, lived under the same roof as Mary, dated her regularly, and intended to marry her. These were three escorts known by name. There were probably many more. In the light of her environment, it is surprising that Mary's reputation was not worse. She had grown to maturity without paternal discipline, without family life, without security. Her beauty had marked her as a perpetual target for adventurous men-about-town. Her job, in a shop patronized solely by males, made her sophisticated beyond her years. Her oppressive financial status and her confinement to a rundown boardinghouse, coupled with a lively personality, encouraged her to accept nocturnal escape with any attractive gallant.

In October of 1838, when she was only eighteen, there occurred a curious interlude in the life of Mary Rogers. On the morning of Thursday, October 4, she failed to appear for work at the cigar store. The same day, her distressed mother found a note from Mary on her bedroom table. The contents of the note, which Mrs. Rogers turned over to the city coroner's office, were never divulged. Three and a half years later, at the time of her death, the *New York Herald* told its readers: "This young girl, Mary Rogers, was missing from Anderson's store . . . for two weeks. It is asserted that she was then seduced by an officer of the U.S. Navy, and kept at Hoboken for two weeks. His name is well known on board his ship."

The reporters who frequented the cigar store, and knew

Mary, quickly filed stories on her disappearance. With one exception, they all suspected foul play. The one exception was an anonymous cynic on the *Commercial Advertiser* who thought that the young lady had gone "into concealment that it might be believed she had been abducted, in order to help the sale of the goods of her employer."

After two weeks the erratic Mary returned to her mother and her job. She had no explanation to offer, beyond remarking that she had "felt tired" and gone to rest with some friends in Brooklyn. When she was shown a copy of the *Commercial Advertiser*, with its snide suspicions of hoax, she became furious. "She felt so annoyed at such a report having got abroad during her temporary absence on a country excursion," said the *Journal of Commerce*, "that she positively refused ever to return to the store." It is not known for certain, however, if she actually quit John Anderson's because her honesty was impugned by the customers, or if she quit simply because her mother, ailing and infirm, required her assistance to help maintain the boardinghouse. But quit she did, in 1839, some months after returning from her mysterious vacation.

Her activities in the three years following are unknown. It is to be presumed that she spent her days cleaning and cooking in her mother's boardinghouse, and her nights supplying diversion for her mother's paid-up roomers. We know that one boarder, Alfred Crommelin, ardently pursued her and was rejected. Her disinterest determined him to remove his person from the boardinghouse. However, he made it clear that if she had a change of heart, he might still be available. Another roomer, the convivial cork-cutter Daniel Payne, had more success. Though a man of limited means, he found ways to entertain Mary and became her most frequent escort. They soon reached an understanding, and Mary began to refuse all outside engagements. Payne was under the impression that they were engaged to be married. But before a date could be determined, another date occurred of more historic importance in the annals of crime.

The Real Marie Roget

Sometime on Saturday morning, July 24, 1841, Mary Rogers visited the office of her rejected suitor, Alfred Crommelin. He was out to an early lunch and his business quarters were closed. From his door, as was the custom, he had hung a slate for messages. On this slate Mary enigmatically scribbled her mother's name. Then she inserted a rose in the keyhole of the door and departed. Crommelin discovered both the signature on the slate and the red rose shortly after lunch, but, as far as we know, did nothing about them. Perhaps he was occupied with his business. Perhaps he was not satisfied with the show of affection. Or perhaps he visited her after all and never confessed it.

The following morning—the now famous morning of Sunday, July 25, 1841—broke hot and humid. It was, the press duly reported, ninety-three degrees in the shade. Many New Yorkers went to church. Many more New Yorkers fled the furnace of the metropolis for the greener pastures of New Jersey and Connecticut. Mary Rogers, too, decided to escape the heat of the city's center. It was ten o'clock in the morning when she rapped on Daniel Payne's bedroom door. He was busy shaving. She called to him that she was going to spend the day at the home of a cousin, Mrs. Downing, whom she frequently visited. Payne, occupied with his beard, called back that he would meet her when she descended from the stage at Broadway and Ann Street at seven o'clock that evening. This was agreeable to Mary, and she promptly left for her cousin's residence on Jane Street two miles away.

Late in the afternoon Payne bestirred himself, went into the city, and dallied at several grog shops where he was well known. When he emerged shortly before seven to keep his rendezvous, he noticed that heavy clouds hung low overhead. There were rumblings of thunder and flashes of lightning. Certain that a rainfall was in store, and aware of Mary's habits, he decided that she would probably spend the night with her relative. He did not bother to go to Broadway and Ann Street. Instead, he returned directly to Mrs. Rogers's boardinghouse and went to bed.

When Payne came down to breakfast in the morning, Mary had not yet appeared. Since it had poured the night before, and since the hour was still early, her absence was not unusual. But when Payne made his way back to the house for lunch and found that Mary had still not appeared, he was disturbed. Mrs. Rogers was also disturbed. She was heard by her colored maid to remark that "she feared she would never see Mary again."

Immediately after lunch Payne set out for Mrs. Downing's place in Jane Street. Upon his arrival he was surprised and agitated to learn that Mary was not there. Nor had she been there the previous day. She had been expected, but had not appeared. Mrs. Downing had not seen her in over a week.

By nightfall Payne and Mrs. Rogers had contacted all of Mary's relatives and friends in the vicinity. None had seen her. None had heard from her. She had disappeared completely. Payne and Mrs. Rogers were now sufficiently alarmed to try other means of inquiry. Payne went to the offices of the *New York Sun*, the most widely read of the cheaper newspapers, and placed an advertisement asking for information about Mary Cecilia Rogers.

The advertisement appeared in the *Sun* on July 27. Among its many readers was Alfred Crommelin, the rejected suitor who had so recently received a rose from Mary. He, too, was troubled by her curious disappearance, her second such in three and one-half years. Crommelin promptly appointed himself a search party of one. He assumed that Payne and Mrs. Rogers had thoroughly scoured the city. He determined to try the outskirts. On Wednesday morning he made his way toward Hoboken, New Jersey. What sent him so far afield, yet with such unerring accuracy, we must deduce for ourselves.

It was a sweltering morning when Crommelin reached Hoboken. He was about to make inquiries after Mary, when he noticed a group of people gathering on the Hudson at a site where spring water was sold for a penny a glass. This site, a cool retreat on the water, was known as Sybil's Cave. Crommelin joined the crowd, and then became aware for the first time of what they were watching. All eyes were on a rowboat, manned by two men, being pulled toward the shore, dragging behind it a body attached to a rope.

What had occurred, only minutes before, was that two sight-seers, James M. Boulard and Henry Mallin, while strolling beside the water, had noticed a human form floating in midstream. The pair had immediately requisitioned the rowboat and headed for the body. Almost simultaneously three men in a sailboat, John Bertram, William Waller, and someone named Luther, had also seen the body, which they had at first thought to be a bag of clothing, and started toward it. The rowboat got there first. The body was that of a disfigured, fully dressed young female. Boulard and Mallin hastily secured a rope to her and pulled her in.

When the unfortunate female at last lay on the beach, Crommelin pressed forward with the others for a better view. Crommelin recognized the corpse at once. "It's Mary Rogers!" he exclaimed. "This blow may kill her mother!"

She was still wearing the costume she had worn four days earlier—flowered bonnet, its ribbon tied under her chin, blue dress, petticoat, pantalets, stockings, and garters. Her face had been badly bashed, and her body bore bruises of violence. From the condition of her corpse, there was every evidence of foul play. Mary's wrists were tightly tied with hemp, and about her throat was wound a strip of lace torn from her petticoat. Edgar Allan Poe, in his graphic account, made it clear that death was caused by strangulation, not by drowning. "The flesh of the neck was much swollen," he wrote. "There were no cuts apparent, or bruises which appeared the effect of blows. A piece of lace was found tied so tightly around the neck as to be hidden from sight; it was completely buried in the flesh. . . . The knot by which the strings of the bonnet were fastened was not a lady's, but a slip or sailor's knot."

Upon the arrival of the Hudson County authorities, the body was promptly transferred from the beach to the small village of

Hoboken. There, Dr. Richard F. Cook, serving as county coroner, hastily performed the autopsy. By nine o'clock that evening the formal inquest began. Crommelin once more identified the corpse as that of Mary Rogers. He spoke of her reputation for "truthfulness, and modesty and discretion," and theorized that she had probably been lured to the Hoboken area by some man. Dr. Cook then testified as to the results of his autopsy. She had been murdered, he stated. She had also been subjected to sexual intercourse, most likely raped, possibly once, possibly many times.

When the witnesses at the inquest had concluded their testimony, the coroner's jury deliberated briefly, then announced that the victim's death had been caused by "violence committed by some person or persons." And thus the mystery of Mary Rogers was officially embarked upon its journey into history.

Mary's mother and Daniel Payne had been notified of the tragedy earlier in the day. The news was brought to them by the man named Luther, who had witnessed from his sailboat the recovery of the body. The day following the inquest, Alfred Crommelin appeared at the boardinghouse to confirm the identification of Mary. He had secured from the Hoboken morgue a flower from Mary's hat, a curl from her hair, a strip of her pantalets, and a garter. These he displayed to the bereaved mother. Mary had been buried hours before. The speedy interment was made necessary by the rapid decomposition of her body due to excessive exposure to water and hot weather.

Though Mary Rogers had vanished on July 25, 1841, and had been found on July 28, no New York newspaper mentioned her murder until August 1. After that, for more than two months she was rarely off the front pages of the popular press.

The sensational publicity accorded the case created wide and feverish interest. Despite this, the police made only desultory efforts to solve it. There was an immediate dispute over the matter of jurisdiction. New Jersey authorities tried to lay the investigation in the lap of the New York police, arguing that Mary had been killed in New York and dumped into the Hudson, and had drifted into the New Jersey area by sheerest accident. The New York police, on the other hand, replied that Mary had been slain off Hoboken, had been discovered near that community and buried there, and that therefore the problem was plainly a responsibility of the New Jersey authorities.

While both states wrangled, the Manhattan press helped resolve the issue by accusing the New York police of shirking their duty, pointing out that Mary Rogers, no matter where she was killed, had been a resident and citizen of New York. At last New York City officialdom bowed to this pressure and reluctantly undertook the case. On Wednesday, August 11, Mary Rogers was exhumed from her Hoboken grave and removed to the Dead House at City Hall Park in New York City. Mrs. Rogers and several relatives were brought to the Dead House, where they positively identified various articles of clothing that had belonged to Mary.

The New York police now had the enigma in their hands. They were neither equipped to solve it, nor, it must be admitted, were they terribly interested. The High Constable of the force, a squat, bald-headed old man named Jacob Hays, was capable enough. He had solved many crimes during his career, and had introduced the techniques of shadowing and the third degree to America. But at the time he was handed the portfolio of the Mary Rogers case, he was sixty-nine years old and approaching retirement. Hays, therefore, turned the case over to his handful of Leatherheads—so-called after the heavy leather helmets they wore—and assigned its perusal to a Sergeant McArdel.

The Leatherheads, who wore no uniforms and carried no firearms, were divided into two groups. The daytime force consisted of two constables from each city ward and a half-dozen marshals. The night force, called the Night Watch, consisted of 146 men. The latter group worked as laborers during the day, then supplemented their salaries by becoming policemen at night. Their pay, as part-time law-enforcement officers, was eighty-seven cents an evening.

Naturally, since they were overworked and underpaid, the Leatherheads had little interest in any new crime that might require extra exertion. Furthermore, many resented any intrusion upon their routine activities, which had been so organized as to give them bonuses above their meager police pay. For, since the city would not raise their wages, a great number of police bolstered their incomes by secretly allying themselves with professional criminals. The standard practice was for thieves to ransack a shop while the Leatherheads turned their backs. Then, when the shopkeepers offered cash rewards for the return of their merchandise, the Leatherheads miraculously recovered the loot, though rarely the looters. Upon collecting the rewards, the Leatherheads split the money with the criminals. Theft was a paying business; murder, unless there was a reward involved, was not. The Mary Rogers case, then, was little more than an unprofitable nuisance.

For almost two weeks after the murder, the police remained inert, while the press fumed and the public boiled. On the day Mary Rogers's corpse was transferred to New York, a committee of angry citizens acted. They sponsored an open meeting and collected $445, to be given as a reward to anyone who apprehended the killer. Shortly after, Governor Seward of New York added an official reward of $750, and the guarantee of a full pardon to any accomplice willing to turn informant.

Now, at last, there was sufficient bounty to spur Sergeant McArdel and his Leatherheads into action. Quickly a long list of suspects was summoned to police headquarters and interrogated. Foremost among these was Daniel Payne. He had known Mary Rogers best, and spoken to her last, before her disappearance. It was felt that he had acted in a suspiciously "unloverlike" manner, presumably because he had not troubled to wait for her at Broadway and Ann Street as he had promised. The police theorized that she might have quit him for another, and that he, in a drunken rage, might have killed her out of jealousy. But Payne, in a detailed statement, was able to account for every hour of the critical Sunday.

The Real Marie Roget

Alfred Crommelin was the next to be questioned. The police, remembering the rose in the keyhole, felt that "there was still some slight tendresse betwixt him and the young lady." Also, Crommelin had been curiously anxious to halt the police investigation. Earlier, he had begged McArdel to drop the case, since a continued inquiry, with its attendant notoriety, might be seriously damaging to Mrs. Rogers's health. Yet Crommelin, like Payne, had an acceptable alibi.

Another of Mrs. Rogers's boarders remained suspect. Dr. Cook had indicated that the bonnet string about Mary's chin had been tied in a sailor's knot, and that there was a sailor's hitch behind her dress, by means of which she had been lifted and dropped into the Hudson. It appeared that, the year before, a young man named William Keekuck had roomed with Mrs. Rogers. Keekuck was now an ordinary sailor in the United States Navy. He was at sea, on the U.S.S. *North Carolina* when the authorities sent for him. The moment his ship docked at Norfolk, Virginia, Keekuck was taken off and hustled to New York for cross-examination. There was indeed some evidence against the frightened sailor. He had boarded his vessel in a great hurry, and very late, the night of July 25. His trousers had been stained, though it was no longer possible to prove that these had been bloodstains. Keekuck admitted that he had dwelt with Mrs. Rogers, and had known Mary, but insisted that he had been only an acquaintance. It was his brother who had been a suitor. Though in New York City on shore leave during July 25, he had not seen Mary Rogers. In fact, he had not seen her since July 3, and was able to substantiate this to the temporary satisfaction of the police; but before he was finally dismissed, William Keekuck was three times hauled off the *North Carolina* for questioning.

Meanwhile, the police were bringing in other promising suspects. Great hopes were held, briefly, over the apprehension of one Joseph M. Morse, a rotund and bewhiskered wood-engraver, who lived in Nassau Street near Mrs. Rogers's boardinghouse. On the Sunday of Mary Rogers's disappearance,

Morse had been seen traveling to Staten Island with an attractive young lady who was not his wife. On the morning Mary was removed from the Hudson, Morse heard about it, left his business at midday, returned home in a frenzied state, had an argument with his wife, beat her up, and departed the metropolis for parts unknown. The authorities were swiftly on his trail. They found him in Worcester, Massachusetts. He had shaved off his beard, purposely lost weight, and was hiding under an assumed name. His prospects, to say the least, were dismal.

Morse was brought back to New York City under guard. There were mutterings in the street of lynch. Morse quickly admitted that he had picked up a comely young lady on the Sunday in question and escorted her to Staten Island. His purpose was not homicidal, but carnal. He had, in fact, shown some ingenuity. He had set his watch back in order to miss the last ferry home. The ruse was successful. Morse then suggested to the young lady that they adjourn to a hotel. She proved amenable. They rented rooms, whereupon Morse made amorous advances, as per plan. These advances, he remarked unhappily, were rejected. He slept the night alone, and returned on the morning ferry to his family hearth and his wood-engraving business. Shortly after, he heard from neighbors of Mary Rogers's Sunday disappearance and death. At once he worried that his attractive companion might have been Mary Rogers. Though he had left her defiant and healthy, he realized that she might have been murdered after his departure, and that he would be discovered and blamed. Without further ado, he fled the suddenly oppressive climate of New York City for Massachusetts.

While the police weighed the veracity of Mr. Morse's little adventure, the penny press publicized it. And luckily for Mr. Morse. For, shortly after, the young lady Morse had abandoned on Staten Island came forward to identify herself and to corroborate his story and her own virginity. The police promptly turned the Sunday Lothario over to the custody and further cross-examination of his waiting spouse.

But the mystery of Mary Rogers still remained unsolved. McArdel and his Leatherheads now abandoned Mrs. Rogers's boarders and the other obvious suspects to concentrate on a line of investigation that had been too long neglected. The police asked themselves the following questions: What had been Mary Rogers's movements after she left the boardinghouse for her cousin's residence? Since she had left at ten o'clock in the morning, while church was out and the streets were filled, who had seen her? And whom had she been seen with? In what direction was she headed? And by what means of transport? These questions, much to the gratification of McArdel, speedily produced an entire new net of suspects and theories.

A stage-driver named Adam Wall was found who thought he had picked up Mary Rogers at the Bull's Head ferry and driven her to a picnic area near Hoboken. Wall said she was accompanied by "a tall dark man," perhaps twenty-six years of age.

Others quickly appeared to support the assumption that Mary had visited Hoboken with a stranger or strangers. In fact, two men told the authorities that they had been walking along the shore, approaching Sybil's Cave, on July 25, when they observed a rowboat land with six young males and a girl. The girl was attractive enough to hold their attention. Minutes after the girl ran off into the near-by woods with her bevy of admirers, another rowboat, containing three anxious gentlemen, drew up. Its occupants inquired of the two visitors if they had seen six men and a girl in the vicinity. When the visitors admitted they had seen just such a group head into the woods, the occupants of the rowboat inquired if the girl had gone willingly or by force. Upon learning that she had gone willingly, the occupants took to their oars and slid away.

Next, several witnesses came forward with the recollection of seeing Mary strolling that Sunday morning toward Barclay

Street in Manhattan. At Theatre Alley, a short lane off Ann Street which once led to the stage door of the Park Theatre, she had been met by a young man "with whom she was apparently acquainted." From the direction she took thereafter, it was thought she could have gone to the Hoboken ferry—or entered the infamous residence of Mrs. Ann Lohman, a notorious and busy abortionist who was known to the carriage trade as Mme Restell.

Actually, there was no direct evidence to connect Mary Rogers's murder with Mme Restell's illegal practices. But whenever there occurred an untimely death in New York, especially one involving a fashionable or beautiful female, there were immediate whisperings against the portly and wealthy English-born Madame. Her record, to be sure, was unsavory. She had been an immigrant dressmaker, had wedded a dispenser of quack medicines named Lohman, and, it was thought, had disposed of him for the inheritance. Thereafter she had lent her talents to birth-control.

Mme Restell's mansion on Greenwich Street was visited by a steady stream of unmarried expectant women, many the mistresses of millionaires and Congressmen. At the time of Mary Roger's death, the Madame's shuttered establishment, nicknamed "the mansion built on baby skulls," had netted her earnings upwards of one million dollars. Shortly after Mary's burial, public feeling against Mme Restell ran so high that crowds gathered about her doorway shouting: "Haul her out! Where's the thousand children murdered in this house? Who murdered Mary Rogers?" On that occasion, violence was prevented only by the quick intervention of the police, who undoubtedly found the mammoth Madame too lucrative a source of income to trouble with such trifles as the corpse of a onetime cigar-counter employee.

The police had just about exhausted their inquiry into Mary Rogers's movements when a new and sensational bit of evidence suddenly came to light. Two young men, the sons of a Mrs. Frederica Loss, who kept a public inn a mile above Hoboken, were beating about the brush near Weehawken on August 25. In the thicket they found a small opening that led into a cramped tunnel or cave. They explored farther, and discovered inside the cave four stones built into a seat. Draped on and about the seat were a silk scarf, a white petticoat, a parasol, a pocketbook, a pair of gloves, and a mildewed linen handkerchief initialed in silk "M. R."

Mrs. Loss's sons immediately gathered up the feminine apparel and brought the find to their mother. She went directly to the Hoboken police, who excitedly contacted their colleagues in New York City. At once the press was filled with woodcuts and stories of Mrs. Loss, her inn, the two of her three sons who had made the discovery, and the opening in the thicket near the cliffs of Weehawken.

This publicity flushed forth a new witness. A stage-driver came forward. He dimly remembered transporting a girl of Mary Rogers's description and a tall "swarthy" man to Mrs. Loss's inn on July 25. This recollection succeeded in stirring Mrs. Loss's own memory. She vaguely remembered the couple. They had had cakes and drinks. Then Mary, or someone like her, and the "swarthy" man had gone off together into the nearby woods overlooking the river. Some minutes later Mrs. Loss had heard a woman's scream from the vicinity of the woods. She had paid no attention. On Sundays the area was filled with gangs of rowdies and loose young ladies who were often vocal.

With the find at Weehawken, all the tangible clues were in. Since the case had not been broken in fact, it could only be solved on paper. Police authorities and amateur sleuths of the city room were soon busy formulating and publishing theories. The overwhelming majority were in accord on Weehawken as the site of the crime. But on the subject of the ciminal's identity there was a great and passionate diversity of opinion.

Who killed Mary Rogers? In the months after her death, almost every literate contemporary was certain he knew. The authorities seemed to lean toward Mrs. Loss and her three sons. Justice Gilbert Merritt, of New Jersey, devoted much time to questioning Mrs. Loss. He believed that she practiced abortion, or permitted her inn to be employed by physicians for that purpose, and that Mary Rogers had died during an operation in one of her back rooms and had been disposed of in the Hudson by her sons. The effects in the thicket, he felt, were only a red herring to divert suspicion. "The murder of the said Mary C. Rogers was perpetrated in a house at Weehawken," Justice Merritt announced, "then kept by one Frederica Loss, alias Kellenbarack, and her three sons, all three of whom this deponent has reason to believe are worthless and profligate characters."

Sergeant McArdel, of the New York Leatherheads, interrogated only the three sons, and found them as undelightful as had Justice Merritt. They were sullen and they were contradictory. But they steadfastly denied that their mother had practiced abortion. When one of them was asked if visitors ever paid their mother fifty dollars for any purpose, he replied: "I never have known any sick person brought to my mother's house to be attended upon." McArdel, too, concluded that Mrs. Loss was guilty of manslaughter, and that her sons were her accomplices in removing the body.

Of all the authorities, Dr. Richard F. Cook held most heartily to his original theory that Mary had been gang-raped and then brutally killed. Again and again he told the press that he was "confident" she had been "violated by six, or possibly eight ruffians; of that fact, he had ocular proof, but which is unfit for publication."

The majority on newspaper row supported Dr. Cook's theory. Murder after murder had been committed by roving bands of rowdies in the New York metropolitan area and among the outing-sites of New Jersey. The weekly *Saturday Evening Post* saw signs of gang violence in the disorder of the thicket, and the *Journal of Commerce* saw the handiwork of street ruffians in the fact that no men's handkerchiefs had been used to strangle Mary. "A piece of one of the unfortunate girl's petticoats was torn out and tied under her chin, and around the back of her head, probably to prevent screams," remarked the *Journal of Commerce.* "This was done by fellows who had no pocket-handkerchiefs."

For weeks the *New York Herald*, which had been crusading against vandals and butcher boys, also championed the gang-rape notion. The *Herald* theorized that Mary and her "swarthy" escort had indeed visited Mrs. Loss's inn for refreshment, and then proceeded to the woods for further refreshment. In the brush they had been set upon by a waiting gang of roughnecks. Mary's escort had been assassinated immediately, and Mary herself slain after she had been attacked. Then both bodies had been shoved into the river. But if this held any probability, what happened to the remains of the "swarthy" escort? As a matter of fact, the body of an unidentified man was found floating in the Hudson five days after Mary's body was recovered. But the man was neither tall nor dark.

The *New York Herald* flirted with one other intriguing possibility. It recalled Mary's first disappearance, three and one-half years before the murder. "It is well known that, during the week of her absence . . . she was in the company of a young naval officer much noted for his debaucheries. A quarrel, it is supposed, providentially led to her return home. We have the name of the Lothario in question . . . but for obvious reasons forbear to make it public." The *New York Herald* was suspecting someone Mary had met through young Keekuck, possibly a superior on the U.S.S. *North Carolina.* Or possibly it was still making allusions to Keekuck himself.

Brother Jonathan was the first of several journals to subscribe to the idea that Mary Rogers had not been murdered at all. Its editors argued that a body in the water only three days, or less, would not be "so soon afloat" and that it would not be "so far decomposed." The corpse fished out of the Hudson at Sybil's Cave must have been in the water "not three days merely, but, at least, five times three days." Therefore, the body could not have been that of Mary Rogers.

On the other hand, if the body had actually been that of

Mary Rogers, then *Brother Jonathan*'s choice for the murderer was Alfred Crommelin. "For some reason," said the journal, "he determined that nobody shall have anything to do with the proceedings but himself, and he has elbowed the male relatives out of the way, according to their representations, in a very singular manner. He seems to have been very much averse to permitting the relatives to see the body."

Daniel Payne fared better than his rival boarder. While there were murmurings about his motives, and about his addiction to drink, all sources agreed that his affidavit concerning his activities on the fateful Sunday was foolproof. Though, as a matter of fact, no original suspect completely escaped judgment in the press. Even the unlucky Joseph Morse, woodengraver and commuter to Staten Island, had his backers. The *New York Courier and Inquirer* had received anonymous letters which made its editors regard Morse as quite capable of "the late atrocity."

Only one publication advocated Mme Restell as a candidate for the Tombs. The *National Police Gazette* doggedly waged a campaign against her. As late as February 1846 the *Police Gazette* was editorializing: "The wretched girl was last seen in the direction of Madame Restell's house. The dreadfully lacerated body at Weehawken Bluff bore the marks of no ordinary violation. The hat found near the spot, the day after the location of the body, was dry though it had rained the night before! These are strange but strong facts, and when taken in consideration with the other fact that the recently convicted Madame Costello kept an abortion house in Hoboken at that very time, and was acting as an agent of Restell, it challenges our minds for the most horrible suspicions."

There was yet one more theory to be put forth. And this, appearing more than a year after the crime, proved to be the most widely publicized and controversial of them all. It was, of course, the theory advanced by Edgar Allan Poe in "The Mystery of Marie Roget," which he expected would give "renewed impetus to investigation."

The Real Marie Roget

In his thinly disguised novelette—he used French names in the body of the story, but identified each character, newspaper, and site with factual footnotes relating to the Mary Rogers case—Poe began by attempting to demolish the pet theories promoted by his predecessors. "Our first step should be the determination of the identity of the corpse," Poe stated, obviously referring to *Brother Jonathan*'s conjecture that Mary Rogers still lived. At great length, and with questionable scientific accuracy, Poe pointed out that a body immersed in water less than three days could still float. "It may be said that very few human bodies will sink at all, even in fresh water, of their own accord." As to the impossibility of decomposition in less than three days: "All experience does *not* show that 'drowned bodies' require from six to ten days for sufficient decomposition to take place." In short, Poe had no doubt that the body recovered at Sybil's Cave was that of Mary Cecilia Rogers.

However, as to the exact scene of the crime Poe was less certain. That the thicket at Weehawken "was the scene, I may or I may not believe—but there was excellent reason for doubt." Poe set down his doubts in detail. If the articles of clothing had been in the thicket the entire four weeks after the murder, they would have been discovered earlier. The mildew on the parasol and handkerchief could have appeared on the objects overnight. Most important, "Let me beg your notice to the highly artificial arrangement of the articles. On the upper stone lay a white petticoat; on the second, a silk scarf; scattered around, were a parasol, gloves, and a pocket-handkerchief. . . . Here is just such an arrangement as would naturally be made by a not-over-acute person wishing to dispose the articles naturally. But it is by no means a really natural arrangement. I should rather have looked to see the things all lying on the ground and trampled under foot. In the narrow limits of that bower, it would have been scarcely possible that the petticoat and scarf should have retained a position upon the stones, when subjected to the brushing to and fro of many struggling persons." Yet, after all these observations against the Weehawken thicket as the scene of the crime, Poe, in the end, concluded that Mary Rogers must have met her end there, after all.

In studying the roll of suspects, Poe felt that there was no evidence whatsoever against Mme Restell or against Morse. He felt that Daniel Payne's deposition to the police vindicated him entirely. As to Crommelin: "He is a busybody, with much of romance and little of wit. Any one so constituted will readily so conduct himself, upon occasion of real excitement, as to render himself liable to suspicion." *Brother Jonathan*'s editors had selected Crommelin as the murderer, said Poe, because, resenting their implications that he had not properly identified the corpse, Crommelin had gone in and brashly insulted the journal's editors. Mrs. Loss was a possibility, but, from her actions, Poe felt that she had played only a secondary part in the crime.

Poe refuted most strongly the popular theory of gang murder. The thicket displayed signs of violent struggle, yet several men would have overcome a frail girl quickly and without struggle. There were evidences that the body had been dragged to the river. One killer might have dragged Mary's corpse, but for several, it would have been easier and quicker to carry her. Nor would a number of assailants have overlooked an initialed handkerchief. Finally: "I shall add but one to the arguments against a gang; but this one has, to my own understanding at least, a weight altogether irresistible. Under the circumstances of large reward offered, and full pardon to any king's evidence, it is not to be imagined for a moment, that some member of a gang of low ruffians, or of any body of men, would not long ago have betrayed his accomplices. . . . That the secret has not been divulged is the very best proof that it is, in fact, a secret. The horrors of this dark deed are known only to one."

This, then, was the essence of Poe's theory. The crime, he insisted, had been committed by a single individual in the thicket at Weehawken. Carefully he reconstructed the murder:—

"An individual has committed the murder. He is alone with

the ghost of the departed. He is appalled by what lies motion-
less before him. The fury of his passion is over, and there is
abundant room in his heart for the natural awe of the deed. His
is none of that confidence which the presence of numbers inevitably inspires. He is *alone* with the dead. He trembles and is
bewildered. Yet there is a necessity for disposing of the corpse.
He bears it to the river, and leaves behind him the other evidences of his guilt; for it is difficult, if not impossible to carry
all the burthen at once, and it will be easy to return for what is
left. But in his toilsome journey to the water his fears redouble
within him. The sounds of life encompass his path. A dozen
times he hears or fancies he hears the step of an observer. Even
the very lights from the city bewilder him. Yet, in time, and by
long and frequent pauses of deep agony, he reaches the river's
brink, and disposes of his ghastly charge—perhaps through the
medium of a boat. But now what treasure does the world hold
—what threat of vengeance could it hold out—which would
have power to urge the return of that lonely murderer over that
toilsome and periolous path, to the thicket and its blood-chilling
recollections? He returns not, let the consequences be what they
may."

And who was this murderer?

He was, Poe decided, an earlier lover. He was the young man
who had eloped with Mary Rogers on her first disappearance
from the cigar store. Three and one-half years later he returned
and proposed again. "And here let me call your attention to the
fact, that the time elapsing between the first ascertained and the
second supposed elopement is a few months more than the
general period of the cruises of our men-of-war." He was,
then, a navy man on shore leave, the very officer the *New York
Herald* stated she had once gone off with. When he came back
to New York, he interrupted Mary's engagement to Payne.
She began to see him secretly. But why did he kill her? Possibly
he seduced her and she became pregnant. He took her to Mrs.
Loss's for an abortion, and she died accidentally. Or possibly
he failed to seduce her, and, on an outing to Weehawken, he

finally raped her. Then, fearing the consequences of the act, he was forced to kill. At any rate, concluded Poe: "This associate is of swarthy complexion. This complexion, the 'hitch' in the bandage, and the 'sailor's knot' with which the bonnet-ribbon is tied, point to a seaman. His companionship with the deceased —a gay but not an abject young girl—designates him as above the grade of the common sailor."

Poe, like the *New York Herald* before him, claimed to know the name of this navy officer. On January 4, 1848, in a letter to an admirer, a young medical student in Maine named George Eveleth, Poe disclosed: "Nothing was omitted in 'Marie Roget' but what I omitted myself:—all that is mystification. The story was originally published in Snowden's 'Lady's Companion.' The 'naval officer' who committed the murder (or rather the accidental death arising from an attempt at abortion) confessed it; and the whole matter is now well understood— but, for the sake of relatives, this is a topic on which I must not speak further."

In 1880 John H. Ingram published a biography of Poe. In it he revealed the name of Poe's suspected "naval officer." The name of the murderer, said Ingram, was Spencer. He did not know his first name, or explain where he had learned his second name. Based on this bit of name-dropping, William Kurtz Wimsatt, Jr., of Yale University, in an investigation of Poe's deductive prowess, attempted to track down the elusive Spencer. He learned that at the time of Mary Rogers's death in 1841 there were only three officers in the United States Navy named Spencer. One was in Ohio at the time Mary vanished in New York; another was infirm; the third was active, and a definite and fascinating possibility. He was eighteen-year-old Philip Spencer, the problem son of Secretary of War John Canfield Spencer. In short, his family was sufficiently influential to hush up any bit of unpremeditated homicide and sufficiently impressive to make Poe admit that "for the sake of relatives, this is a topic on which I must not speak further." Philip Spencer, it might be added, was quite capable of carrying on an affair with Mary and seeing her to an abortionist, or of killing her under different circumstances. Three months before the murder he had been expelled from his third school, Geneva College (now Hobart College), for "moral delinquency." He drank too much and he absented himself from classes too often. Where did he spend his time of truancy? In New York, and with Mary? We do not know. But we do know that in the year following her death he was caught and convicted of planning, and almost executing, the only mutiny in American naval history. Returning from a training cruise to Africa aboard the brig *Somers*, Acting Midshipman Philip Spencer chafed at the conditions on the vessel. He conspired with two subordinates, Boatswain's Mate Samuel Cromwell and Seaman Elisha Small, to kill his superiors and convert the *Somers* into a pirate ship. His plot—though the seriousness of his intention later became a matter of great controversy—was exposed in time by Captain Alexander Mackenzie, and young Spencer, hooded and manacled, was hanged from the main yardarm with his unfortunate companions.

While the publication of Poe's "The Mystery of Marie Roget" created a brief flurry of interest in Mary Rogers, it must be remarked that this interest was confined largely to readers of *Snowden's Ladies' Companion*. By 1842 the Leatherheads had given up their hope of obtaining the cash reward and had reverted to their old, less complex practice of restoring stolen merchandise. By 1844 the Leatherheads had been replaced by the more efficient, better-paid Municipal Police, and High Constable Jacob Hay was in retirement. As for the press, it had turned to matters of more topical interest. With each passing month, as the Mary Rogers case receded in time, the chances for its solution became more difficult. For one thing, popular interest, always fickle, had subsided, and with it the pressure that stimulated police activity. For another, the mortality rate among the suspects had mounted in rapidity—and violence.

On Friday, October 8, 1841, Daniel Payne followed his

betrothed to an early grave. On that morning a boatman, walking down a path to the Hudson River at Weehawken, passed the much-publicized thicket. He saw a man stretched on the ground. The man was Daniel Payne. Beside him was an empty bottle of laudanum. He was alive when the boatman reached him, but lapsed unconscious and never recovered. Two days later a coroner's jury agreed that he had committed suicide, but decided that his death might also be attributed to "congestion of the brain, brought about by irregular living, exposure, aberration of the mind." His friends announced that from the day he learned of Mary's death Payne had lived almost exclusively on a diet of rum, and had probably drunk himself to death.

A month later Mrs. Loss was also dead. One of her sons had been tampering with a loaded gun, when it accidentally discharged. The bullet struck her. As she lay dying, she summoned Justice Gilbert Merritt. She said she had a statement to make concerning the fate of Mary Rogers. According to the *New York Tribune*, Mrs. Loss made the following deathbed confession:

"On the Sunday of Miss Rogers's disappearance she came to her house from this city in company with a young physician, who undertook to procure for her a premature delivery. While in the hands of the physician she died, and a consultation was then held as to the disposal of her body. It was finally taken at night by the son of Mrs. Loss and sunk in the river. . . . Her clothes were first tied up in a bundle and sunk in a pond . . . but it was afterward thought that were not safe there, and they were accordingly taken and scattered through the woods as they were found."

After Mrs. Loss's death, her sons were closely questioned. They refused to confirm their mother's confession. The authorities also discredited it, and it was soon forgotten.

On April Fool's Day, 1878, Mme Restell, hounded by Anthony Comstock and fearing a jail sentence (she had once served a year on Blackwell's Island), donned a diamond-studded nightgown and stepped into her bathtub. Minutes later she was dead by her own hand. She had cut her throat. "A bloody ending to a bloody life," was Comstock's epitaph. The *Police Gazette* only regretted that she had expired without a word about Mary Rogers.

In the more than one hundred years that have passed since the death of Mary Rogers, every other suspect went to his grave in silence. Yet not one was permitted to rest in peace. For the mystery of Mary Rogers provided too fascinating and gruesome a game to be affected by any time limit. Though the $1,195 cash reward may have long since expired, the pursuit of a solution continued to hold rewards of its own. The reason is plain: a solved crime is a mere spectator sport, but an unsolved one remains an invitation to participate.

"There is no more stimulating activity than that of the mind, and there is no more exciting adventure than that of the intellect," Willard Huntington Wright once remarked. "Mankind has always received keen enjoyment from the mental gymnastics required in solving a riddle." Few unsolved crimes, it is true, have possessed those elements of murder most foul, yet complex, with clues and suspects sufficient, yet bizarre and simple, to provide riddles of enduring quality. But there have been a handful that managed to meet all specifications. The destruction of Andrew and Abby Borden, in Fall River, Massachusetts, was such a riddle. The shooting of Joseph Bowne Elwell, the bridge expert, in his New York apartment, was another. The discovery of Starr Faithfull on a Long Island beach fulfilled the stringent requirements. And certainly the savage slaying of Julia Wallace in a London suburb while her husband, William Herbert Wallace, searched, or pretended to search, for an insurance prospect at the nonexistent Menlove Garden East has, in a few decades, become "the perfect scientific puzzle."

However, the mystery of Mary Rogers, more than most, has stood the test of time as a mental exercise because it offers a challenge provided by only a few other unsolved murders. While it had the standard ingredients—the beautiful victim known to celebrities, the provocative clues from sailor's knot to the arrangement of apparel at Weehawken, the colorful collection of suspects ranging from lovers to abortionists—it also had the genius of Edgar Allan Poe. Thus, when we transport ourselves in time back to that sweltering July morning in 1841 and begin the game and the hunt, we not only compete with the police and press of the period, but we challenge the analysis and deduction of the world's first great detective-story writer. In short, we have the added excitement of pitting ourselves against Poe.

Ever since Poe's death in 1849, armchair amateurs at detection have begun the game by attempting to discredit the master's theories before proceeding with their own. Will M. Clemens, who visited Sybil's Cave and the Weehawken thicket in 1904 for *Era Magazine*, decided that "the confessions mentioned by Poe are of doubtful authenticity." Edmund Pearson, after studying contemporary accounts, concluded that "Poe, in writing fiction about the case, was in the position of being able to depart from fact when he liked, and adhere to it when it suited his purpose; that he was first and last a romancer, and a devotee of the hoax; and that the theory that he actually solved the mystery of the death of the real Mary Rogers is not proven, and is very doubtful." Russel Crouse, after pondering "The Mystery of Marie Roget," stated: "As an actual aid in the solution of the crime it is of no more use than the less literary contributions of the stupid and bungling police of the day. For Poe's ratiocination stems from untrustworthy and highly controvertible rumor rather than from fact."

Several other commentators on crime have been less harsh with Poe. They have seen some merit in his deductions, and allowed for the possibility of his being proved right in the future. A quarter of a century ago Winthrop D. Lane reopened the case for *Collier's* magazine. He announced that if Mrs. Loss's deathbed confession was correct, it vindicated Poe completely. "He absolved Payne and Crommelin of complicity," said Lane. "He said no gang did the murder. He advanced the idea of a fatal accident under Mrs. Loss' roof (though he had no idea of the nature of the accident)—and here he made an extraordinarily shrewd guess. He thought the articles of clothing might have been placed in the thicket to divert attention from the real scene—and here he was exactly and uncannily correct."

William Kurtz Wimsatt, Jr., after his own probings into the case, doubted that it would ever be solved. But he had no doubt that if new evidence were uncovered, it would be evidence generally in support of Poe's theories. "We shall know the truth only if it was somewhat as Poe and Ingram say, if there was a confession by a man of influential family, if this was known as an inside story, and if someone on the inside wrote the secret down in a document which survives and is to come to light." If this document revealed the murderer as a naval officer, possibly the son of a Secretary of War, then Poe would have triumphed entirely over his critics. "For all his idle argument about bodies in the water," wrote Wimsatt, "his labored inconsistency about the thicket and the gang, for all his borrowing of newspaper ideas, or (where it suited him) indifference to newspaper evidence, despite the fact that he was so largely wrong and had to change his mind, he did fasten on the naval officer."

But if not Poe's naval officer, then who else?

As early as 1869 a mystic and lecturer, Andrew Jackson Davis, who had been acquainted with Poe, presented his own solution to the Mary Rogers case in the form of a novel called *Tale of a Physician*. Davis thought Mary had become pregnant by a wealthy lover, who then took her to a New York City abortionist, probably Mme Restell. When Mary died on the table, the lover paid off and fled to Texas.

In 1904 Will M. Clemens still had the opportunity to interview several of Mary's contemporaries about Hoboken. Most of these elders felt that Mary and her "swarthy" escort had both been murdered inside Mrs. Loss's inn by her three unrestrained sons, for purposes of either rape or robbery. In 1927 Allan Nevins thought that the responsibility for the death of

Mary Rogers "was not the work of Payne but of another lover." Nevins believed that Mary had been seduced, and had died of an illegal operation. In 1930 Winthrop D. Lane located the original records of Mary Rogers's inquest in the dusty basement of the Hudson County Courthouse. After reading these and pursuing other evidence, Lane pointed the finger of guilt at Mrs. Loss. He regarded her dying confession of the crime as the truth.

"Mrs. Loss' confession," wrote Lane, "has had a curious history. It seems to have failed to get itself accepted as the truthful explanation of the affair. . . . And yet it is the most likely explanation. Why should she make such a confession if it were not true? She was on her deathbed—and had nothing to gain unless it was a clear conscience. A mother is not likely to implicate her son in so serious an affair unless there is some powerful reason. It is less likely that she lied than that others, for reasons entirely unknown to us, failed to make use of the confession."

The reason, perhaps, that the confession was not fully acted upon was that its existence was of doubtful authenticity. After the *New York Tribune* reported Mrs. Loss's dying statement to Justice Merritt, the Justice promptly wrote an open letter to the *Courier and Enquirer* denying the confession and stating that the *Tribune*'s story was "entirely incorrect, as no such examination took place, nor could it, from the deranged state of Mrs. Loss's mind." The *Tribune* replied that it had obtained its story from two of Justice Merritt's magistrates. The *Herald* challenged the *Tribune* to print the names of the magistrates. The *Tribune* retreated into hurt silence.

Like all the others who have studied the facts of the case, I, too, have played the game. Among the major suspects, my choice for the most suspicious is Alfred Crommelin. I believe that Mary Rogers was his mistress at the time she was engaged to marry Payne. Why, then, the rose in his keyhole? Because she wished to tell him, before aborting his child, that she still loved him. And how, then, his fortuitous arrival at Sybil's

Cave? Because he knew where her body had been disposed of by the abortionist, and he knew where it might be found, and wished to be immediately on hand to identify it and see that it received Christian burial. But how, then, did Crommelin have an alibi for the Sunday? Quite logically because he was not present when Mary died, but with friends, who established his alibi.

To my mind, the most stimulating aspect of the Mary Rogers affair is the broad scope of possible suspicion. A damaging indictment can be constructed against almost anyone remotely connected with Mary Rogers. There is no limit to the boundaries of one's fancy or surmise. Consider the oft-overlooked John Anderson, tobacconist, who was Mary's employer. He was beside her for long hours each day. He walked her home. He had, surely, an eye for a well-turned ankle. It was thought, on newspaper row, that he had encouraged her first disappearance. Had he perhaps encouraged her second also?

In 1887 the *New York Tribune* reported that John Anderson had hired Edgar Allan Poe, whom he had long known as a customer, to write "The Mystery of Marie Roget" in order to divert suspicion from himself. While this tidbit opens up delightful possibilities, its veracity is certainly to be questioned. It appears that Anderson lived on to a senile old age. After his death in 1881, his will was contested on the grounds of legal insanity. The fight was still in the New York courts during 1901, when Mary Rogers made a ghostly appearance before the bar. In the tug-of-war involving Appleton *vs.* New York Life Insurance Company, it was revealed that old Anderson had claimed he knew who killed Mary Rogers. He knew, he told relatives, because she told him. She had often appeared before him as a nightly apparition, and during one such nocturnal tête-à-tête she had revealed the name of her murderer. Unfortunately, Anderson kept the name "a spiritual secret."

Among other periphery suspects, in a category with the Broadway tobacconist, I would be inclined to include the seemingly harassed Mrs. Rogers, proprietress of the historic roominghouse on Nassau Street. An impoverished old woman, to be sure, and ailing, of course. Yet how did she manage to maintain her house? The boarders seem to have been so very few and far between. Certainly there must have been another steady source of income. The son in South America? Possibly. Or Mary?

Does it strike a blow at motherhood and country to suggest that Mrs. Rogers, out of fear of bankruptcy, employed the beautiful cigar girl for the pleasure of her guests—and of visitors to her vacant rooms? Assuming this premise, it is not beyond the realm of possibility that Mary was trapped in pregnancy, and that her mother took her to an abortionist, under whose instruments Mary expired. Then it would have been Mrs. Rogers, grief-stricken, who disposed of the body with the aid of Crommelin or another.

Or was the secret murderer of Mary Cecilia Rogers one of the most illustrious names in literature? Was the murderer Edgar Allan Poe himself?

Poe knew Mary Rogers when he dwelt in New York City, and in the half-year before her death he frequently traveled from Philadelphia to New York. Might he not have seen her again? Not at the boardinghouse, not he, a married man. But at cafés or hotels—or on outings to New Jersey. She was beautiful and gay, and would have served as a welcome escape from the neuter Virginia and the dominating Maria Clemm and the hounding Graham. And of course he would have attracted her. He had some social station; he was published; he was brooding and brilliant.

Might not Poe have been the "swarthy" gentleman who accompanied Mary to Weehawken? And there, in the thicket, in one of his drunken, narcotic rages, might he not impotently have attempted rape, or even actually raped her, and then been forced to silence her forever? His record of alcoholic rage with women is well known. It is a fact that in July 1842, bleary with drink, he took a ferry to New Jersey to see his old Baltimore sweetheart, Mary Devereaux, who was then a married woman. Poe, his eyes bloodshot, his stock under his ear, was already in

Mary Devereaux's house, waiting, when she returned from a shopping-trip with her sister—most fortunately with her sister. Poe fell upon her, screaming: "So you have married that cursed ——! Do you love him truly? Did you marry him for love?"

Mary Devereaux held firm. "That's nobody's business; that is between my husband and myself."

But Poe pressed after her. "You don't love him. You do love me. You know you do."

While, on this occasion, Poe was finally pacified and sent packing, he may not have left Mary Rogers so easily.

But all of this, I confess, is speculation. As to actual evidence that Edgar Allan Poe murdered Mary Rogers? I can only repeat once more that we are playing a game. . . .

After Mary Cecilia Rogers was removed from the Dead House in mid-August of 1841, she was buried in the New York City metropolitan area. No one knows today the exact location of her final resting-place—except that she may be found still in the pages of "The Mystery of Marie Roget."

VII

The Real Robinson Crusoe

"The person I speak of is Alexander Selkirk, whose name is familiar to men of curiosity, from the fame of his having lived four years and four months alone in the island of Juan Fernandez."

SIR RICHARD STEELE

On January 26, 1709, two English vessels, the *Duke* and the *Duchess*, privateers six months out of England, rode a Pacific downpour and gale somewhere off the coast of Chile, while the unhappy crews worked the storm-lashed ships and grumbled. Their complaints were directed less against seasickness or the scarcity of enemy prizes than against the absence of water and the increase of scurvy among their number. That night Captain Woodes Rogers, aboard the *Duke*, noted in his log:

"We spoke with our Consort who complains their men grow worse and worse, and want a Harbour to refresh 'em; several of ours are also very indifferent, and if we don't get ashore, and a small Refreshment, we doubt we shall both lose several Men. We are very uncertain of the Latitude and Longitude of Juan Fernandez . . . and being but a small Island, we are in some doubts of striking it."

Juan Fernández, named after the Spanish navigator who had accidentally discovered it in 1563 and dwelt on it raising goats and pigs, was actually a group of three volcanic islands—Santa Clara, Más Afuera, Más a Tierra—lying in the Pacific Ocean about 360 miles west of Valparaiso. Though their precise loca-

(216)

tion was uncertain, Captain Rogers, in desperate need of a safe and quick landfall, continued to search for them, on advice of William Dampier, his pilot.

Dampier, during two earlier trips of sack and piracy around the world, had employed Juan Fernández several times as a repair station, his last visit having been less than five years before. Now, at fifty-seven, unable to obtain his own ship due to a consistent record of discontent and mutiny under his previous commands, Dampier had signed on as pilot for the more efficient Woodes Rogers.

Though Dampier's skill as a commander may have once been at fault, his memory of geography was still the best. Five days later Captain Rogers was able to rapidly scrawl in his log: "At seven this morning we made the Island of Juan Fernandez."

The speedy location of mountainous Juan Fernández undoubtedly helped preserve many members of Captain Woodes Rogers's expedition. It also preserved, as we shall see, the life of one who was to become the most popular prototype in all literature.

Late the following afternoon, February 1, Captain Rogers navigated his vessels to within four leagues of the largest island of the group, Más a Tierra, and lowered a longboat containing the boat physician, two officers, and several crew members. As they rowed toward shore, darkness fell quickly and they were soon lost to sight. While Captain Rogers peered into the night toward the craggy silhouette of the island, he was suddenly startled to observe "a Light" on the shore.

Captain Rogers was filled with anxiety. His first hope was that the light had come from his own longboat. But he quickly realized that its glow had been too powerful. Disturbed, Captain Rogers ordered the quarterdeck gun fired, a signal for the longboat to return, and then ordered lanterns hung about the ship to guide the small craft back. After midnight the longboat returned. Its occupants also had seen what they characterized in the plural as "the Lights."

Captain Rogers summoned his staff to conference. The consensus opinion held that French or Spanish were occupying the island and that the lights were those of enemy warships in Cumberland Bay. The question, then, was whether to flee or fight. Rogers considered only briefly. Without water, he faced an epidemic or a mutiny. He gave orders to prepare for an engagement at daybreak.

When dawn arrived on February 2, 1709—memorable day— Captain Rogers had his two ships on the move, out of sight of the main bay, preparing for a surprise assault on the French or Spanish. A stiff wind was whipping up from the island, recorded Captain Rogers, "when we open'd the middle Bay, where we expected to find our enemy, but saw all clear, and no Ships in that nor the other Bay next the N.W. End. These two bays are all that Ships ride which recruit on this Island, but the middle Bay is by much the best. We guess'd there had been Ships there, but that they were gone on sight of us."

It was now high noon. A yawl with six men at the oarlocks, as well as one of the expedition's sponsors, Captain Thomas Dover, a onetime English doctor who had fought witchcraft and been censured for advocating extensive use of mercury, and another officer, "all arm'd," headed toward the distant bay and the beach beyond. When after several hours the yawl did not return, Captain Rogers's concern grew. At last he launched his "Pinnace with the Men arm'd, to see what was the occasion of the Yall's stay; for we were afraid that the Spaniards had a garrison there, and might have seiz'd 'em."

The pinnace had not been gone long when it was seen returning swiftly to the *Duke*. It had left for the island shore with eight men. It was returning with nine.

"Immediately our Pinnace return'd from the shore," Captain Rogers noted in his journal, "and brought abundance of Crawfish, with a Man cloth'd in Goat-Skins, who look'd wilder than the first Owners of them. He had been on the Island Four Years and four Months, being left there by Capt. Stradling in the *Cinque-Ports*; his Name was Alexander Selkirk, a Scotch man, who had been Master of the *Cinque-Ports*, A Ship that came here last with Capt. Dampier, who told me that this was the best Man in her; so I immediately agreed with him to be a Mate on board our Ship. 'Twas he that made the Fire last night when he saw our Ships, which he judg'd to be English."

When Alexander Selkirk mounted the deck of the *Duke* and stood before its astonished Captain and crew, he looked like nothing quite human. Four years and four months of solitary confinement to the desert island had transformed a civilized, twenty-seven-year-old son of a churchgoing Scotch cobbler into a wild-eyed, bearded, leathery thirty-two-year-old savage. He wore cap, coat, and breeches of goatskin, all crudely stitched together with thongs of goat. His shirt was of linen sewed with the worsted of discarded stockings. His feet were bare, and the soles almost as hard as the deck upon which he stood. "It was some time before he could wear Shoes, after we found him," said Captain Rogers. "For not being us'd to any so long, his feet swell'd when he came first to wear 'em again."

Rogers questioned the castaway, but had difficulty understanding him. "He had so much forgotten his Language for want of Use, that we could scarce understand him, for he seem'd to speak his words by halves." In the twelve more days the ships remained at anchor, Selkirk found his tongue, and was soon relating his adventure in his old Fife accents.

He had been marooned on Más a Tierra early in October 1704, he explained, at his own request, after strong disagreement with Captain Thomas Stradling, his superior on the *Cinque Ports*. Stranded on the primitive island, Selkirk had successfully fought loneliness, rats, and the elements. He had escaped hunger by chasing down wild goats, after tiring of turtle and fish, and later had taken to cultivating turnips. He had escaped capture by a Spanish landing-party through his swiftness of foot, and he had escaped insanity by improvising dances with his pet cats, bellowing Scotch psalms aloud, and fashioning tools out of a stock of iron on hand.

After his deliverance by Captain Rogers, Selkirk, soon nicknamed Governor by the men, took crew members on an escorted tour of his thirteen-mile-by-four-mile domain. He showed off the two grass huts, lined inside with goatskins, which he had built; he showed off the notched tree which had been his calendar; he indicated the high hill, with the path he had worn toward its summit, from which for most of his fifty-two months he had kept daily lookout for ships on the horizon. To prove his agility, Selkirk raced the crew's pet bulldog in chase of a goat. The bulldog fell exhausted, but Selkirk continued over the crags until he brought down the kid.

On the afternoon of February 14 the English vessels, fully repaired, their holds filled with water and meat, weighed anchor, prepared to go about their assigned business for their distant Bristol backers. As the crews watched Juan Fernández recede, Alexander Selkirk was among them. He had exchanged his hairy goats' suit for the uniform of an English seaman, and, at Dampier's recommendation, he was serving as Second Mate on the *Duke*.

But Selkirk did not see Great Britain for almost three years more. The *Duke* and the *Duchess* battled and plundered off Peru and California, and then sailed for Guam and Batavia before rounding the Cape of Good Hope with rich cargoes. When Selkirk reached the Thames again and saw the skyline of the city of London, he had been promoted to Sailing Master of a vessel captured off California and renamed the *Batchelor*, and was himself eight hundred pounds the richer in prize shares. He took a carriage to London in the company of Captain Dover, his immediate superior, and arrived in the city an utter stranger after an absence abroad of eight years, more than half of them spent in isolation.

Selkirk did not remain a stranger to London very long. He returned to the city October 14, 1711. Within a year he was one of its most prominent personalities. For this fame he had to be grateful, if grateful he was, to the literary propensities of two of his rescuers.

Selkirk settled in London. He rented rooms from Katherine and John Mason. Of this pair we know only that Mason was a tailor and that his wife was referred to by Selkirk as his "love-ing friend," whatever that may mean. It would be two and one-half years before Selkirk finally returned to his native village of Largo and his family. Why he remained so long in London and later in Bristol before attempting a reunion with his closest relatives, we can only conjecture. He may have been too moody to face the chatter of his kin. That he was strange and withdrawn, we have on the word of the gregarious, cherubic Sir Richard Steele, an author who, for all his naïveté, was a man of quick perceptions.

"When I first saw him," wrote Steele, "I thought if I had not been let into his character and story I could have discerned that he had been much separated from company from his aspect and gesture; there was a strong but cheerful seriousness in his look, and a certain disregard to the ordinary things about him, as if he had been sunk in thought. . . . Though I had frequently conversed with him, after a few months' absence he met me in the street, and though he spoke to me, I could not recollect that I had seen him; familiar discourse in this town had taken off the loneliness of his aspect, and quite altered the air of his face."

We may be sure it was not only "familiar discourse" that made Selkirk more convivial. After long abstinence on Más a Tierra, Selkirk had rediscovered the pleasures of the bottle. By September 1713 there was a warrant out for his arrest in Bristol. He had, while in an intoxicated condition, assaulted a shipwright named Richard Nettle, punched the poor man about, and left him somewhat damaged.

Yet it is likely that there was an even better reason for Selkirk's extended stay in London and then in Bristol. Originally, it may be true, he was held immobile by his depressive frame of mind, and later attracted by the taverns and gay spots of London and Bristol. But the greater probability is that he remained in England because he had become a celebrity, and because he enjoyed his new eminence.

Captain Woodes Rogers had taken his Sailing Master in hand

shortly after they disembarked at Erith. Rogers knew that he had a curiosity, a conversation piece, and he escorted him about town, introducing him to friends and hostesses and journalists, and encouraging him to recount his experiences on the desert island. In 1712 Captain Rogers introduced Selkirk to his friend Sir Richard Steele in a London coffeehouse. Steele, ever alert for a story, wished to publish an interview with Selkirk at once, but held off a year out of deference to the literary plans of Captain Rogers.

The early eighteenth century seems to have been a period when every literate Englishman who went to sea went with a poniard in one hand and a pencil in the other. Publishers encouraged these logs, journals, and memoirs of freebooters, buccaneers, and privateers because the public wanted them. The fashion for factual adventure was not unlike that of more recent times, when one had only to fail to climb a Tibetan peak or frighten a Ubangi to find a vast audience. William Dampier, a cutthroat and pirate if ever there was one, gained respectability and set the literary standard in 1697 with his *New Voyage Round the World*. In it he admitted exploring, killing, and looting with one eye on a possible best-seller. "Forseeing a necessity of wading through rivers frequently in our land-march," Dampier noted, "I took care before I left the ship to provide myself a large joint of bamboo, which I stopt at both ends, closing it with wax, so as to keep out any water. In this I preserved my journal and other writings from being wet, tho' I was often forced to swim."

Captain Woodes Rogers was no exception to this kill-and-tell mania. During squalls, plagues, sea battles, and explorations he meticulously kept up his journal, expanding notations made in the *Duke*'s log. His journalist's eye was keen, and he savored Selkirk as his *pièce de résistance*. His writing friends, Steele among them, though permitted to meet and talk to Selkirk, were led to understand that they must hold off until Rogers's journal was in the bookshops.

In 1712, not many months after returning to London, Captain Woodes Rogers published *A Cruising Voyage round the World*. With care and effective detail he told the adventure of the "Man cloth'd in Goat-Skins, who look'd wilder than the first Owners of them." Though unadorned, his sailor's prose was often undramatically effective, and the essential story came through—the story of man overcoming nature, of a civilized human being's struggle to remain civilized, of the virtue and pleasures of being alone in paradise. It was this last escapist note that sounded wide appeal. For Rogers made it plain, as Steele would after him, that Selkirk had been happier on his island kingdom than on his King's sceptered isle.

"By this one may see," wrote Captain Rogers, "that Solitude and Retirement from the World is not such an unsufferable State of Life as most Men imagine. . . . We may perceive by this story the Truth of the Maxim, that Necessity is the Mother of Invention, since he found Means to supply his Wants in a very natural Manner, so as to Maintain his Life, tho not so conveniently, yet as effectually as we are able to do with the help of all our Arts and Society. It may likewise instruct us, how much a plain and temperate way of living conduces to the Health of the Body and the Vigour of the Mind, both which we are apt to destroy by Excess and Plenty, especially of strong Liquor, and the Variety as well as the Nature of our Meat and Drink: for this Man, when he came to our ordinary Method of Diet and Life, tho he was sober enough, lost much of his Strength and Agility."

Almost simultaneously with the publication of Captain Rogers's book, there appeared a rival book concerning the same voyage, penned by another member of the expedition with a literary bent. This account, in two volumes, was entitled *A Voyage to the South Sea and round the World*, and it was written by Captain Edward Cooke. In Cooke's pages Selkirk was relegated to the merest mention, and favor was given to a variety of gales and a raid on Guayaquil. Cooke recorded "the Light" on shore, and added: "All this stir and apprehension arose, as we afterwards found, for one poor naked Man who passed in our Imagination at present, for a Spanish Garrison, a Body of Frenchmen, or a Crew of Pirates." It is generally thought that Cooke overlooked including the full drama of Selkirk's condition and rescue because of some reportorial deficiency. More probably, he deferred to his superior officer. Once Captain Rogers had the castaway in print, Cooke felt free to insert his version of the "poor naked Man" in subsequent editions appearing later that same year.

And now, at last, Sir Richard Steele was free to enter the trials with his own version. When he had first met Selkirk, he was publishing, in collaboration with Joseph Addison, *The Spectator*. By 1713, though an elected member of Parliament and much engrossed with mistresses, he had launched a paper of his own, *The Englishman*, which survived three years. He filled the entire issue of *The Englishman* dated 1–3 December, 1713, with a classic recital of Alexander Selkirk's tribulation. "I had the pleasure frequently, to converse with the man soon after his arrival in England in the year 1711," he wrote. "It was a matter of great curiosity to hear him, as he is a man of good sense, give an account of the different revolutions in his own mind in that long solitude. When we consider how painful absence from company, for the space of but one evening, is to the generality of mankind, we have a sense how painful this necessary and constant solitude was to a man bred a sailor, and ever accustomed to enjoy and suffer, eat, drink, and sleep, and perform all offices of life, in fellowship and company."

Those readers in the British Isles who had not read or heard about Alexander Selkirk from the works published by Captain Rogers and Captain Cooke in 1712 certainly read or heard about the Scotchman's "long solitude" with the appearance of Steele's article. There is little doubt that through these publications Selkirk became, for eighteen months, a man of mark. But he might soon have been forgotten had not one of his readers been an alert, prolific, irrepressible pamphleteer named Daniel Defoe.

The Real Robinson Crusoe

No authority on the life of Defoe has ever doubted that "the father of English journalism," who drew heavily from topical events for his chapbooks and novels and who dashed off the true lives of adventurers, prostitutes, and bandits, first became acquainted with Alexander Selkirk in Captain Woodes Rogers's *A Cruising Voyage*. Defoe may have read the added versions presented by Captain Cooke and Sir Richard Steele. He may have personally met Selkirk in London or Bristol, through Rogers, and interviewed Selkirk and seen his notes. But that he first became aware of Selkirk in the pages of Captain Rogers seems without argument.

At any rate, if Captain Rogers saw a story in Selkirk's lonely island adventure, Daniel Defoe saw a better one. And thus the seed was planted for the creation of the best-known character in all fiction—Robinson Crusoe.

Though Defoe had his prototype and his story as early as 1712, he did not write it until late in 1718 or early in 1719. To understand this protracted gestation one must realize something of Defoe's position and activity in those intervening years, and in the years preceding.

Defoe was fifty-two years old when he first heard of Alexander Selkirk. He had lived many lives before that, and seen and experienced much, yet it was his knowledge of the rough Largo castaway that would serve him best and make him immortal.

Defoe was the son of a butcher. Jonathan Swift called him "an illiterate fellow, whose name I forget," yet Defoe was conversant with Latin, French, Spanish, Italian, and Greek. Before turning to writing, he was employed by a hosiery-importer and spent two years on the continent of Europe. He took up the quill in 1703, wrote a satiric pamphlet called *The Shortest Way with the Dissenters*, and was soon the object of a $250 reward. Besides the sum offered for his capture, there was published the only description we have of him:

"He is a middle aged, spare man, about forty years old, of a brown complexion, and dark-brown colored hair, but wears a wig; a hooked nose, a sharp chin, gray eyes, and a large mole near his mouth."

When he was finally brought to the bar, his sentence was severe. He was fined two hundred marks; ordered to stand thrice in the public pillory, his neck and wrists clamped between wooden blocks, in Cornhill, Cheapside, and Temple Bar; and confined to Newgate Prison for a period of fifteen months. From Newgate he published, three times a week, his eight-page scandal sheet, *The Review*, which eventually inspired Addison and Steele to bring out *The Tatler* and *The Spectator*.

Defoe was released from Newgate earlier than he had expected, by the Earl of Oxford, on the condition that he serve as a government spy in Scotland for two years. One wonders if he was ever in Largo, and if there he met a family named Selcraig whose son had gone off to sea with an expedition headed by Captain William Dampier.

By 1712 Defoe was still deeply engrossed in politics. He was serving as a secret agent for the Earl of Oxford under the pseudonym of Claude Guilot. He was performing as a political propagandist, in the *Review*, for Queen Anne. He had a large home in Stoke Newington and funds enough, for the first time, to adequately support his wife, Mary, and their seven children. He was too busy to bother about Alexander Selkirk. He put the castaway off for a time of more leisure or a time of want. The leisure, enforced, and the time of want came all too soon. Within six years Defoe's world had crashed about his feet. With Queen Anne's death he lost much of his royal patronage. His meager savings disappeared in speculations. His ill-health increased, and with it his debts.

At fifty-nine he was writing everything and anything. And then he remembered Alexander Selkirk, and he wrote that, too.

No one knows precisely how many pamphlets and books he produced before 1718. It is thought that his novel based on Selkirk was the 292nd full-length manuscript to flow from his pen. More conservative estimates have credited him with from

210 to 254 published works in a lifetime of seventy-two years. But one thing is certain: had he died before sixty, he would have been remembered by a handful of curiosity-hunters as a hack. Fortunately he lived, and the title he put to paper late in that harried year of 1718 was:

The Life and Strange Surprizing Adventures of Robinson Crusoe, of York, Mariner: Who lived Eight and Twenty years, all alone in an un-inhabited Island on the Coast of America, near the Mouth of the Great River of Oroonoque; Having been cast on Shore by Shipwreck, wherein all the Men perished but himself. With an Account how he was at last strangely deliver'd by Pyrates. Written by Himself.

Though the novel of shipwreck and isolation would be written hurriedly, the preparations for it were careful. We know that Defoe did extensive general research, not only from the accuracy of the story itself, but from notes the author made, which may still be seen in the Guildhall Library. A typical extract from these notes reads: "Goats: plenty . . . Fish: abundance, Split and Salt . . . The fat of young Seals good as Olive Oil." Defoe, who always possessed a large library, read Captain Dampier's account of a journey around the world, Sir Walter Raleigh's narrative on Guiana, Robert Knox's *Historical Relation of Ceylon*, and Richard Hakluyt's *Voyages*. More specific research was obtained some time before when Defoe transacted business with a Captain Thomas Bowry, of the East India Company, who showed him maps of Juan Fernández.

In all his writings Defoe never once mentioned meeting Selkirk, or even referred to the prototype by name, though in a preface to *Robinson Crusoe* he spoke of "a man alive, and well known, too." The generally accepted story is that Defoe did meet Alexander Selkirk in the city of Bristol during 1713 at the residence of Mrs. Damaris Coysgarne, better known to history by her later name, Mrs. Damaris Daniel.

The groundwork for the meeting, if ever it took place, was probably laid by the indefatigable Captain Woodes Rogers. He was a close friend of Major Nathaniel Wade, the Town Clerk of Bristol, whose daughter was Damaris Daniel. Mrs. Daniel was destined for a lively matrimonial career. She married three wealthy men: the first a merchant, John Coysgarne, who died in 1740; the second a linen-draper, Joseph Beck, who died before 1752; and the third an ironmaster named Thomas Daniel. When Captain Rogers brought his confused celebrity, Selkirk, to Bristol for a rest, he probably introduced him to his friend Major Wade and to the Major's daughter, Mrs. Damaris Daniel, who was dwelling at 16 St. James's Square with her merchant husband. There is evidence that Daniel Defoe was in Bristol at the very same time, lodging at a public house but often accepting the sociabilities of Mrs. Daniel, an old acquaintance. Thus, it is supposed, as an amusement, or perhaps to give her friend Defoe a journalistic piece, Mrs. Daniel brought together Defoe and Selkirk.

In her later years Mrs. Daniel told one of her grandsons that "Selkirk handed over his papers to Defoe." She also revealed to a friend, Joseph Harford, who in turn passed it on to his family, that "Selkirk had informed her that he had placed his papers in Defoe's hands."

For more than two centuries scholars have debated the probability of a meeting between Defoe and Selkirk in Bristol. R. L. Megroz, the Selkirk biographer, regards the meeting as a myth. Walter Wilson, who did a three-volume biography of Defoe, and Professor James Sutherland, a Defoe scholar, have considered the meeting a likely possibility.

Whether the creator of Robinson Crusoe obtained his inspiration and materials from the real Robinson Crusoe directly, by conversing with him in Bristol, or indirectly, by reading about him in London, we may never know. But by late 1718 Defoe was busily engaged in developing *The Life and Strange Surprizing Adventures of Robinson Crusoe, of York, Mariner,* fashioned after Alexander Selkirk, who was by then a member of His Majesty's Navy on leave in the Pall Mall section of London.

When the book was done, Defoe submitted it to his bookseller-publishers as a work of non-fiction. This was a period when the novel, unless an allegory, was in ill-repute. Defoe thought he would have a better chance if the narrative was understood to be factual. According to the tradition, *Robinson Crusoe* was rejected by one prominent publisher after another. It is thought that as many as twenty turned it down. At last a publisher was found. He was William Taylor, located "at the Sign of the Ship in Pater-Noster-Row," which was a London alley. Taylor printed the book and issued it on Saturday, April 25, 1719. The first edition was fifteen hundred copies, priced at five shillings a copy.

A half-year later *Robinson Crusoe* became the first novel ever to be serialized. Defoe placed it with *The Original London Post; or Heathcote's Intelligence*, a magazine which appeared three times a week. Robinson Crusoe went to sea in *Heathcote's* on October 7, 1719, and thereafter appeared in sixty-five consecutive issues of the periodical.

The story fell like a bombshell on its vast reading audience. The critics and literati got to it, but not until later. They regarded Defoe as an untalented hack, and did not take him seriously until the volume became the talk of London. Crusoe's first audience was the lower middle class, the shopkeepers, clerks, soldiers, sailors, serving-wenches, housewives who escaped poverty and monotony in the sensations of pamphlets and cheap books. In the middle-class Robinson Crusoe's lone fight for survival against all odds, they saw themselves.

"I was born in the year 1632, in the city of York, of a good family," *Robinson Crusoe* begins. The portrait of Crusoe that emerges in his own words is shrewdly conceived. He is made out neither superior nor heroic. He is made out the average Englishman, quite practical, quite dull, yet intelligent and persevering. He goes to sea, is captured by the Moors, manages to escape to Brazil, where he becomes a prospering tobacco-grower. When he is induced to lead a 120-ton ship to Guiana in order to acquire slaves cheaply, he runs into a storm off the Orinoco River. The vessel is smashed on a sandbar, and all hands perish except Crusoe. He swims to a near-by island and survives.

During his first thirteen days as a castaway he recovers from the wreckage of the boat a quantity of food and rum, a carpenter's chest, two rifles, two barrels of gunpowder, a variety of clothing, a hammock, some rope, and other materials. "A less skilled writer," Professor Sutherland has pointed out, "would have set him on the island with only a jack-knife."

Robinson Crusoe's twenty-eight years on the desert island, eighteen without sight of another mortal, are too familiar to recount in detail. His melancholy, his prayers, his invention, his explorations, his construction of a log fortress, his foraging for green limes and grapes, his taming of wild goats, his clumsy fashioning of a shovel and of pottery, all are as much a part of the memory of most adults as the memory of playing house in childhood. And then, after almost two decades of utter isolation, that most dramatic and terrifying moment in all literature:

"It happened one day about noon, going towards my boat, I was exceedingly surprised with the print of a man's naked foot on the shore, which was very plain to be seen in the sand. I stood like one thunderstruck, or as if I had seen an apparition. I listened, I looked round me; I could hear nothing, nor see anything. . . . I came home to my fortification, not feeling, as we say, the ground I went on, but terrified to the last degree, looking behind me at every two or three steps, mistaking every bush and tree, and fancying every stump at a distance to be a man."

After this warning the cannibals arrived, and then came the battle with them and the rescue of the "comely, handsome fellow" called Friday, who is converted by Crusoe from a Pagan who diets on human beings to a less carnivorous Protestant. Friday is soon followed by his father and a fugitive Spaniard. "My island was now peopled," Crusoe reflects, "and I thought myself very rich in subjects. And it was a merry reflection which I frequently made, how like a king I looked."

The best part of Defoe's tale is told, and so now an English ship appears. Mutineers bring the Captain ashore, but Crusoe contrives to rescue him and help him recover his ship. Crusoe returns to his native England. Most of his family have passed away. Crusoe marries, has three children, lives in prosperity, returning only once to his desert island, which the English mutineers and Spaniards have developed into a thriving colony.

Crusoe's story was not entirely fashioned after Alexander Selkirk's life. There were numerous differences, which may have grown out of Defoe's natural creativity, or may have been made desirable by Selkirk's presence in London at the time of the writing and publication. Robinson Crusoe was a level-headed English tradesman; Selkirk was a hot-tempered Scotch sailor. Crusoe was shipwrecked off Brazil (thereby inspiring a ridiculous insistence from Tobago that it was Crusoe's island) and marooned against his wishes; Selkirk was left stranded off Chile at his own request. Crusoe was isolated eight-and-twenty years; Selkirk was alone four years. Crusoe acquired the company of Friday; Selkirk had no companionship at any time. Crusoe faced the threat of black savages; Selkirk fled from a Spanish landing-party.

But the main concept of the story, and the numerous realistic details that made it a delight, were borrowed without change from Selkirk. On his desert island, which closely resembles Juan Fernández, the fictional Crusoe fears loneliness, sea lions, and rats, as did the living Selkirk. Crusoe finds companionship in cats, goats, and the Bible, as did Selkirk. Crusoe creates shelters, goatskin clothing, and crude tools, as did Selkirk.

The Life and Strange Surprizing Adventures of Robinson Crusoe was an immediate best-seller. The first edition was followed in seventeen days by a second, which in turn was followed in twenty-five days by a third. And by August 8, three and one-half months after publication, there was a fourth edition. The publisher, William Taylor, made one thousand pounds' profit on the book. And the sequels must have netted him considerably more, for when he died of fever in 1724 he left an estate in excess of thirty thousand pounds. Defoe, it is believed, received royalty of ten pounds for every thousand copies of *Robinson Crusoe* sold. While the book and its sequels may have given him some brief measure of security, he was deeply in debt in 1731 when he died of an apoplectic stroke in a Ropemaker's Alley lodging-house, where he had been in hiding from enemies and creditors.

But while Defoe lived, the demand for more Robinson Crusoe was so great that he immediately went to work on a sequel. The second volume, Part II, appeared in August 1719. In it Defoe sent Robinson Crusoe back to his desert island to visit with the Spanish settlers, then plunged him into further adventures in China, India, Siberia, Russia, and Madagascar. The sequel was well received. Its immediate sales were greater than those of the first volume, with two editions in 1719 and two more in 1722. Publisher Taylor thought that this public enthusiasm deserved the reward of yet another sequel. Thus, in August 1720 a third volume, called Part III, made its way into the bookshops. This last was entitled *Serious Reflections During the Life and Surprizing Adventures of Robinson Crusoe: With His Vision of the Angelick World. Written by Himself.* Defoe had run dry of ideas for further physical adventures, and so in Part III he confined Crusoe's roamings to his thoughts and philosophies. It was a hodgepodge of Defoe's old pamphlets strung together, and it was a bore. Its sale was only fair, and, mercifully, Crusoe did not venture beyond the Angelick World.

Though Defoe's public gave him their unanimous approval, his fellow writers and their publishers did not. The most devastating thrust was made by one Charles Gildon, who attacked Defoe with a pamphlet entitled *The Life and Strange Surprizing Adventures of Mr. D----- De F--, of London, Hosier, Who Has Lived Above Fifty Years by Himself in the Kingdom of North and South Britain.* The dyspeptic Mr. Gildon strongly challenged the factuality of Defoe's book. Furthermore, he listed its inconsistencies and errors. In this he was joined by other journalistic pygmies whose creativity was limited to scavenging great works for small blunders. It was pointed out that before swimming to the shipwreck to recover supplies Crusoe stripped naked. Yet, once on the ship, he said: "I went to the bread-room and filled my pockets with biscuit." Crusoe had a pipe and box of tobacco, yet complained that he wished he could smoke. Crusoe was without salt for his bread, yet tried to instruct Friday in the use of salt for his meat.

This was the meanest carping by envious critics. The public ignored it, though Defoe seemed to take much of it to heart. He corrected all errors in subsequent editions of his book. And to the charges that it was not a true story, that no such person as Crusoe existed, he retorted that he had meant the book as an allegory. The tale was true, he argued, insofar as it was symbolic of the misfortunes of his own life, with the shipwreck a veiled representation of his own bankruptcy. This was surely the sheerest balderdash, but it served to silence the Gildons.

The success and fame of *Robinson Crusoe* grew and spread in Defoe's own lifetime, and in the centuries after. And through the years it was read by everyone. Alexander Pope, Dr. Samuel Johnson, and Wilkie Collins praised it. In more recent times Sir Winston Churchill confessed copying "the method" of Defoe for his own books. And Virginia Woolf thought the reality of Crusoe, especially to young readers, almost obliterated Defoe. "It never occurred to us that there was such a person as Defoe, and to have been told that Robinson Crusoe was the work of a man with a pen in his hand would either have disturbed us unpleasantly or meant nothing at all."

But if everyone (or, let us say, almost everyone), in Defoe's time and since, read *Robinson Crusoe*, there is cause to wonder if the one person, besides the author, most responsible for the book ever read it. The speculation is irresistible. Alexander Selkirk was in London during the appearance of *Robinson Crusoe*. Did he ever—uncomfortably, as we would imagine—enter a bookshop in the neighborhood of St. Dunstan's, request the desert-island story, and put down his five shillings? We shall never know. But the fact remains that he did not have to read it to enjoy it, for he had already lived the story first in a brief life often more exciting than the one Defoe devised for Robinson Crusoe of York.

He was born Alexander Selcraig in 1676. His birthplace was a thatched house in the small seaside fishing-village of Largo, situated in the Fife district of Scotland. The thatched house was razed in 1868, and in a niche of the new one, on the site of his birthplace, a remote relative seventeen years later placed a stone statue of Robinson Crusoe, which may be seen to this day by tourists laden with golf clubs on their way to the near-by St. Andrews course.

His parents were John and Euphan Mackie Selcraig, and they had been wedded nineteen years before his birth. In those prolific years they produced seven consecutive boy children, and Alexander was the seventh. The elder Selcraig maintained a shoemaking establishment under the family roof. His children found him a good provider, but a stern and God-fearing father. The paternal discipline, however, seemed to have little effect on the youngest son, except to inspire constant revolt.

Alexander had no interest in schooling, beyond the subject of geometry. He was more interested in the lore of sailing, which he learned from neighboring fishermen in Largo Bay. His major extra-curricular activity involved a predilection toward disorder and mayhem. At the age of thirteen, armed with a club, he followed his oldest brother and several other young delinquents in a Sunday-morning assault upon the crowded Presbyterian Church. When he was nineteen, he was summoned to appear before the church elders "for his undecent beaiver in ye church." But the elders were forced to announce Alexander's non-appearance, since he had "gone away to ye seas; this business is continued till his return."

At odds with his family, and probably to avoid church punishment, Alexander had run off to sea at nineteen, exactly as Crusoe was to do later. He was gone six years. It was thought that he served on a Dutch-built ship sent to the West Indies by the Company of Scotland, a corporation in competition with

England's East India Company. He returned from that voyage with only a fund of experience and a secondhand pistol.

Immediately he was in trouble again. According to the Largo church records, he engaged in a violent free-for-all fight with members of his family. The disagreement was provoked by Alexander's moronic brother, Andrew, who had been sent to fetch fresh water from the family well and returned instead with salt water from the sea. Alexander drank it down and spluttered, a performance which sent Andrew into gales of laughter. Whereupon Alexander grabbed up a staff and began to belabor his brother, who shouted for help. The elder Selcraig rushed into the room in time to prevent Alexander from snatching up his pistol. Alexander turned on his father, just as his older brother John arrived with his wife. While Alexander and John wrestled, John's wife separated them, screaming at Alexander: "You false loon, will you murder your father and my husband both?" By this time neighbors had reported the brawl to the kirk authorities. Alexander was haled before the entire church congregation. He sullenly admitted his error in conduct, was rebuked from the pulpit and dismissed.

After two more years of similar extroversion and chastisement, Alexander came to realize that the boundaries and climate of Largo were too restrictive for his animal spirits. He cast his glance toward broader and less inhibited horizons. The newspapers were filled with notices of the celebrated Captain William Dampier, who was about to embark on a privately financed expedition to the South Seas in search of gold-laden Spanish galleons. Alexander Selcraig was intrigued. Oppressed as he was by his elders, both in home and in kirk, and desirous as he was to make his fortune quickly, he abruptly left Largo for the docks of London. It would be almost a dozen years before he would see his native heath again.

Had young Selcraig known more about the commander with whom he wished to cast his fortune, he might well have remained longer in Largo. Captain William Dampier was a pirate by nature and deed, and his activities were condoned only because he confined his depredations to enemy shipping. With this cloak of legality and a facile pen, he continued to promote backing for every kind of buccaneering venture. Though his record as a leader combined inefficiency with sadism—he had once lost a ship through poor seamanship, and once been court-martialed for cruelty to a junior—he managed, late in 1702, after exploiting his talents in a best-seller, to obtain backing for one more privateering venture. By early 1703 the austere *London Gazette* was able to announce: "Captain William Dampier, being prepared to depart on another voyage to the West Indies, had the honour to kiss Her Majesty's hand, being introduced by His Royal Highness the Lord High Admiral."

It was Dampier's intention to take two ships to Peru, and there to lie in wait for galleons carrying Lima gold. He assured his backers that if this program failed to net them six hundred thousand pounds in loot, he would then continue to the South Seas in further pursuit of riches. To spearhead his attack, he acquired, for his personal command, a twenty-six-gun vessel known as the *St. George*. For her consort, he enlisted the *Fame*, under the leadership of Captain John Pulling.

But even as the crews were being signed on, Dampier fell into an argument with Pulling. As a result of this, Pulling withdrew from the expedition. Desperate for a hasty replacement, Dampier settled upon the *Cinque Ports*, an erratic 120-ton barque with sixteen guns and a good-natured chief named Captain Charles Pickering.

For the long voyage that lay ahead, Pickering decided that his small vessel would require a crew of sixty-three persons. He descended to the London docks to interview seamen, and among the first he met was a husky twenty-seven-year-old Scot who gave his name as Alexander Selkirk. This was, indeed, our old friend from Largo, the ebullient Alexander Selcraig. He had left behind his family name, not wishing to sully it further with the taint of piracy. On the London wharf his aggressive manner, sturdy physique, and obvious experience immediately im-

The Real Robinson Crusoe

pressed Captain Pickering. Alexander was signed on the *Cinque Ports* as Sailing Master.

In short days the *Cinque Ports* joined Dampier's *St. George* at Kinsale, on the Irish coast. Five weeks more were spent in preparation, and in September of 1703 the expedition put to sea. During the twenty-one days it took the two ships to reach the Cape Verde Islands, Sailing Master Selkirk realized that he was in for a bruising voyage. The fact that the *Cinque Ports* was overcrowded and overage, that the cabins were filthy, the water foul, the cuisine putrid, was the least of it. A far greater peril was that of personality. Selkirk was at immediate odds with his superiors, just as they were at odds with one another.

Hostility engulfed the boats like a tropical squall. While Selkirk respected Captain Pickering, he disliked Pickering's superior, Dampier, and despised his own immediate superior, Lieutenant Thomas Stradling. Yet Selkirk might have survived the expedition, and kept his temper in check, and lost Robinson Crusoe for posterity, had Captain Pickering continued in command. But shortly after the Cape Verde Islands were left behind, misfortune struck. Pickering contracted tropical fever and died. The despised Lieutenant Stradling was promoted to the captaincy of the *Cinque Ports*.

Meanwhile, Dampier ordered his vessels around Cape Horn to the Juan Fernández group, which he felt would serve as an excellent base from which to intercept enemy shipping. Rounding the Horn, a severe storm blew up. The *St. George* was parted from the *Cinque Ports* in the waves and spray, and the *St. George* presumed her consort lost. When at last Dampier limped into Cumberland Bay and anchored off the deserted Más a Tierra, he found the battered *Cinque Ports* waiting.

In the next weeks, while casks were filled with fresh water and food was gathered and the vessels were heeled over and scrubbed, Selkirk continued his running argument with Captain Stradling over harsh treatment of the crew. At last, after Selkirk promised to lead their revolt, forty-two crewmen voted to abandon the *Cinque Ports* and remain ashore. For two days this rift persisted, until Captain Dampier was induced by Stradling to speak to the rebels. Dampier went ashore and lectured the holdouts at length on the wealth that was so near at hand. Once more, vision of gold triumphed over integrity. Beneath the weight of Dampier's eloquence, the mutiny was broken.

Before further unrest could be generated among the seamen, an enemy ship intervened. It was on February 29, 1704, while five crewmen of the *Cinque Ports* were foraging the island on assignment, that a French ship was sighted on the horizon. Dampier forgot the five crewmen and gave chase. After a seven-hour engagement, the French ship slipped away toward the mainland to summon assistance. Dampier and Stradling, instead of returning to Más a Tierra to pick up the waiting crewmen, agreed to abandon the five and set sail for Peru. Selkirk and his crew vigorously protested this heartless act, to no avail.

The next two months were busy ones. A pair of Spanish vessels, heavy with gold, tobacco, and indigo, were captured off Peru. A fifty-ton bark was run down, and timber, rope, and turtle shell were taken off her. Another Spanish ship was caught and emptied. On April 27 the *St. George* and *Cinque Ports* were anchored off the village of Santa María. Dampier, Stradling, and 102 crewmen, in three longboats, took off in the night to raid and sack the community. At daybreak they were sighted by Indians, who rushed to spread the alarm. The entire town was armed and waiting when Dampier and his men rowed into sight. After brisk firing from the shore, the raiders withdrew, capturing, in their retreat, a 150-ton Spanish craft filled with brandy, marmalade, and linen.

Back on board again, Stradling informed Dampier that he opposed the risks taken for the small prizes involved. He was, he said, after bigger game and thought he could accomplish more alone. Dampier had no choice but to permit his defection. The crews of the two ships were informed of the separation and given their choice of remaining with Dampier or Stradling. Five on each vessel changed over. Selkirk saw the choice as

one between two evils. Both commanders were intolerable—
but Dampier was inefficient to boot. Selkirk decided to remain
with Stradling.

On May 19, 1704, the ships parted company. The *St. George*
sailed for the waters off Peru. The *Cinque Ports* headed for
waters off Central America. But Central America produced few
prizes, and the *Cinque Ports* was soon in need of victuals and
repair. Stradling pointed his craft toward Juan Fernández, and
by September 1704 he reached the anchorage of Más a Tierra.
A landing-party went in search of the five crewmen earlier
abandoned. Two were found hiding in the hills. The other three
had been made captives of the French.

During the next weeks Stradling had his leaky vessel hastily
patched while provisioning it with water, meat, and greens. By
early October the boat was only partially mended, when the
impatient Stradling gave orders to sail. The crew grumbled,
and Selkirk took their protests and his own to Stradling. Selkirk
argued that the *Cinque Ports* was still in precarious condition,
riddled as it had been by shot and smashed by heavy seas, and
he insisted that the sailing be delayed until repairs could be
properly concluded. Stradling was adamant. The *Cinque Ports*
was leaving at once. Selkirk replied that if it left at once, it
would do so without its Sailing Master. He asked to be put
ashore. As he later told Sir Richard Steele, he preferred "to
take his fate in this place than in a crazy vessel, under a dis-
agreeable commander." To his surprise, Captain Stradling com-
plied at once, directing that a longboat be readied to move
Selkirk and his effects to the desolate beach.

As subsequent events proved, Selkirk was entirely correct in
his argument that the *Cinque Ports* was unseaworthy and required additional attention. Long after, Selkirk learned that the
Cinque Ports, wallowing toward Panama, had run ashore off
Colombia, then Spanish territory. The entire crew was imprisoned, and many died of ill treatment. Stradling, after being
held captive in Lima, was transferred to further incarceration
in Spain.

In making his rash demand to be set ashore, there is little doubt that Selkirk expected, as on a previous occasion, to be accompanied by other crew members who resented as strongly their Captain's impetuosity. In this expectation Selkirk was to be disappointed. For, to the Englishmen on the crew, the wind-swept, primitive island held more terrors than their over-crowded, ancient boat. Not one of Selkirk's sympathizers volunteered to join him and his sea chest in the bobbing longboat.

Stradling personally sat at the helm of the longboat as its oarsmen rowed the sulky Sailing Master toward the lonely beach. Touching shore, Selkirk left the others and waited while his hurriedly gathered, meager effects were dumped on the land beside him. As the others prepared to depart, Selkirk must have glanced about him at the forbidding, tangled vegetation, the barren hills behind, and the thundering loneliness of his new home. Here, it is true, there was no cruel authority, no rotting planks that might give way to the first heaving waves, but there appeared an unseen danger far greater—the danger of naked aloneness in the terrible unknown.

The longboat was pulling away, back toward the bustling haven of the *Cinque Ports*, when Selkirk had his one ripping moment of remorse. He suddenly called out for the longboat to return and remove him. Stradling remained implacable, determined to punish Selkirk as an object lesson to the rest of his restless crew, and the longboat continued to withdraw. Casting all pride and restraint aside, Selkirk renewed his pleas, bellowing after the longboat. Stradling would not reconsider. Instead, as John Howell reported in 1829, the Captain "shouted taunts as the desperate man waded into the water calling after his comrades."

Toward dusk, the forlorn Selkirk still stood on the empty shore, watching as the *Cinque Ports* weighed anchor and moved slowly out of the great bay. As the sight of its sail diminished, Selkirk admitted, "his heart yearned within him and melted at parting with his comrades and all human society at once."

And now he was alone.

The Real Robinson Crusoe

It must have been as the earth was the day after Creation. Night was lowering swiftly. And as Selkirk turned to face his fearful future, the only sounds, beyond the beating of his heart, were the waves rolling in at his feet, and the wind in the brush, and the eerie bleating and howling of invisible monsters.

We have no record of Alexander Selkirk's first night on his deserted island. We know only how the fictional Robinson Crusoe spent *his* first night, and since his first actions may have been based on Selkirk's, they are worth noting. "For a while I ran about like a madman. Night coming upon me, I began, with a heavy heart, to consider what would be my lot if there were any ravenous beasts in that country, seeing at night they always come abroad for their prey. All the remedy that offered to my thoughts at that time was to get up into a thick bushy tree like a fir, but thorny, which grew near me, and where I resolved to sit all night, and consider the next day what death I should die; for as yet I saw no prospect of life. . . . I went to the tree, and getting up into it, endeavoured to place myself so as that if I should sleep I might not fall; and having cut me a short stick like a truncheon for my defence, I took up my lodging, and having been excessively fatigued, I fell fast asleep. . . . When I waked it was broad day, the weather clear, and the storm abated."

The first day of the first week of his more than two hundred solitary weeks on Más a Tierra, Alexander Selkirk took stock of his stores. His worldly goods were much fewer than Robinson Crusoe's. On his person he wore linen shirt, breeches, long woolen stockings, and buckled shoes. In his sea chest were additional pieces of clothing, some bedding, a kettle, a hatchet, a knife, a few pounds of tobacco and pipe, "a flint and steel," several mathematical instruments, a Holy Bible and "other books of devotion, together with pieces that concerned navigation." Then, too, he had a firelock, one pound of powder, and a considerable quantity of bullets.

His immediate necessity was food. He had brought from the *Cinque Ports* sufficient nourishment for two full meals. He was immediately driven to find sustenance. He had neither the courage nor the spirit to go hunting at first. He confined himself to the near-by beach, picking up shellfish and turtle. He started a fire by setting pimento wood upon his knee and rubbing the pieces together. He boiled the shellfish, which were as large as lobsters, and found them to make delicious broth. He gorged himself on turtle, so much so that later he could not stomach turtle except in jelly form. Yet, from the first day, and for many days, he did not eat regularly, but only when he was famished. The reason for this was that he had fallen into a deep, depressive lethargy.

Ennui and fear dominated his first eight months on the island. He attempted little in the way of storing food, building shelter, finding occupation, or exploration. "He diverted and provided for himself as well as he could," he told Captain Rogers, "but for the first eight months had much ado to bear up against Melancholy and the Terror of being left alone in such a desolate place." He admitted to Steele that during this early phase he even considered suicide. "The necessities of hunger and thirst were his greatest diversion from the reflections on his lonely condition. When those appetites were satisfied, the desire of society was as strong a call upon him, and he appeared to himself least necessitous when he wanted everything; for the supports of his body were easily attained, but the eager longings for seeing again the face of man, during the interval of craving bodily appetites, were hardly supportable. He grew dejected, languid, and melancholy, scarce able to refrain from doing himself violence."

Fear was as paralyzing a factor as solitude. Selkirk found a cave and fortified it with stones. Night after night he sat huddled in this cave, close to his sweet pimento fire, musket in hand, fighting off sleep lest he be overwhelmed by beasts of prey. He cringed at the throaty mating-calls of giant sea lions— "very large Mouths, monstrous big Eyes, and a Face like that of a Lion, with very large Whiskers, the Hair of which is stiff

enough to make Tooth-pickers"—who crowded the beach of
the bay in great mass "to whelp and ingender."

His sole diversion was his Bible. In the years before, he had
hated the pious elders of his home kirk and the unbending
religiosity of his parents, but now he reached for faith with the
clutching desperation of a dying man. And it was this recovery
of faith that saved his sanity.

It was the turning-point in his life as a castaway. The Good
Book gave him good companions and men of courage, and al-
layed his fears. Long after, in the presence of Captain Rogers,
"He said he was a better Christian while in this Solitude than
ever he was before, or than, he was afraid, he should ever be
again." In London, he remembered how he overcame the crisis,
and he tried to explain it to Steele. "By degrees, by the force
of reason and frequent reading the Scriptures, and turning his
thoughts upon the study of navigation, after the space of eighteen months he grew thoroughly reconciled to his condition.
When he had made this conquest, the vigour of his health,
disengagement from the world, a constant cheerful, serene sky
and a temperate air, made his life one continual feast."

Reinforced by his new faith, and by prayer, Selkirk moved
out of his dungeon cave into the open. Instead of hiding from
life, he would face it like a civilized man. Instead of regarding
his personal island as a hell filled with hidden terrors, he would
regard it as a paradise put at his exclusive disposal. He began
his new life by seeking shelter befitting a man of possession and
station.

He began by constructing "two Hutts." Actually, it is
thought, he had to build only one completely. The remnants of
another, one of the few landmarks of previous habitation on the
island, existed not far from the beach. The remnants had been
erected by an earlier castaway, a Mosquito Indian named
William, who had been a part of Captain Dampier's crew in
1681. William had been left behind on Más a Tierra, by accident, for three years and two months before Dampier re-

turned to rescue him. Selkirk probably knew his story well
(though future generations would not, since the Indian was
served by no Rogers or Steele—or Daniel Defoe).

It was the Indian's hut that Selkirk rebuilt and employed as a
kitchen for preparation of his meals. A larger hut he constructed
completely with his own hands. The walls were made of pimento trees. The roof was laid with long grass. Its interior was
lined and carpeted with the skins of goats. Its situation was
most agreeable. It stood on a rise before a large woods and,
said Selkirk, was "fanned with continual breezes and gentle
aspirations of wind, that made his repose after the chase equal
to the most sensual pleasures." Into this larger dwelling Selkirk
moved his sea chest and personal effects. And here he spent his
happiest hours reading his Bible, his volumes of devotion, his
nautical books, and often singing psalms aloud before the hour
of retirement.

With his places of domicile established, he now turned his
attention to other basic needs. He determined to dine regularly
and with variety, and to protect his stomach against a time of
illness or famine. Wearied of shellfish and turtle, he turned to
catching a half-dozen other kinds of sea food, including silver-
fish and cavallos. But the unremitting diet of fish, without salt,
made him suffer attacks of diarrhea.

Firelock under his arm, he began to explore his private
thirteen-mile domain. He made his way through thick forests,
saw blackbirds on the wing and hummingbirds no larger "than
a large Humble Bee," came across springs with fresh water,
and from a distance he studied the three-thousand-foot volcanic
mountain known as El Yunque, which he found too formidible
to traverse. Best of all, he found the variety of edibles he required.

Three miles inland, Selkirk came across cabbage trees and
water cresses. Acres of turnips, sowed long before by Dampier's men, stretched before him. There were black plums,
radishes, a pimento fruit to use as seasoning, and "also a black

The Real Robinson Crusoe

Pepper call'd Malagita, which was very good to expel the Wind, and against Griping of the Guts."

For meat he had the wild goats. They were everywhere. At first he shot them and cooked what he needed. But, he said, "when his Powder fail'd, he took them by speed of foot; for his way of living and continual Exercise of walking and running, clear'd him of all gross Humours, so that he ran with wonderful Swiftness thro the Woods and up the Rocks and Hills." He was able to run uphill with such speed that he was capable of capturing quantities of wild goat far beyond his immediate requirements. Some of the kids he kept in a stockade for pets. Other kids he lamed in one leg, to retard their running ability when they grew up. He was, of course, protecting his future against starvation. He knew that if he fell ill, or grew infirm and slow with years, he would not be able to catch his dinners unless the objects of his hunt were equally slackened in speed.

During four years on Más a Tierra, Selkirk notched a record of five hundred wild goats captured and killed. He slit the ears of other goats and released them. In 1741, thirty-two years after Selkirk had departed the island, Commodore George Anson, on a round-the-world cruise with six navy ships, arrived on Más a Tierra. His crew went ashore, and the first wild goat they downed had its ears slit. "We concluded," reported the Commodore's chaplain, "that it had doubtless been formerly under the power of Selkirk. This was indeed an animal of a most venerable aspect, dignified with an exceedingly majestic beard."

While pursuit of the goats, as well as consumption of their meat, did much to preserve Selkirk's health, the quest of one such animal almost cost him his life. It was his only serious accident during his entire stay on the island. Once, climbing a hill, he saw a goat and gave chase. "He pursu'd it with so much Eagerness," wrote Captain Rogers, "that he catch'd hold of it on the brink of a Precipice, of which he was not aware, the Bushes having hid it from him; so that he fell with the Goat down the said Precipice a great height, and was so stunn'd and bruised with the Fall, that he narrowly escap'd with his Life, and when he came to his Senses, found the Goat dead under him. He lay there about twenty-four hours, and was scarce able to crawl to his Hutt, which was about a mile distant, or to stir abroad again in ten days." Discussing the same accident with Steele, Selkirk related that he "lay senseless for the space of three days, the length of which he measured by the moon's growth since his last observation."

As he gained in health and comfort and in knowledge of his surroundings, his fears dissipated completely. Instead of shrinking from the sea lions bleating on the beach, Selkirk approached and studied them. Some were indeed monsters—"above 20 foot long," thought Selkirk, weighing no less than "two Tun" —and extremely aggressive. Often, "like an angry Dog," one would attack him, but he would beat it off with a stick. He observed that their tails lashed an adversary to the ground, while their jaws "were capable of seizing or breaking the limbs of a man." He learned that by placing himself between head and tail, he could avoid being struck while dispatching the sea lion with his hatchet. He found their flesh "as good as English Lamb," and their oil a satisfactory substitute for butter in the frying of meats.

A short time later, another terrible foe was overcome. The island, Selkirk discovered, was filled with rats which through the years had invaded it from anchored ships. The rats shredded his clothes when he was out of his large cabin, and at night they gnawed at his feet. It did not take Selkirk many months to find the antidote. For not only rats had come off passing ships, but cats also. These felines roamed wild. Selkirk trapped them in great number, tamed them with goat meat, bred them, and soon had hordes of kittens. Thereafter, the cats lay about his bed "in hundreds"—and the rat invasion was ended.

In his third and fourth years on Más a Tierra, Selkirk's daily routine was a busy one and satisfying. He prepared three meals a day. He hiked into the hills. He picked fruit. He pursued goats. He returned for regular periods of prayer and of reading aloud, the latter so that he might not lose his faculty of speech. He spent long hours taming kids, "and to divert himself would now and then sing and dance with them and his Cats." He made new conveniences, scooping out a coconut shell to serve as a drinking-cup, and hammering a section of iron hoop into a knife.

Laboriously, too, he made new attire. Though his father had been a cobbler, he had not himself learned the trade. When his shoes wore out, he was satisfied to go barefoot. For garments, he dried the hairy skin of goats and stitched the strips together.

Yet, in Eden, for the first man, nothing is easy. To say that Selkirk "stitched" the strips of goatskin together is over-simplification itself. How did he do it? And with what? Where were the scissors and needles and threads? With his knife he sliced thin thongs of leather from the skins, and sinews from the goat. These were his threads. He had found some nails. These were his needles. Thus he stitched and tacked together cap, coat, and breeches. In his sea chest he found spare linen. He fashioned the linen into the parts of a shirt, then unraveled worsted from his used stockings, and with nail and wool sewed his last shirt, which was threadbare on his back when Captain Rogers found him.

Daily he added to his calendar of time. With nautical instru-ments he scanned the heavens, observed the changes of the moon, and cut into a tree the passing of each day, with special markings for each memorable occurrence.

Daily, too, he made his way to the two-thousand-foot sum-mit of his lookout, adjusted his spyglass, and searched the empty horizon for signs of rescue. Several times in the fifty-two months he saw the distant sails of ships. They passed without drawing closer. On one occasion two vessels neared the bay, anchored, and sent a longboat in toward the beach. Selkirk was confused—at once excited, at once fearful. He could not make out the nationality of the ships. If they were Spanish, he must hide, because "he apprehended they would murder him, or make a Slave of him in the Mines." If they were French, they would still be his enemies, but they would not be as cruel. And, then, they might be English, his own people at last. The chances were two out of three in his favor. He made his decision.

Firelock in hand, Selkirk went down to the open beach and exposed himself. But he had guessed wrong. As the longboat neared the shore, he saw that its occupants were in the uniform of Spain. He turned to run for his life. As he told Captain Rogers:

"The Spaniards had landed, before he knew what they were, and they came so near him that he had much ado to escape, for they not only shot at him but pursu'd him into the Woods, where he climb'd to the top of a Tree, at the foot of which they made water, and kill'd several Goats just by, but went off again without discovering him."

Even Defoe's imagination was hard put to create any scene in fiction as suspenseful and comic as the actual image of the goatskin-clad Scot crouched breathless in the branches and foliage of a sandalwood tree while a group of chattering conquistadors of the New Granada relieved their bladders on the base of the tree below.

Beyond this one narrow escape and the accident in falling from the precipice, the months passed peacefully and lazily. The seasons were reversed at this latitude. Spring came regularly in October and November, and then cool breezes tempered the summer heat, and one July there was a snowfall. It was a lovely life, leisurely and free from care, and it mellowed the once wild Sailing Master and made him think that he might never want to leave his kingdom, after all. "This manner of life grew so exquisitely pleasant," wrote Steele, "that he never had a moment heavy upon his hands; his nights were untroubled and his days joyous, from the practice of temperance and exercise."

When he took to his bed, the night of January 31, 1709, surrounded by his pet cats, it is likely that Selkirk fell into a sound sleep without care or worry. He had only another typical pleasant summer's day waiting for him. He could not know that his island idyll was ended.

We do not know the hour of the following day that he once more attained his lookout and, from force of habit, brought the spyglass to his eye. But we know what sight was magnified in his glass. Four leagues off shore stood the *Duke* and the *Duchess* under the command of Captain Woodes Rogers. Their parentage was plain. Selkirk could see that they were English.

The vessels were too far out to be attracted by any sign Selkirk could make in broad daylight. He returned to the beach and impatiently waited for nightfall. The moment it was dark, he lit a series of bonfires—"the Light" Captain Rogers saw from his deck and "the Lights" that made the startled Captain Thomas Dover turn tail in his longboat. Selkirk waited for a response. Beyond the boom of a cannon from the *Duke* and the appearance of distant lanterns, there was none.

It is probable that Selkirk remained tensely awake through the long, impatient night. With daybreak he could see that the great bay was empty. The ships had disappeared. His spirits must have been shattered, but before noon the *Duke* and the *Duchess* reappeared, preparing for their phantom fight. Now they moved in closer and dropped anchor, and one ship lowered a yawl.

In a frenzy of excitement, Selkirk waited at the water's edge as the small craft drew closer. Captain Dover, the eccentric physician, once more led the landing-party, accompanied by seven men. We are told that Selkirk waved at them. Then, as they came ashore, he scrambled to offer them fresh water and shellfish, and, uttering incoherencies, he pressed upon them a stew of goat meat. While they ate and watched their half-civilized host in animal skins, Selkirk sped up a near-by incline, caught a darting goat, threw it over a shoulder, and returned to present it to his countrymen.

There are several versions relating Selkirk's reaction to being rescued from his island. Steele understood that he met the offer with "greatest indifference." Captain Dover reported that the castaway declined to leave on any ship commanded by Captain Dampier. On the other hand, Captain Cooke wrote that Selkirk, hearing the roll of officers on the vessels, stated that he had "an irreconcilable aversion" to one with whom he had served on the *Cinque Ports*, but agreed to go aboard only because Dampier— "for whom he had a friendship"—was an officer. Whatever the truth, when the pinnace came in search of the yawl to learn what had occasioned the delay, Selkirk willingly accompanied it back to the *Duke*. He submitted to an interview with Captain Rogers, rejecting rum for water as he told the story of his four years and four months, speaking "his words by halves." In turn, he questioned the Captain and learned of the destruction of the *Cinque Ports*. He learned also, for the first time, of the great events that had occurred between 1704 and 1709 in the world beyond Más a Tierra, of Scotland's union with England, of the Earl of Marlborough's glorious victories over the French at Blenheim and Ramillies, of the invasion of Russia by the youthful Charles XII of Sweden and of his eventual defeat. Before the day was done, Selkirk had agreed to forgo the solitary pleasures of Utopia for the more strenuous life in the community of men. He signed on as Second Mate of the *Duke*.

When the *Duke* and her consort sailed out of Cumberland Bay on February 14, 1709, Alexander Selkirk looked upon the rugged outlines of his island home for the last time. Unlike Crusoe, he never returned. Más a Tierra did not remain a desert island long. After Commodore Anson's visit, during which the venerable goat with the marked ear was found, England considered taking possession of the island for a military base. But Spain anticipated this move, and in 1750 established her own garrison on Más a Tierra. More than a half-century later, after Chile won its independence, it took over the island, converting it into a prison for political offenders. In more recent years, after the prison was removed, Chilean settlers colonized the island, raising livestock and exporting shellfish. Today about three hundred colonists remain, and, at last report, Chilean geologists announced that Más a Tierra was in danger of disappearing into the sea unless steps were taken to halt erosion created by constant winds.

As Selkirk withdrew from the island, he could not know that the two-thousand-foot peak which had served so long for his lookout would one day be memorialized by his countrymen. In 1868 a party of English naval officers from the H.M.S. *Topaze* established a tablet on the lookout site: "In memory of Alexander Selkirk, mariner."

At the time of his last glimpse of Más a Tierra, we may be sure Selkirk's mind was less on immortality than on temporal matters. He had left his home in Largo seven years before in poverty and disgrace. He would, he prayed, return affluent and respected. His dream was in the hands of Captain Woodes Rogers.

Few veteran seamen, in 1709, practiced legal piracy more efficiently than Captain Rogers. His merchant backers had invested 14,000 pounds in his talents. In the year following the rescue of Selkirk, Captain Rogers parlayed their investment to the sum of 170,000 pounds. En route to Peru, Rogers captured and added to his expedition a sixteen-ton Spanish craft he renamed the *Beginning*. Shortly after, he ran down a fifty-ton bark, which he named the *Increase* and turned into a hospital ship with Selkirk as its Sailing Master. Next he determined to raid the wealthy city of Guayaquil, Peru. He approached the city and sent two Spanish prisoners in with a demand for forty thousand pieces of eight. The authorities made a counter offer of thirty-two thousand pieces of eight. Impatient with the bickering, Rogers and seventy crew members charged the community. Spanish cavalry resisted briefly and ran. Rogers and his men proceeded with their pillage.

Lieutenant Connely of the *Duchess* and "Mr. Selkirk the late Governour of Juan Fernandez" headed a detail assigned to strip jewelry from Guayaquil's beautiful Spanish noblewomen. Selkirk apparently acquitted himself in an unusually restrained manner. As Captain Rogers reported it:

"Our Men got several Gold Chains and Ear-Rings, but were

otherwise so civil to them, that the Ladies offer'd to dress 'em Victuals, and brought 'em a Cash of good Liquor. Some of their largest Gold Chains were conceal'd and wound about their Middles, Legs, and Thighs, etc., but the Gentlewomen in these hot Countries being very thin clad with Silk and fine Linnen, and their Hair dressed with Ribbons very neatly, our Men by pressing felt the Chains, etc., with their Hands on the Outside of the Lady's Apparel, and by their Linguest modestly desired the Gentlewomen to take 'em off and surrender 'em. This I mention as Proof of our Sailors Modesty and in respect to Mr. Connely and Mr. Selkirk."

This modesty contributed considerably to the twelve hundres pounds' worth of jewelry acquired by the English in the raid. Besides the jewelry, Rogers took with him from Guayaquil 25,000 pieces of eight, 230 bags of flour, 150 bales of drygoods, a large quantity of food and arms, several small ships—and the yellow-fever germ. The last, caught during the raid, swept the expedition, and soon 140 crewmen were in the hospital ship.

Meanwhile, the *Duke* and *Duchess* and their captive vessels plowed the Pacific toward the American west coast. Off California, a high-decked Spanish galleon, the *Nostra Seniora de la Incarnacion Disenganio*, was captured in three hours. It was renamed the *Batchelor* and placed under the command of Captain Dover, who selected Selkirk for his Sailing Master. Shortly after, another, larger Spanish galleon was engaged. But this one had sixty cannon. After a day's battle, during which Rogers was badly wounded in an ankle, the English privateers withdrew.

It was early in 1710 when Rogers gave the order to leave Spanish waters and head for home. After calling at Guam and Batavia, the expedition reached the Cape of Good Hope late in December. There the privateers held over three months, then joined an English convoy going to England. Selkirk, we are told, "often beguiled the time by relating to his brother officers his adventures upon the island."

The Real Robinson Crusoe

When he reached London in mid-October of 1711, Selkirk had been gone eight years, one month, and three days. He found London little changed, still possessing its easy, countrified air, its famous landmarks towering over the low roofs of the city, its coaches bumping noisily over the warren of cobbled streets. But if London had not changed, Selkirk certainly had. He had seen it last a ne'er-do-well of twenty-seven; now he was a minor celebrity of thirty-five and, by his standards, wealthy.

Of the 170,000 pounds prize money the expedition earned, one half went to its Bristol backers and the other half stayed with the crews. Captain Rogers received 14,000 pounds, and Sailing Master Selkirk received 800 pounds, a considerable sum in those days. As to Selkirk's celebrity, his island adventure had intrigued officers and crew in the long journey home. Now it delighted London. He lingered for two and one-half years, meeting people, drinking heavily, and wenching. He was often the subject of the darkest moods. But when at last he began to recover his humor, as Sir Richard Steele noted, he turned his face toward home.

It was a Sunday morning in the bright spring of 1714 when Alexander Selkirk dismounted from a carriage before the thatched Selcraig cottage in Largo. He had returned in style. He wore a gold-laced coat and breeches, most likely taken from a Spanish galleon. In his pockets were hundreds of pounds. Beside him were his old sea chest and firelock, badges of his recent distinction. But his long-deferred entrance was marred by the fact that no one was at home. Then he remembered that it was Sunday. Leaving his effects behind, he hurried up the hill to the church—for a better entrance.

"As soon as he entered and sat down," wrote John Howell, who had heard the story from relatives, "all eyes were upon him; for such a personage perhaps had seldom been seen within the church at Largo. He was elegantly dressed in gold-laced clothes; besides, he was a stranger, which in a country-church is a matter of attention to the hearers at all times. . . . After remaining some time engaged in devotion, his eyes were ever turning to where his parents and brothers sat, while theirs as often met his gaze; still they did not know him. At length, his mother, whose thoughts perhaps at this time wandered to her long-lost son, recognized him, and, uttering a cry of joy, could contain herself no longer. Even in the house of God she rushed to his arms, unconscious of the impropriety of her conduct and the interruption of the service. Alexander and his friends immediately retired to his father's house to give free scope to their joy and congratulations."

The pleasures of homecoming were short-lived. Within a week Selkirk had lapsed into his earlier state of deep depression. He took a room with his eldest brother John and his sister-in-law. He was rarely seen in his room. It irritated him to speak to his family, or recount his adventures to the curious. Each morning he left his brother's residence early, with food in hand to last the entire day. He returned late at night, ignoring relations and their guests. His only interest, in the house, was in training and cavorting with his sister-in-law's two cats. Remembering what he had accomplished with his pets on Más a Tierra, he taught the Selcraig cats "to dance and perform many little feats." Once when the cats waited his return at night, he nodded at them, remarking: "Were children as docile and obedient, parents would all be happy in them."

His days were spent in hiking and sailing. He had acquired a handsome boat. In good weather he took it out into Largo Bay or to Kingscraig Point and silently fished. More often he went for solitary strolls through the secluded, romantic valley of Keil's Den. Finally, and most oddly, he began to construct a cave such as he had first dwelt in on Más a Tierra.

He dug the cave high on a hill that rose behind his father's house. He furnished it with a roof and terrace and a few effects, and when the weather was too poor for walking or fishing, he would retire to the cave and stare gloomily out over the bay below. Sometimes his parents found him weeping. Once when they begged him to pull himself together, he exclaimed: "Oh, my beloved island! I wish I had never left thee! I never was before the man I was on thee! I have not been such since I left thee! And, I fear, never can be again!" He never ceased regretting his return to civilization. England "could not, he said, with all its enjoyments, restore him to the tranquillity of his solitude."

And then one day he met Sophia Bruce, and his life as a recluse came to an end. He was hiking through Keil's Den, on his way to the ruins of Balcruivie Castle, when he first saw her. She was tending a cow on her father's property. He watched as she picked wildflowers and sang a rural lay. Her loneliness, as well as her person, attracted him. He came into the open and addressed himself to her, and their acquaintance was begun. After that, he neglected his cave and his boat for a daily rendezvous in Keil's Den. He found Sophia, whose parents were poor and whose three uncles were ministers, an "innocent" lass, yet "amiable."

He kept his love, and his meetings, secret. Neither his family nor his friends knew of his female companion, "for he felt ashamed, after his discourses to them, and the profession he had made of dislike to human society, to acknowledge that he was upon the point of marrying, and thereby plunging into the midst of worldly cares."

Fearful of his family's "jests," he proposed to Sophia that they elope to London and there wed. She was agreeable. They left Largo suddenly, one day late in 1716. They soon had a comfortable apartment in the Pall Mall section of London. They were not yet man and wife, in the eyes of the law, when Selkirk decided to go to sea again. Restless, bored with inactivity, he suddenly enlisted in the English navy. He was assigned to the H.M.S. *Enterprise*. But before setting forth, he made a will, naming as his beneficiary "my loveing and well beloved friend, Sophia Bruce, of the Pelmel, London, spinster." Later Sophia would insist that she had legally become Mrs. Selkirk before he boarded the *Enterprise*, "on or about the fourth day of March."

By the beginning of 1719 Selkirk was back from his naval

cruise. He remained with Sophia in Pall Mall all the rest of that year, the year that saw the appearance and popularity of an octavo volume bearing the woodcut of a castaway in goatskins, entitled *The Life and Strange Surprizing Adventures of Robinson Crusoe, of York, Mariner.*

In 1720, again anxious to be on the move, Selkirk signed on H.M.S. *Weymouth* as Lieutenant, though some sources believe he went as First Mate. In November, or earlier, he took his farewell of Sophia and traveled to Plymouth to join his ship. But there was a delay, which would prove fatal to poor Sophia. The *Weymouth*, being prepared to hunt down pirates and slave-runners off Africa, was not yet ready to sail. Selkirk loitered about Plymouth. It must be presumed that he drank a good deal, and, drinking one day in a public house kept by the "gay" widow Candish, he fell in love again.

Frances Candish was attractive, flirtatious, and frank. Selkirk wooed her, but for a few weeks she resisted. At last she accepted his proposal. They were married on December 12, 1720, and, before sailing, he prepared a new will in her favor.

The *Weymouth* put to sea shortly after, and made the African Gold Coast safely. The pirates proved an elusive quarry. There were several landings, for supply, and during one of these some members of the crew were captured by natives, but finally rescued. As a consequence of these stops, however, malaria and yellow fever invaded the ship. From June until November, while the *Weymouth* pushed down along Africa, as many as three or four crewmen died in a single day.

On December 13, 1720, as the *Weymouth* drew closer to the pirates, another death was entered in its log. The entry read: "Alexr. Selkirk, DD . . . P.M. Alexr. Selkirk Deceased." Like so many of his shipmates, he had undoubtedly died of the fever. Three months later the pirates were caught and hanged. And in 1722 the *Weymouth* was back in England with the news that the real Robinson Crusoe was dead.

There was an unhappy aftermath. In Plymouth, Frances Candish Selkirk applied for probate of her husband's will. In

London, Sophia Bruce Selkirk applied for probate of her husband's will. Since each claimed the late Alexander Selkirk as her legal husband, the issue went to court. Frances called Sophia "a person of very indifferent character and reputation" and said that Selkirk had merely been "a boarder or lodger with her." Sophia called Frances a criminal opportunist who knew "the said Alexander was then a marryed man, and not a single Person, and was at the time of such Marriage Much Overcome or Intoxicated with Liquor."

Both parties in the dispute were asked to produce their marriage certificates. Frances Candish displayed proof of her union, but Sophia Bruce could find no proof. Thus the case was resolved, and Frances Candish, twice widowed and already wedded a third time to a tallow-chandler in Plymouth named Hall, became the legal Selkirk heir. In 1724 Frances Candish journeyed to Largo to claim Selkirk's properties and his inheritances from his parents, who were by then both dead. She took what was legally hers, though she had no interest in the desert-island relics, and departed into history. Of Sophia Bruce we know no more after her judicial defeat, beyond the fact that she remained some time in London and was destitute, and tried once to secure charity from a Westminster clergyman.

As for Selkirk, he lay at the bottom of the Atlantic sea. All that remained of him were the tangible evidences of his great adventure. The gold-laced suit, the worn sea chest, the coconut cup—mounted on silver, and once stolen by a peddler for the silver, but later returned—they were with the family in Largo. Also left behind was the sturdy musket, on which he had carved his name and the picture of a seal on a rock and a rhyme:

> *With 3 drams powther*
> *3 ounce haill*
> *Ram me well & pryme me*
> *To Kill I will not faile.*

These were his legacy, all that existed of four years and four months on Más a Tierra. These, and Robinson Crusoe.

Selkirk had fulfilled himself only on his lonely island. His story, like Defoe's, was a hymn to man's indestructibility. And in that brief victory he found, for the first time and the last, true happiness. His tale is a tale with a moral. Sir Richard Steele saw the moral clear, after he had seen Selkirk, and he wrote it down for all to read and to remember:

"This plain man's story is a memorable example that he is happiest who confines his want to natural necessities; and he that goes further in his desires, increases his want in proportion to his acquisitions; or, to use his own expression, 'I am now worth eight hundred pounds, but shall never be so happy as when I was not worth a farthing.'"

VIII

Hardly Coincidental

"*All the characters in this book are fictitious. Any resemblance to persons living or dead is purely coincidental.*"

FROM AN OLD SAYING

Once, when a correspondent asked Gustave Flaubert to identify the real-life Mme Emma Bovary, he replied rather testily: "*I am Mme Bovary!*"

And, to be sure, there was some truth in his reply. He had drawn much of Emma Bovary's character, and some of her story, from his imagination, his experience, his reading, and his fantasies based on observation. His instincts about French women in general—"suffering and weeping at this very instant in twenty villages of France"—were personal contributions of his very own.

Yet, as we know from existing evidence, though some of Mme Bovary was derived from the recesses of Flaubert's own creativity, more of her was derived from the actual Mme Delphine Delamare, the dissatisfied and faithless young wife of a country doctor in Ry, France.

If choice had to be made and credit given, I would say that Mme Delamare, and not Monsieur Flaubert, was more nearly Emma Bovary.

Why did not Flaubert acknowledge his literary debt? As I remarked at the outset of this examination, there are several reasons why an author will not admit to a *roman à clef*. Sometimes he believes that the characters have become too much his own to credit to any outside inspiration. Sometimes he does not wish to detract from his own invention. Sometimes he fears the more painful aftermaths of lawsuit, assault, and anger. Therefore, in the great majority of instances, novelists like Flaubert never concede their debt. They simply do not recognize its existence. They remain silent.

It was not always so. For the insistence by modern novelists and their publishers that any resemblance of their characters to persons living or dead be blamed on the laws of coincidence is a precaution and ritual of rather recent vintage. In times past, in the last century and before, writers and their publishers rarely bothered to put into print such defensive camouflage. There were heartier men in those days, and fewer lawyers (and statutes of libel), and authors drew portraits of real persons with reckless abandon—and often admitted it.

Of the six prototypes I have saved to sketch in my final chapter, three were openly acknowledged by their debtors. Two authors remained silent as to their sources. And only one, Flaubert, made public denial. Had I the space to recount in detail the half-hundred more prototypes who deserve mention for their forgotten contributions to literature, most of them citizens of the eighteenth and nineteenth centuries, I think it would be evident that the average of acknowledgment given them by authors maintains. But for my restricted gallery, six more personalities will suffice.

As usual, within the limitations set down at the outset, I have made my selection on the basis of personal interest. The models in the pages that follow are those that struck my fancy—and I am reassured in the knowledge that they also struck the livelier fancies of Gustave Flaubert, Alexandre Dumas *fils*, Frederick Marryat, Edward Bulwer-Lytton, Wilkie Collins, and Charles Dickens.

"*I* am Mme Bovary!"—any resemblance to persons living or dead is purely coincidental.

Purely coincidental? Hardly coincidental, as we shall see . . .

. . .

Hardly Coincidental

There are no statistics, unfortunately, on the occupations or backgrounds that have supplied the greatest number of prototypes to writing men. But it would seem to me, in tracking down the originals of great characters developed in the last few centuries, that an extraordinary number were notorious women, scandalous women, scarlet women—sometimes prostitutes, courtesans, and mistresses, but more often lightly domesticated ladies of lively libido or secret loves. These women of erratic virtue consistently inspired novelists to fashion their memorable *femmes fatales* of fiction.

Mlle Manon Porcher, arrested by French authorities for "scandalous and public debauchery" and for theft, was deported with other convicts to the colony of Louisiana. She was followed by a young nobleman named Avril de La Varenne, who married her. In the hands of Antoine François Prévost d'Exiles—the Abbé Prévost—Manon Porcher became the immortal Manon Lescaut.

La Paiva, a beautiful courtesan of the Second Empire, lived in retirement in the Parc Monceau section of Paris. Émile Zola sought an introduction and interviewed her, as well as other women of her class. "I cannot invent facts," he explained. "I absolutely lack the faculty for inventing plots or stories." Or, he might have added, characters. La Paiva and her friends became the celebrated Nana.

In 1916, in Hawaii, W. Somerset Maugham met a medical missionary and his bluenosed wife, and then he met a prostitute who was being driven off Iwelei after a raid. She was, he noted in his journal, "plump, pretty in a coarse fashion, perhaps not more than twenty-seven; she wore a white dress and a large white hat, and long white boots from which her calves, in white cotton stockings, bulged." She was, of course, destined to become Sadie Thompson.

Thus, women of easy morals have, through the years, provided material for men of letters. Let us examine two more of these women in greater detail, two who inspired the fictional heroines of *Madame Bovary* and *Camille*.

Gustave Flaubert's inspiration for Mme Emma Bovary—
"the most complete woman's portrait I know in the whole of
literature, including Shakespeare and including Balzac," Émile
Faguet has stated—came to the author when he was thirty years
old and uncertain of his literary future. Until then his career
had been confused and unpromising. "I went to school when I
was only ten," he would say, "and I very soon contracted a
profound aversion to the human race." During his formative
years he suffered falling in love with a married woman almost
twice his age, he suffered studying law in Paris, and he suffered
a fit of epilepsy.

Shortly after his father, Dr. Achille-Cleophas Flaubert, a
successful Rouen physician, purchased a two-century-old
mansion on the Seine, called Croisset, young Flaubert turned
his full-time attention to writing. For nine months a year, he
wrote six hours daily in the study overlooking the river. The
other three months he spent in Paris seeking experience. One
Parisian experience, the most involved he was to have with a
woman, began when he met Louise Colet, a poetess. She was
extremely attractive, with her fair hair worn in ringlets and her
large, soft eyes and her throaty voice, and she had a husband
and a lover at the time Flaubert met her. In a month she became
Flaubert's mistress—though the excitement of her submission
delayed Flaubert's ability to consummate the union for some
time. Thereafter, for several years Louise was Flaubert's correspondent, literary conscience, and, in the end, the bane of his
existence.

In 1851, after a trip to Egypt, Palestine, and Greece, Flaubert penned the first draft of *The Temptation of St. Anthony*.
Upon its completion, he sent for his two closest friends, Maxime du Camp, editor of the *Revue de Paris*, and Louis Bouilhet,
a shy peasant poet. Flaubert told them he was going to read to
them from the manuscript of his newest work. For almost four
days, reading aloud eight hours a day, Flaubert enacted *The
Temptation*. He finished his reading on a midnight, and waited

for the verdict. One of the pair said: "We think you ought to throw it in the fire and not speak of it again."

The following afternoon, deeply discouraged, Flaubert joined du Camp and Bouilhet in his garden. He complained to them of his artistic barrenness. He had several new historical ideas in mind, but he wasn't sure of them. He had no desire to return to the desk in his study. What he needed, he thought, was a fresh subject.

At this point Maxime du Camp cautioned him: "As soon as you feel irresistibly drawn towards this poetic soaring, you must choose a subject in which it would be so absurd that you will be forced on your guard and compelled to drop it." Then du Camp added: "Take some workaday subject, one of those episodes bourgeois life is full of, and compel yourself to handle it in a natural tone."

Flaubert complained that he knew no such episodes of bourgeois life. Suddenly Louis Bouilhet spoke. "Why not write the story of Delamare?" he asked.

Flaubert sat up. "Now, that's an idea!" he exclaimed.

Bouilhet continued speaking. He had intended for some time to mention the Delamare idea to Flaubert. It had first occurred to him during a visit to Flaubert's mother while Flaubert was abroad. On arriving at Croisset, Bouilhet had found another guest, an elderly, sorrowful provincial woman who was introduced to him as Mme Delamare. She dwelt in poverty in a near-by village, caring for herself and a very young granddaughter who had been left in her charge. Her son had recently committed suicide, and since her son had once studied under Dr. Flaubert, she was finding consolation in the company of the great doctor's widow. It was then that Bouilhet placed the old lady in his memory, recalled the tragedy of the Delamares, and thought what a fine realistic piece it might make for Gustave Flaubert. Did Flaubert remember the tragedy? He did indeed.

Eugène Delamare had been a plodding medical student, studying surgery at the Rouen hospital under Flaubert's father. He was a mediocre undergraduate. He failed in several critical examinations, and did not have the funds to obtain special tutoring or extend his time in the hospital. Unable to obtain his diploma as a full doctor, Delamare became a licensed medical officer, an *officier de sante*.

Shortly after, Delamare married a widow older than himself —an act with much precedence in the French provinces—and took a job as health official in a rural community called Ry. When his wife died, Delamare met an attractive seventeen-year-old blonde girl named Delphine Conturier. She was the youngest daughter of one of his patients, a well-off farmer who possessed considerable property at near-by Blainville-Crevon. She had been educated at the Ursulines, a finishing-school in Rouen, and her head was filled with reveries evoked by romantic novels. On August 7, 1839, she became the second Mme Delamare.

At the start, Delphine had been excited by the prospect of marrying a mature medical man. Soon she found Delamare a bore and the small community oppressive. Flaubert sensed, or possibly repeated, her feelings exactly when he showed Emma Bovary's growing distaste for Dr. Charles Bovary. Mme Bovary had imagined an impulsive, stimulating lover, set against a world of gondolas and tropical vistas. Instead she had a dullard whose conversation was "as flat as a street pavement. . . . He could not swim, he could not fence, he could not handle firearms. . . . Her innermost heart, however, was waiting for something to happen. Like shipwrecked sailors, she turned a despairing gaze over the solitude of her life, seeking some white sail in the far mists of the horizon. . . . But nothing happened to her; God had willed it so! The future was a dark corridor, with its door at the end shut fast."

Delphine Delamare had a high regard for her own intellect and beauty, and she had only contempt for her bourgeois husband. She determined to have a more stimulating life. She began to spend money extravagantly on clothes, and Delamare was soon deeply in debt. When this became tiresome, she began to invite the attentions of other men, first a farmhand, then a notary clerk, then—anyone. As Flaubert wrote of her fictional counterpart: "She recalled the heroines of the books that she had read, and the lyric legion of these adulterous women began to sing in her memory." Secretly, in fields, hotels, and back rooms, Mme Delamare accepted the attentions of lover after lover, desperate for the ideal that did not exist. She neglected her husband, her little daughter, her friends and neighbors, her visits to Mass, as she indulged herself in sensuality.

Old Mme Delamare tried to warn her son. But he adored Delphine and laughed at his mother. The spending and the nymphomania continued. At last, during the early dawn of March 6, 1848, in the ninth year of her marriage, when her credit was gone and her appearance less attractive to admirers, Delphine Delamare committed suicide by swallowing arsenic. Several months later the grief-stricken Delamare learned the full extent of his wife's extravagances, and learned for the first time of her infidelities. Shocked beyond reason, he killed himself, leaving his small daughter to the care of his impoverished mother.

When Bouilhet reminded Flaubert of this provincial tragedy, he went on to remind him of more. As Francis Steegmuller recounted it: "He reminded him of the black-and-yellow striped curtains in young Madame Delamare's parlor, which had first caused her to be thought pretentious and extravagant by her mother-in-law and her neighbors and had been gossiped about all over Normandy; of the way she had instructed her peasant servant to address her in the third person; of her prettiness, her chic, her haughtiness and nervousness, her at-homes on Friday afternoons which she herself was the only one to attend, the unpaid bill she had left at a lending library in Rouen. He recalled Delamare's heavy appearance and manner, his good-natured mediocrity, his satisfaction with his situation in life, the confidence, almost the affection, with which he was regarded by his country clients."

Flaubert realized at once that the Delamares were almost perfect for his pen. He hated the destructive romanticism and mediocrity of the bourgeois in the provinces. He knew Normandy and he knew these people. Two things bothered him. The story was vulgar and the people commonplace. Nevertheless, Flaubert could not resist. Despite his mother's entreaties that he refrain from ever mentioning the Delamares as his models, for fear the elderly Mme Delamare might be offended, Flaubert proceeded to mold Emma and Charles Bovary out of the lives of Delphine and Eugène Delamare—with a touch of Louise Colet added.

The novel went slowly, six pages a week. "I itch with sentences that never appear," he told Louise. "What a heavy oar the pen is." He worked seven hours a day, every day, for fifty-five months. He allowed Maxime du Camp to publish it first, as a six-part serial, between October and December of 1856. The publication churned up a tempest. "As soon as the first chapters had appeared," said du Camp, "our subscribers rose in wrath, crying that it was scandalous, immoral. They wrote us letters of doubtful courtesy, accusing us of slandering France and disgracing it in the eyes of the world. 'What! Such women exist? Women who deceive their husbands, pile up debts, meet their lovers in gardens and hotels? Such creatures exist in our lovely France, in the provinces where life is so pure? Impossible!' "

After being tried and acquitted of writing pornography, Flaubert permitted Michel Levy to publish *Madame Bovary*. It appeared in April 1857, in two volumes, and sold fifteen thousand copies in sixty days. Though Louise Colet, having by then fought with Flaubert, thought the book read as if penned by a traveling salesman, the critical acclaim was otherwise unanimous. Sainte-Beuve announced: "He has style." Charles Baudelaire thought it "a marvel." Victor Hugo sent his congratulations. And though Flaubert, in his crotchety and lonely old age, tired of its notoriety—"I should like to find some way of making a lot of money so that I could buy up every copy of

Hardly Coincidental

Madame Bovary in existence, throw them all into the fire, and never hear of the book again"—it went into edition after edition and attained the stature of a classic. Delphine Delamare could not know it, but in her death she had finally fulfilled her most romantic dreams.

At almost the same time that the provincial courtesan who inspired *Madame Bovary* was struggling to escape the captivity of her mean village in Normandy, a more worldly courtesan was struggling to maintain her precarious position in Paris. Marie Duplessis, the original model for Marguerite Gautier, heroine of *Camille*, started lower and rose higher than Delphine Delamare.

The prototype for the lady of the camellias was born Rose Alphonsine Plessis in Nonant, France, on January 15, 1824. She later changed her name to Marie Duplessis because it sounded less common. On her father's side, her grandmother had been a streetwalker and her grandfather a licentious priest. Her father, a peddler who later opened a draper's shop in Nonant, was a drunkard and a brute. Eventually Marie's mother separated from him, obtained employment as maid to an English family, and placed Marie and a sister with cousins.

When Marie was nine, her mother died. Marie was returned to the custody of her father, who permitted her to roam about unrestrained and wild. Some short time after, it was said, she "left her virtue, together with her petticoat, underneath a bramble bush in a hedge." She was thirteen when her father became aware that she had the face of an angel and the body of Salome. He decided to capitalize on these commodities. For a small sum of cash he turned her over to a wealthy, lecherous friend, Plantier, aged seventy, who used her as he wished and then abandoned her in Paris. She briefly sought refuge with relatives who owned a grocer's shop, then acquired shabby quarters of her own among the dissolute students of the Latin Quarter. She supported herself as a messenger for a corsetmaker, as a clerk in a hat store, and as a girl of the streets.

We have a picture of her in this period, as recollected by a young playboy and theater-manager named Nestor Roqueplan. One evening, ascending the steps of the Pont Neuf, he saw standing before a vendor of fried potatoes "a pretty girl, of delicate appearance and very dirty. She was munching a green apple which she did not seem to care about. Fried potatoes were what she wanted. I bought her a bag of them." Less than two years later Roqueplan saw her again. She was transformed into a splendid young lady, and was escorted by the handsome Duc de Guiche-Gramont, who was to become a Foreign Minister of France. "He had with him, hanging on his arm, a very charming lady, most elegantly dressed, who was no other than my little *gourmande* of the Pont Neuf. She was now known as Marie Duplessis."

Her rise had been rapid. It had its real beginnings on a Sunday in her sixteenth year, when she accompanied two girl friends to a restaurant in Saint-Cloud. The proprietor, dazzled by her beauty, invited her to return the next week—alone. Soon she was his mistress, installed in an apartment in the rue de l'Arcade. For the first time, she had the necessities of life. In short months she would have its luxuries, too. One evening she was seen at the theater by Count Ferdinand de Monguyon, and overnight she abandoned her restaurateur for royalty. Next she was seen at a dance by the Duc de Guiche-Gramont. He made a better proposition than the Count and whisked her off to the spas of Germany for the summer.

To more rapidly gain her material needs, she accepted lovers in great number. According to the newspaper *Figaro*, she was at one time supported by a syndicate of seven ardent admirers. The seven gentlemen pooled their money to keep her, and each was given a separate night of the week to visit her. "They symbolized their collective devotion by combining to present her with a magnificent dressing-table containing seven drawers."

Marie Duplessis had long graduated from the Latin Quarter and was finally established in a lavish suite of rooms at 11

Boulevard de la Madeleine. The rooms, with their walls draped in heavy silk, were exotically and romantically furnished. In the anteroom were rare plants growing out of lacquered boxes; in the salon were pieces of rosewood furniture, Venetian mirrors, ornaments of solid silver, and a magnificent Pleyel piano; in the dining-room were rare tapestries and Dresden china; in the boudoir were the six-foot dressing-table, leather-bound volumes of Alfred de Musset, Victor Hugo, and Abbé Prévost, velvet and satin curtains, and a great wardrobe filled with gowns designed by Mme Palmyre.

By 1844, when Marie was twenty, there were still multiple lovers, but one man in particular was paying for the luxuries in the boulevard de la Madeleine. Marie had met the Count de Stackelberg at the baths of Bagnères. He had been the Russian Ambassador to Vienna. He was married, wealthy, and eighty years of age. He was later represented in the novel *Camille* as the elderly Duc de Mauriac. In the novel he befriended Marguerite Gautier and sponsored her because she so closely resembled a daughter he had lost. Their fictional relationship was platonic. Dumas assured us this was not so in fact. "The story of the consumptive daughter whose double the Duke discovered in Marie Duplessis is sheer invention. The Count, in spite of his great age, was not an Edipus looking for an Antigone, but a King David looking for a Bathsheba."

Though the discreet old Russian paid the bills, purchased carriages and horses for Marie in England, and rented boxes for her at all the best Parisian theaters, he was not able to give her the love she desired. For this facet of her needs—her extreme romanticism and intense sensuality—she looked elsewhere. Foremost among her young lovers was the witty Viscount Édouard de Perregaux, who had been a member of the French cavalry in Africa and was now a member of the Jockey Club in Paris, and who attended her regularly when the Russian was occupied with his wife.

Many descriptions of Marie Duplessis in her twentieth year, with all Paris at her feet, still exist. Jules Janin remembered, after her death, that she "was tall, very slight, with black hair, and a pink and white complexion. Her head was small; she had long enameled eyes, like a Japanese woman's, but they were sparkling and alert. Her lips were ruddier than the cherry, her teeth were the prettiest in the world; she looked like a little figure made of Dresden china." For all her depravity and nymphomania, her lovely young face continued to bear the look of a startled virgin. Dumas recalled it well when he wrote in *Camille:* "How it was that her ardent life had left on Marguerite's face the virginal, almost childlike expression, which characterized it, is a problem which we can but state, without attempting to solve it."

Men were moved by her candor, her flashes of gaiety, her tact, her graceful fragility, and, above all, her worldly weariness, brought on by the pointlessness of her existence and her growing attacks of tuberculosis. It was remarked that she "made vice decent, dignified and decorous." She enjoyed her clothes and servants, her two spaniels, her carriage outings to the country, her visits to the opera and the theater. She enjoyed, too, gambling at cards, drinking, and off-color stories. She longed for solitude, security, and true love—but these she never had for any length of time. Her trademark, of purity, of elegance, of beauty, was the white camellia. She had a fresh vase of them in her apartment daily. She carried them in small bouquets when riding in the Champs-Élysées or sitting in the Opéra.

Alexandre Dumas *fils* saw her first in 1842, when he was eighteen and unsuccessful and she was eighteen and famous. He was strolling in the Place de la Bourse one afternoon when a rich blue carriage, drawn by two splendid bays, halted at the curb. She stepped down and entered a shop. She wore an Italian straw hat, cashmere shawl, and India muslin dress. She had her dogs on leash, and a bouquet of camellias in a gloved hand, and she had a wondrous smile. He was instantly smitten.

But he held little hope. She was the child of millionaires, the beloved princess of pleasure betrothed to the mighty. He was the illegitimate son of a great father, and nothing more. He was struggling to become a writer in the shadow of his fat, childlike parent. The elder Dumas was prodigious. He bragged that he had produced five hundred children, fought twenty duels, written enough to fill twelve hundred volumes (including *Monte Cristo* and *The Three Musketeers*), and earned and spent five million dollars. Alexandre Dumas *père* would have known at once how to manage Marie Duplessis. Alexandre Dumas *fils* was helpless.

However, less than two years later he met Marie and made her his mistress, and through her found his fame and fortune. "On a fine day in September 1844 I had been to Saint-Germain-en-Laye to see my father," young Dumas recalled afterwards. "On my way there I had met Eugène Dejazet, the son of the famous actress. We had ridden together in the beautiful forest of Saint-Germain, and returned to Paris for dinner, and gone to the Variétés, and were seated in the stalls, Marie Duplessis was in the stage box on the right-hand side. She was alone there, or rather, she was the only person one could see there, sniffing at a bouquet, nibbling sweets from a bag, hardly listening to the performance, looking about her in all directions, exchanging smiles and glances with three or four of our neighbors, leaning back from time to time, to chat with an invisible occupant of her box, who was no other than the aged Russian Count S."

Then Dumas had a stroke of luck. Marie often waved to a stout woman in an opposite box, whose name was Clemence Prat. She was a hat-maker who dwelt near Marie Duplessis and who often served as Marie's procuress. Dumas's companion, Dejazet, knew Mme Prat and went to speak to her. He returned with exciting news. After the theater, Count de Stackelberg was taking Marie directly to her suite. He would leave immediately. They would wait in the street, and then enter and join Marie and Mme Prat for supper.

It was midnight when Dumas and his friend entered the salon. Marie Duplessis, in a brocade gown, was at the piano. Champagne was served, and then supper. Mme Prat told a coarse story. Marie laughed, fell into a fit of coughing, rushed into her bedroom. Dumas followed. When he realized how ill she was, he begged to continue seeing her so that he might care for her. What transpired next Dumas reported faithfully, word for word, in his novel. Marie, or Marguerite, considered his proposal and then studied him.

"So you are in love with me? Say it straight out, it is much more simple."

"It is possible; but if I am to say it to you one day, it is not today."

"You will do better never to say it."

"Why?"

"Because only one of two things can come of it. . . . Either I shall not accept: then you will have a grudge against me; or I shall accept: then you will have a sorry mistress; a woman who is nervous, ill, sad, or gay with a gaiety sadder than grief, a woman who spits blood and spends a hundred thousand francs a year. That is all very well for a rich old man like the duke, but it is very bad for a young man like you, and the proof of it is that all the young lovers I have had have very soon left me."

Their hectic affair lasted one year, and it ended for the very reasons about which she had cautioned him. In a few months, after escorting her to dances and gambling-casinos and buying her expensive gifts, Dumas was almost out of funds. He tried his luck at baccarat to win more, and lost all. He borrowed and he fretted. He became insanely jealous of her Russian Count and insisted she give him up. She said she would if he paid all the bills. Thereafter he was bitterly silent.

Meantime, her consumption grew worse. She tried hypnotists and she tried George Sand's doctor, to no avail. At Dumas's insistence, she gave up night life and champagne, and went on summer outings with him and drank goat's milk. She accompanied him to the country for a week, but the silence and the fresh air and the wild life suddenly bored her. She returned to Paris, to her old dissipations, and one night when she had com-

plained that she was too exhausted to see him or anyone, Dumas
watched a lover enter her rooms.

In a cold fury, Dumas sat down and wrote her a note:

My Dear Marie, I am neither rich enough to love you as I could
wish, nor poor enough to be loved as you wish. Let us forget,
therefore, you a name which must be very nearly indifferent to
you, I a happiness which has become impossible for me. It is
superfluous for me to tell you how sorry I am, for you know
how much I love you. Good-by, then. You have too tender a
heart not to understand why I am writing this letter and too
much intelligence not to forgive me for writing it. *Mille sou-
venirs.* A.D.

Marie Duplessis did not reply. And she was soon too busy,
and too ill, to care. She had seventeen months of life left. She
lived them to the hilt. Franz Liszt was in Paris for a series of
concerts. Marie ordered her doctor, who knew the musician,
to bring him to one of her receptions. Liszt came and was con-
quered. He called her Mariette and cared for her, and she loved
him. When he prepared to depart on a tour, she wrote him: "I
know I shan't live. I'm an odd kind of girl, and I can't hold on
to this life that's the only kind I know how to lead and that I
can't endure. Take me away. Take me anywhere you like. I
won't worry you. I sleep all day, in the evening you can let me
go to the theater, and at night you can do what you want with
me." He promised to take her with him to Turkey later in the
year, but by then she was seriously ill. Liszt never saw her
again. When it was too late, he regretted that he had not been
at her bedside. "I would have tried to save her at any price," he
said.

Meanwhile, Marie's old suitor Viscount de Perregaux
pressed his love and begged her to dismiss all other men. She
replied: "Do you want to do me an injury? You know perfectly
well that what you propose would be very damaging to my
future, which you seem resolved to make miserable and sad."
What de Perregaux next proposed was marriage. In a fit of self-

pity, mingled with fear of desertion by friends in her worsening illness, she went with de Perregaux to London. They were married at the Kensington Registry Office on February 21, 1845. But Marie was not meant for marriage, and in even this one attempt at respectability she was cheated by the law. France did not recognize the legality of the union. It was just as well. She could not endure de Perregaux. She left him, though retaining the title of Countess and stamping de Perregaux's coat of arms on her writing-paper and dinner service.

Wracked with coughing and weakness, she went to Weisbaden for the cure. There was none. She returned to Paris, a wan cameo, and a reporter from *Le Siècle* saw her with her camellias at the opera for the last time. "She looked as though she had come from her tomb to reproach all the brilliant young fools and the Ninons of the day for having abandoned and forgotten her."

De Perregaux did not forget her. She had begged his forgiveness, and he was beside her bed as she lay staring at the Virgin on her dressing-table. She recognized her Viscount at last. "You have come to see me. Good-by. I am going away." Théophile Gautier reported the rest. "For three days, feeling herself slipping down into the gulf that awaits us all, she held tightly to the hand of her nurse as though she would never let go. But she was forced to let go in the end, when the angel of death arrived. By a last effort of youth, recoiling from destruction, she rose to her feet as though to escape; then she gave three loud cries and fell forever." It was February 3, 1846. She was twenty-three years of age.

She lay in a coffin surrounded by camellias. The old Russian Count, supported by his valet, saw her put to rest in the Cemetery of Montmartre. Two weeks later de Perregaux purchased a better plot of ground. He had her disinterred in the rain. Alexandre Dumas, who had just returned from Spain and Africa, was with de Perregaux as the slight body was placed in the permanent grave and the monument engraved with marble camellias was set over it forever.

Hardly Coincidental

For young Dumas the affair was not yet ended. There was a much-publicized auction of Marie's luxurious effects. Dumas attended it, then wrote an elegy to her. Still that was not enough. The virginal face, the magnificent body, haunted his waking dreams. Five months later he was at work on a novel, *La Dame aux camélias*. The heroine was Marie Duplessis, re-named Marguerite Gautier. The hero was himself, though the fictional name Armand Duval had only his initials. The story was their story, idealized but faithful to the facts and to Marie's background and character. The novel was written in four weeks. The first edition of twelve hundred copies, published by Cadot, was given a wide and sensational press, and it sold out at once. Beyond his thousand-franc advance, Dumas made little on it. He wished to make more. Someone suggested a play. He tried collaboration with a friend of his father's. The collabora-tor sought to make *Camille* the story of Marie and her Russian. Dumas objected. He decided to attempt the play on his own. He completed it in eight days and read it to his father, who was tearful. He took it to a theater. The management accepted it, but went bankrupt before production. When this happened a second time, Dumas gave up.

On New Year's Day, 1851, walking alone in the rain, Dumas found himself outside the Cemetery of Montmartre. He en-tered and sat before Marie's grave. He remembered later that he wept—over his defeats, his depression, and over her. He re-turned to his quarters, reread the play, rewrote it, and tried again. It opened in the Vaudeville Theatre, just a half-dozen years, almost to the night, after Marie's death. The audience cried and cheered, and Dumas wired his father: "Great, great success. So great that I felt I was at the *première* of one of your works." And his father replied: "My best work, my dear child, is yourself." Among the thousands who saw, and were moved by, the play was the popular Italian composer Giuseppe Verdi, who was inspired to create his opera *La Traviata*, which was produced in 1853.

Dumas married twice after his affair with Marie Duplessis.

In old age he became obsessed with the wickedness of prostitution, and proposed to the government that all unmarried women be drafted and taught trades in state schools and that all women of the streets suffer deportation to the colonies. Yet when he died in 1895 and was buried in the Cemetery of Montmartre, onlookers insisted upon snatching white camellias from his grave and placing them on the grave of Marie Duplessis. Despite the author's last tirades against women of pleasure, Frenchmen remembered what Dumas the younger had forgotten —that such a woman had made him famous, and had made romance flower just a moment longer in a world grown material and somewhat dreary.

While it may be that the greatest number of colorful heroines have been derived from the company of ladies who have lived lives of notoriety, it is quite possible that the greatest number of memorable heroes have been patterned after gentlemen who lived lives of high adventure. These were men who courted danger and violence, on land and on the sea, in every corner of the globe. For the most, their exploits have been forgotten and they have disappeared into relative anonymity, excepting as they survive under pseudonyms in the pages of classical and popular fiction.

Such a man, for example, was the strapping New England shoemaker Enoch Crosby, who had served as one of General George Washington's first espionage agents. His secret history was made public in 1831 with the appearance of a 216-page factual book entitled, *The Spy Unmasked; or, Memoirs of Enoch Crosby, Alias Harvey Birch, The Hero of Mr. Cooper's Tale of the Neutral Ground; Being an authentic account of the secret services which he rendered his country during the Revolutionary War. (Taken from his own lips, in short-hand)*. The slender volume included a dedication to James F. Cooper, Esq., whose "pen first immortalized the subject of the following Memoir," and an autographed engraving of the prototype captioned with the legend: "the true Harvey Birch, Hero of *The Spy*." With a peddler's pack on his back and his true identity sewed into the lining of his vest, Enoch Crosby served John Jay's Committee of Safety by mingling with disloyal Tories and exposing them. Almost a half-century later, when the ancient John Jay recounted his agent's daring deeds to James Fenimore Cooper, Crosby served fiction as well by inspiring the popular hero of *The Spy: A Tale of the Neutral Ground.*

Though Cooper had credited his inspiration to John Jay, the creator of *Uncle Tom's Cabin* insisted that she owed her debt to an even higher authority. When a visitor asked to shake the hand that had penned the immortal book, Harriet Beecher Stowe replied that her hand had not written the story.

"If you didn't write it, then who did?" asked the startled visitor.

Mrs. Stowe lifted her gaze. "God wrote it. I merely wrote His dictation."

Conceding this collaborative effort to the Lord, the name of one of His flock must be added if the full roll of credits for *Uncle Tom's Cabin* be cited. Josiah Henson, a Maryland slave who had suffered deeply in bondage, made a thrilling escape by underground railway to Canada, established an all-Negro Utopia in Ontario, and chatted with Queen Victoria in London, was the prototype for old Uncle Tom. Mrs. Stowe, in earlier days, when her mind was less clouded, admitted as much. She had met Henson in 1850 at her brother's house in Boston, and had read his seventy-six-page memoir, which "furnished me many of the finest conceptions and incidents of Uncle Tom's character." The resultant volume sold three million copies in the United States alone and provoked Abraham Lincoln to welcome Mrs. Stowe to the White House with the question: "Is this the little woman whose book made such a great war?"

Among men of violence, First Mate Owen Chase, of the ill-fated whaler *Essex*, may have done less than Josiah Henson in the cause of liberty, but he did considerably more than Henson for the cause of world literature. In November 1820 the 238-ton *Essex* was smashed and sunk in the Pacific by a mammoth sperm whale. Chase and five others began their long travail at sea in a twenty-seven-foot open boat. They drifted forty-five hundred miles in ninety-one days. Three died, and those who were spared were reduced to cannibalism to survive. At Chase's suggestion, they separated the limbs of the last dead man, cut his flesh into strips, and ate him. They were rescued by a ship out of London, taken to Chile, and then returned to Nantucket in June 1821. Young Herman Melville read Chase's slender book, *Narrative of the Most Extraordinary and Distressing Ship Wreck of the Whaleship Essex*, and once thought he saw Chase visiting aboard the *Acushnet*—and *Moby-Dick* had its Captain Ahab.

There have been many hundred Owen Chases in the hidden history of literature, though few, it must be admitted, inspired characters as majestic as Ahab. I should like to recount in more detail the adventure saga of one of these prototypes, a man of action who inspired the hero of *Peter Simple*.

It was Frederick Marryat, the seaman turned writer, who fashioned his Captain Savage in *Peter Simple* after the dramatic figure of the outspoken, redheaded, six-foot Thomas Cochrane, the tenth Earl of Dundonald. As a boy, young Frederick Marryat, moved by the sight of Lord Nelson's state funeral and bored by his mathematics tutor, ran off to sea three times. At last Marryat's father relented and employed his influence with Lloyd's of London, and his connection with a relative in the West Indies who knew Lord Cochrane, to enlist the fourteen-year-old lad on the frigate *Imperieuse*, a 38-gun captured Spanish vessel which had been placed under Cochrane's command.

Young Marryat, with his cocked hat, frilled shirt, white breeches, dirk, and sea chest, all gifts of his father, went to Plymouth in September 1806, bowed before the thirty-one-year-old Lord Cochrane, and had his name entered in the books as a First-Class Volunteer. Less than two months later the *Imperieuse*, with its crew of 284, put to sea, and Marryat was launched on his career as a writer.

It was not a pleasure cruise. Marryat learned this three days later. "At midnight, in a heavy gale," he wrote, "so dark that you could not distinguish any object, however close, the *Imperieuse* dashed upon the rocks between Ushant and the Main. The cry of terror which ran through the lower decks, the grating of the keel as she was forced in; the violence of the shocks which convulsed the frame of the vessel; the hurrying up of the ship's company without their clothes; and then the enormous waves which again bore her up and carried her clean over the reef, will never be effaced from my memory." The terror of the angry seas was soon followed by the first terror of combat. Yet both of Marryat's fears were swiftly overcome by the strong competence of his Captain. His respect and admiration soon became unquestioned hero-worship. In four months, against the French in the Mediterranean, the *Imperieuse* destroyed or captured a brig, a privateer, six gun-vessels, and fifty merchant ships, and laid waste to a portion of Barcelona.

Young Marryat returned to London with three stomach wounds, considerable prize money, and a desire for more action under Lord Cochrane. He was soon to have his wish. Eleven French ships, intended for the West Indies and Martinique, lay bottled up in the Aix Roads, protected by shore batteries on their flanks and a mile-long boom of spars, beams, tubs, and cables at the center. They were being held in check by a fleet of thirty-four English vessels under the cautious Lord Gambier. Cochrane's assignment was to rip this protective boom and open up the French ships to attack.

The *Imperieuse* joined the blockading English fleet, and Cochrane prepared for his commando raid. A brig was converted into a suicidal fire ship. It was filled with fifteen hundred barrels of gunpowder, on the top of which were piled three thousand hand grenades and hundreds of shells. On the black, windy night of April 11, 1809, Marryat and four others guided the fire ship toward the French inlet. "It seemed to me like entering the gates of hell," Marryat remembered. A fuse was lit. Marryat and the others leaped off the fire ship into a four-oar dinghy they had been towing. The explosion was to take place in fifteen minutes. Unexpectedly, it occurred in seven minutes, when the dinghy was only two hundred yards off. The fire ship's casks of gunpowder, its grenades and shells, blew up, shredding the French boom and tearing it from its moorings. The French boats were thrown into the wildest disorder. Some ran aground and others attempted to escape upriver.

Lord Cochrane signaled his superior, Lord Gambier, to attack. Gambier refused to move in for the kill. In a fury, Cochrane allowed his *Imperieuse* to drift under the French cannon, using this as a ruse to make Gambier come to his rescue and fight. Still Gambier remained immobile. "The French Admiral was an imbecile," Napoleon Bonaparte told an English visitor, "but yours was just as bad. I assure you that if Cochrane had been supported, he would have taken every one."

Nevertheless, the attack on the Aix Roads was hailed as a victory in England. Lord Cochrane was made a Knight of the Order of the Bath. Lord Gambier was about to receive the official thanks of Parliament, when Cochrane stepped in and challenged his superior's right to receive it. Gambier demanded a court-martial on Cochrane's charge of neglect. The nine-day trial was held on a ship at Portsmouth. Gambier's naval friends silenced Cochrane with legalities, and doctored evidence in favor of the accused. Gambier was acquitted, and rather than permit himself to be exiled to a poor assignment, Cochrane chose to persist in his battle against incompetence and corruption in Parliament.

Frederick Marryat continued his seafaring career without his idol. At the age of twenty-three, he was placed in command of his own naval vessel. When it was thought that a submarine was being fitted out in Brazil or a pirate vessel in Louisiana to rescue the captive Napoleon from Saint Helena, Marryat was instructed to have his ship, the *Beaver*, patrol the lonely isle. At seven o'clock in the morning following the Emperor's death, Marryat came ashore to gaze at his corpse and sketch his face. In Marryat's thirty-eighth year, after a quarter of a century in the navy, he tendered his resignation to the Admiralty, after being assigned as gentleman-in-waiting to the Duke of Sussex. That very year, 1830, he published his first novel, *The King's Own*. But he still had the image of Lord Cochrane in mind. As he wrote a friend: "I am puzzled upon the variety of works which I have commenced upon which to finish. I therefore go on adding up matter for *Peter Simple* one day." Meanwhile, he purchased an interest in the *Metropolitan Magazine*, a monthly devoted to "Literature, Science and the Fine Arts." In 1832 he took the journal over completely and converted it into a magazine publishing stories of nautical interest, most of them written by himself. It was in the pages of *Metropolitan*, between June 1832 and December 1833, that he first serialized his long ode to Lord Cochrane and the *Imperieuse*, who were made to appear in fiction as Captain Savage and the *Diomede*. After serialization, the novel *Peter Simple* was issued between book covers in three volumes.

It was, Christopher Lloyd has remarked, Marryat's "masterpiece." It was also his most popular novel. The story of Peter Simple, black sheep of a noble family, who went to sea under a daring Scot named Captain Savage, and who won for himself the hand of a lovely French lass named Celeste while helping Savage blockade the French fleet, swept all England. It was read by sailors, tradesmen, schoolboys, and its realistic dialogue and whirlwind action enthralled King William IV and Samuel Coleridge. It influenced generations of landlubbers and sent them to sea. Passages of *Peter Simple* were required reading in the British Navy. Joseph Conrad perused it and went before the mast, as did Admiral von Hipper. It made the muscular Marryat his reputation and his fortune. Thereafter, his novels earned him an income in excess of twenty thousand pounds, and his payment for stories equaled the best sums received by Carlyle.

Most important, Marryat felt that in *Peter Simple* he had given Lord Cochrane the immortality due him. Even at forty, Marryat still saw his mentor through the worshipful eyes of a fourteen-year-old. Thus, his description of Captain Savage:

"A sailor every inch of him. He knew a ship from stem to stern, understood the character of seamen and gained their confidence. He was besides a good mechanic, a carpenter, a rope-maker, sail-maker, and cooper. He could hand reef and steer, knot and splice: but he was no orator. He was good tempered, honest and unsophisticated, with a large proportion of common sense and free with his officers."

This was the Captain that Marryat had known and loved. But there was more to Lord Cochrane's character and career than appeared in *Peter Simple*. As a matter of fact, few prototypes in literature have had backgrounds as heroic, controversial, and diverse as Cochrane had in his eighty-five years of life.

Thomas Cochrane was born in Annsfield in 1775. His mother was the daughter of a frigate captain. His father was a hard-drinking, eccentric inventor who extracted by-products from coal and who discovered an improved means of salting herring. Cochrane made his debut at sea at the age of eighteen. He was assigned to a frigate commanded by an uncle, and distinguished himself by suffering a court-martial and a reprimand for insulting a superior officer. Despite his outspoken manner and quick Scotch temper, his talents for seamanship and command were not to be denied. At twenty-one he was a naval lieutenant, and at twenty-five he had the captaincy of his own vessel.

It was in 1800 that Thomas Cochrane was given full charge of six officers and eighty-four men aboard the 158-ton sloop *Speedy*. It was, Cochrane averred, "a burlesque on a vessel of war." It carried fourteen small guns. Larger cannon would have burst it apart at the seams. Cochrane made it topheavy with sail, intending to rely on agility instead of fire power. In thirteen months off Spain, the *Speedy* took fifty enemy vessels, five hundred prisoners, and seventy-five thousand pounds in prize money. Against more powerful ships, Cochrane used every stratagem he could conceive. Once, trapped by a bristling enemy boat, he ordered a Danish insignia and yellow quarantine flag run up, and explained that his craft had just left an African plague zone. Off Barcelona, he had his most spectacular success.

He decided to engage a huge and forbidding Spanish frigate, the *El Gamo*, which was manned by 319 crewmen against his own 54, and which catapulted broadsides of 190 pounds against his own 28 pounds. He hoisted the Stars and Stripes, and before the deception was discovered, he was alongside the *El Gamo* with his grappling-irons. His men, their cutlasses in their mouths, their faces blackened with tar, leaped shrieking onto the deck of the Spanish ship. As the battle went hand-to-hand, Cochrane hacked down the *El Gamo*'s flag. The Spaniards thought their commander had surrendered, and quit, and Cochrane was master of their ship with a loss of three men.

Though the Admiralty frowned upon his impetuous tactics, the English public adored Cochrane. Soon his victories aboard the *Imperieuse*, which Marryat heralded in fiction, enhanced his reputation further. But when he lost the court-martial proceedings against Gambier, he determined to turn his combative talents against corruption inside England. He had himself elected to Parliament, and battled relentlessly for naval reform.

Then, suddenly, his world tumbled about him. In February 1814 a man named R. Du Bourg arrived in England from France with the sensational announcement that Napoleon Bonaparte had been defeated. The next morning, on the heels of the rumor, Omnium stock jumped five points. Before the rumor was discredited, Lord Cochrane's broker had unloaded 139,000 pounds' worth of Omnium stock for Cochrane at a huge profit. The authorities quickly investigated. They learned that Du Bourg had visited Cochrane the day the rumor was spread.

On June 8, Cochrane, Du Bourg, and six others were put on trial for conspiring to boost the stock market through dissemination of false information. Cochrane fought valiantly to prove that Du Bourg was a friend of his uncle's and had merely come to him for a change of clothes. As to the selling of the stocks, he pointed out that he had been liquidating them regularly in that period. Nevertheless, he was found guilty. "I cannot feel disgraced while I know that I am guiltless," he told the court. He was sentenced to a year in jail, to one hour in the public pillory, and to a fine of a thousand pounds. For fear of riots, the government withdrew the pillory punishment. Cochrane went to jail. He was drummed out of the navy, expelled from Parliament by a vote of 140 to 44, and deprived of his knighthood. The Admiralty was having its revenge for Gambier.

Once Cochrane escaped his cell, spent several weeks with his bride of two years, and was then rearrested trying to address the House of Commons. Upon his release from prison, Cochrane felt himself a sailor without a ship and a man without a country. He was angrily determined to regain his reputation and fortune. He offered his services to the navies of the world. In the next ten years, three foreign governments bid for his genius, and he served them all in their fights for freedom.

In August 1818, accompanied by his wife and five-year-old son, he sailed for Chile, to become Admiral of its seven-ship navy and its two hundred seamen. For $8,000 a year, he led the Chileans in their revolt against Spain. His greatest victory was won in 1820, when he slipped into the harbor of Callao on the night of a fiesta and with fourteen small boats surrounded and captured the 44-gun Spanish flagship *Esmeralda*.

In 1823 Lord Cochrane transferred his talents to the service of Emperor Dom Pedro I of Brazil. Taking over seven rotting vessels and an undisciplined and inexperienced crew of sailors, he defeated a Portuguese fleet of thirteen ships, riddled an enemy convoy of sixty merchantmen (only thirteen reached Lisbon), and "succeeded in freeing an area twice the size of Europe."

His last performance in his long, bitter comeback was staged in Greece, which was still fighting for independence against Turkey. Lord Cochrane was paid fifty-seven thousand pounds —much of which he invested in a Greek loan that ultimately netted him a hundred thousand pounds' profit—to command the Greek sea forces. In three months he was able to capture only two Turkish vessels. The Greeks, he wrote to friends in Paris, "are collectively the greatest cowards (not excepting the Brazilians) I have ever met with."

Hardly Coincidental

He was fifty-three when he returned to London in 1828. Four years later he was pardoned by the government, and given the rank of Rear-Admiral in the British Navy. In 1841 his knighthood was restored. In 1860 he was buried with honors in Westminster Abbey. Unfortunately, lusty old Marryat, already in his grave a dozen years, could not enjoy the storybook vindication of his storybook Captain Savage.

A special place in literature, I suppose, should be set aside for those adventurers and men of action who lent their talents to the pursuit of crime—and criminals. I refer to the obscure murderers and officers of the law, the hunted and the hunters, whose moments of glory inspired classic killers and sleuths of fiction.

We know that the story of Jean Valjean, hero of Victor Hugo's *Les Miserables*, was "based upon that of a real man." The real man was Pierre François Gaillard, known to the Sûreté as Lacenaire, a mediocre philosopher-poet who received much sympathy when he was jailed for theft in 1829 and less when he cold-bloodedly stabbed to death an old bachelor and his aged mother for five hundred francs in 1834. We know also that the characters in a more recent novel, Rachel Field's *All This, and Heaven Too*, were derived from the principals involved in the Praslin murder. On an August night in 1847, in the bedroom of a Paris mansion, the renowned Duke de Praslin slashed and shot the Duchess de Praslin. It was thought that the Duke performed this liquidation out of affection for Miss Field's great-aunt, Mlle Deluzy, who had been a governess in the Praslin home and had been much admired by the Duke.

In the years between Lacenaire and the Duke de Praslin, and before and since, there have been innumerable other slayers, as well as investigators, whose activities animated interesting characters of fiction. Two such prototypes—a poisoner and a detective who were responsible for memorable characters in *Lucretia* and in *The Moonstone*—have proved particularly fascinating

The poisoner was Thomas Griffiths Wainewright, a man of delicate and sensitive tastes, an author, a friend of Charles Lamb, William Hazlitt, and Thomas De Quincey. He was, said Oscar Wilde, "not merely a poet and a painter and an art-critic, an antiquarian and a writer of prose, an amateur of beautiful things, and a dilettante of things delightful, but also a forger of no mean or ordinary capabilities, and as a subtle and secret poisoner almost without rival in this or any age." By eliminating three of his relatives, and perhaps several of his acquaintances, Wainewright attracted the literary curiosity of Charles Dickens and Edward Bulwer-Lytton. Dickens memorialized Wainewright as Julius Slinkton in *Hunted Down*, but did a poor job of it. Bulwer-Lytton drew the poisoner as Gabriel Varney in *Lucretia*, and here the portrait was worthy of the model.

Actually, Edward Bulwer-Lytton, by background and taste, was the author most perfectly suited, in his time, to attempt a fictional biography of Wainewright. His grandfather, out of sheer exuberance, wrote a play in Hebrew, and then burned it when he could find no actors who could speak Hebrew. His father was a general who expired prematurely. Bulwer-Lytton published his first poems at seventeen. He took a hiking-trip through England at twenty-one, met a murderer whom he found "gentle and courteous," and escaped assassination by another murderer whom he found less courteous. He went to France and impressed Parisians with the fit of his lavender trousers and his agility at whist. After graduating from Cambridge at twenty-three, he married Rosina Wheeler, the beautiful, temperamental, and somewhat vulgar niece of an Irish officer. His mother disapproved, and cut off his allowance. It was Bulwer-Lytton's loss, but literature's gain. He turned to authorship for his livelihood. He wrote everything from plays to orations, earning and spending as much as three thousand pounds a year, and in 1834, two years before separating from his wife, he published *The Last Days of Pompeii*. His primary fascination, encouraged perhaps by his marriage, was with the subject of murder. He had written three novels on crime, and been soundly criticized for his morbidity. Nevertheless, in 1846 he began to prepare a fourth.

"I had long had in my mind an exposition of certain vices," he wrote a friend. "While occupied with these ideas I became acquainted with the lives of two criminals; it was through their cultivation that I thought to trace the phenomena of their crimes." The two criminals were, of course, Thomas Griffiths Wainewright and his wife, Frances Ward Wainewright.

Wainewright's downfall, as Bulwer-Lytton very well knew, had been caused by his efforts to collect benefits on the insurance policies of his victims. But, as any less literate policy-holder might have told him, insurance companies are not separated from their profits so easily. They fought Wainewright, defeated and exposed him, and, in the end, were indirectly responsible for convicting him on a charge of forgery. It was to these benevolent organizations that Bulwer-Lytton turned for added detail on the actual life of his intended model.

We have no record of Bulwer-Lytton's inquiries to Mr. Henry P. Smith of the Eagle Insurance Company, but we have two of Mr. Smith's obliging replies dated May 1846. In the first reply, Mr. Smith wrote Bulwer-Lytton: "I will collect and send you all the Wainewright papers. There is no record of the forgery, that is, of the offence which sent him to Australia, because my duty directed my enquiries solely to the insurances —that is to the deaths. He forged five powers of attorney to put himself into possession of the capital of a sum in which he had a life interest, and was allowed by the Bank to plead guilty to the second plea—that of uttering the forged document— which saved his life. You are perhaps aware that Wainewright was a writer, a contributor to *The London Magazine*, I think, under the name of James Weathercock, and that he edited a poem of Marlowe's, which edition is in the Forster's library. In these works your skilful glance may exercise itself in detecting the poison among the flowers, and therefore I name them to you." In his second letter, Mr. Smith added: "On making further search, I found a list of the contents of the forfeit trunks, and this led me to a second packet of papers and books which had escaped my first enquiries. . . . There is no proof of the nature of the posion used, but the general medical opinion of the time pronounced it to be strychnine. . . . Mr. Thompson tells me that Wainewright confessed that he employed strychnine and morphine, and you will gather more of his history from the additional briefs and their notes, now sent to you."

With these documents on his desk beside him, and his first-hand knowledge of Wainewright, who was still alive in the penal colony of Hobart Town, Edward Bulwer-Lytton proceeded to create the character of Gabriel Varney for his novel *Lucretia; or, The Children of Night*. And if Varney, that man of "effeminate beauty," was as a character credible, it was only because Wainewright was as a human being utterly incredible.

Thomas Griffiths Wainewright was born in October 1794. His birth caused the death of his mother at twenty-one, and his father, an attorney, died shortly after. Wainewright was sent to live with his maternal grandfather, Dr. Ralph Griffiths, at spacious Linden House, Turnham Green, England. Few prodigies have been blessed with so fascinating a grandparent. Not only was Dr. Griffiths the publisher of *The Monthly Review*, but he was also the publisher of *Fanny Hill, The Memoirs of a Woman of Pleasure*, characterized by Anthony Comstock as "the most obscene book ever written." Dr. Griffiths had found a former civil servant, John Cleland, a writer of sorts who had been with the East India Company in Bombay, languishing in debtor's prison, and induced him to create a two-volume story of pornography in 1748. Cleland had undertaken the project with enthusiasm. His heroine, Frances Hill, hired at fifteen as a maid in a London household, found herself accompanied to bed by her mistress, who passionately kissed her. Related the fictional Fanny: "Encouraged by this, her hands became extremely free, and wander'd over my whole body, with touches, squeezes, pressures, that rather warm'd and supriz'd me with their novelty, than they either shock'd or alarm'd me." What occurred thereafter earned Cleland twenty guineas and Dr. Griffiths ten thousand pounds, though the book remained an under-the-counter rarity in Anglo-Saxon countries for two centuries—and continued to be a best-seller in France, where the English edition may still be purchased for the trifling sum of six hundred francs.

This literary obscenity allowed Dr. Griffiths to raise his grandson in style. And when he died in 1803, at the age of eighty-three, he left the nine-year-old Wainewright 5,200 pounds, with the provision that he live on the interest and never touch the capital. Wainewright's uncle, George Edward Griffiths, took over Linden House and the education of the restless young boy. After attending Charles Burney's Academy at Hammersmith, Wainewright went into the Guards as an orderly officer. He despised army life, consumed ten shots of whisky every evening, and at last decided that his vocation was authorship. His revolt against army life took the form of an illness that helped him obtain his discharge. For a short period he suffered a nervous breakdown, "ever shuddering on the horrible abyss of mere insanity," he said.

But he recovered, and immediately he began to write. In three years he published fifteen essays on art, acting, music, ballet, and engravings in the *London Magazine*, which also published Charles Lamb, Thomas Hood, Thomas De Quincey, and William Hazlitt. His pieces appeared under the pen names Janus Weathercock, Cornelius Van Vinkbooms, and Egomet Bonmot, and while they were gossipy and frivolous, they glittered with wit. Lamb thought Wainewright's writings "capital" and regarded him as the periodical's "best stay." He was at his finest on the subject of art. De Quincey thought him an honest critic because he "spoke for himself and was not merely a copier from books." He liked Da Vinci, Turner, Constable, and Blake. Generally, he preferred the old masters to the moderns. "Things that spring up under my nose dazzle me. I must look at them through Time's telescope."

He also attempted to paint. Between 1821 and 1825 one of his oils was exhibited at the British Institution and a half-dozen more at the Royal Academy. He apparently had some talent, since William Blake thought one of his Academy pictures "very fine."

His wit and culture attracted friends. He adored Charles Lamb, of whom he wrote: "His talk without affectation was compressed, like his beloved Elizabethans even unto obscurity. Like grains of fine gold, his sentences would beat out into whole sheets." Lamb returned his adoration and spoke often of the "kind, light-hearted Wainewright." As a matter of fact, De Quincey met him first across Lamb's dinner table, and years later remarked with wonder: "Amongst the company, all literary men, sat a murderer."

At this stage, Wainewright's appearance gave little promise of his subsequent notoriety. He dressed in the height of fashion, and was much complimented for his antique cameo breastpin and his lemon kid gloves, and for the extraordinarily large ring (which would be remembered long after) that he wore beneath one glove. "In person," his friend B. W. Proctor wrote, "Wainewright was short and rather fat, with a fidgety, nervous manner, and sparkling, twinkling eyes, that did not readily disclose their meaning. These, however, had no positive hardness or cruelty. His voice was like a whisper, wanting in firmness and distinction. A spectator would at first sight have pronounced him thoroughly effeminate had not his thick and sensual lips counter-balanced the other features and announced that something of a different nature might disclose itself hereafter."

His tastes were exquisite, those of a connoisseur of all things, but his tastes were beyond his purse. It was this, in the end, that led to his downfall. His library was lavishly decorated with a pomona-green chair, a lamp of antique Roman materials, a bit of Florentine majolica, a Greek vase, a Michelangelo engraving, and an ivory crucifix. His books, some studded with rubies, included rarities on the occult arts, astrology, and toxicology. He collected expensive hothouse plants and costly proof engravings.

He was constantly in debt. First, there was the support of his wife. He had married Frances Ward in 1821. "A sharp-eyed, self-possessed woman," Proctor called her, "dressing in showy flimsy finery. She seemed to obey Wainewright's humours and to assist his needs; but much affection did not apparently exist between them." Then, he entertained frequently. He had his friends, Lamb, John Forster, William Macready, to dinner and served them the choicest foods and wines. And he continued to indulge his taste for personal luxuries.

In 1825, to supplement his income, he embarked upon his life of crime. "It was death to stand in his path," the Chambers' Edinburgh *Journal* reported. "It was death to occupy the very house with him. Well might his associates join in that portion of the Litany which prays to be delivered from battle, from murder, and from sudden death, for sudden death was ever by his side." Before murder, Wainewright first indulged in the more innocuous—but, in his case, more fatal—crime of forgery. Since the legacy of 5,200 pounds from his grandfather carried with it the provision that he not be permitted to touch the capital sum, the money was held in trust by four men, and Wainewright received only the interest, paid him by the Bank of England. The inequity of this arrangement preyed upon Wainewright. At last he decided to rectify the injustice. He forged an order, in the names of the four trustees, which requested that the Bank of England transfer 2,259 pounds of the capital to him immediately. The Bank of England paid off, and the forgery was not discovered for a half-dozen years.

This money, easily gained, was easily spent. By 1829 Wainewright was again in serious financial straits. Forced to give up his London apartments, he moved fourteen miles out of town to Linden House, there to dwell with George Edward Griffiths, his uncle. In short months he made an astute observation. His uncle was terribly old, too old to enjoy the lovely Georgian mansion. The house might better serve those capable of fully appreciating it. Without further qualm, Wainewright poisoned his uncle and inherited Linden House. There are two schools of thought on the method Wainewright employed to dispatch his relative. Some believe that Wainewright inartistically deposited strychnine in the old man's coffee. Others, knowing better his æsthetic sensibilities, said that he carried crystals of a tasteless East Indian poison known as nux vomica in his ring, and released the solution while serving the old man his dinner.

Linden House proved a white elephant. It required a thousand pounds a year for minimum maintenance. Despite this burden, Wainewright thoughtfully assumed the care of his wife's mother, Mrs. Abercrombie, and his wife's two half-sisters, Helen and Madeleine Abercrombie. Though still plagued by the necessity for income—he had mortgaged Linden House for living-expenses, and owed money for food and coal —he now assumed yet another responsibility. His young and quite attractive sister-in-law, Helen Abercrombie, a charming innocent, was planning a trip. She was also involved in a lawsuit, in an effort to obtain title to certain properties owed her. Wainewright advised her that no trip could be taken, and no chancery lawsuit won, unless she had insurance on her life. Helen obliged. She obtained short-term insurance from two companies for six thousand pounds at a premium cost of a mere seventy-eight pounds. Later, with Wainewright's encouragement, Helen took out twelve thousand pounds' more insurance with other companies, naming her sister Madeleine and Wainewright as the beneficiaries.

It was in August 1830, while the last insurances were being applied for, that a voice of dissent was heard. Wainewright's mother-in-law, Mrs. Abercrombie, felt there was too much ado about insurance. It may have been, also, that the old lady was becoming suspicious of Wainewright. Her objections troubled the master of Linden House. It was, no doubt, to alleviate her upset that Wainewright finally emptied a dose of strychnine into her coffee. And Mrs. Abercrombie's objections were heard no more.

Hardly Coincidental

The primary target, however, was still Helen Abercrombie. Under extreme financial pressure, Wainewright moved her and Madeleine and his wife to an apartment in London. On the night of December 14, 1830, Wainewright escorted the three women to a play. They returned home for a late supper and dined on lobsters and porter. Wainewright's heavy ring was much in evidence. Before daybreak, young Helen was suffering fever, headache, and partial blindness. A doctor was summoned. He induced her to vomit and gave her sedatives. For six days Wainewright solicitously watched over her and supervised her meals and drink. On December 20, while Wainewright and his wife were outdoors sketching, Helen consumed a bowl of jelly, suffered severe convulsions, and died. A family nurse, in attendance, gloomily remarked that old Mrs. Abercrombie had passed on in exactly the same way. Wainewright suggested an autopsy, but it revealed nothing. Many years later a friend asked Wainewright: "How did you have the cold-blooded barbarity to kill such a fair, innocent, and trusting creature as Helen?" Wainewright thought a moment, then replied in the best of cheer: "Upon my soul, I don't know, unless it was because she had such thick ankles."

Immediately, Wainewright prepared to collect the wages of sin. The several insurance companies were not ready to pay off. They claimed that Helen Abercrombie had made false statements in her applications and that her policies were therefore invalidated. In a fury of frustration, Wainewright sued for the eighteen thousand pounds. It took five years for the suit to come before a jury. In June 1835 the trial began. The insurance companies argued that the late Helen Abercrombie had been used by her brother-in-law in an attempt to pay his debts. They hinted murder. The result was a hung jury. In December the suit was tried again. This time the jury found against Wainewright and for the companies.

Wainewright was not on hand for the verdict. Two years before, hounded by creditors, he had abandoned his wife and fled to France. It was said, though never proved, that he con-

(293)

tinued his avocation of homicide. According to rumor, Wainewright persuaded a friend, a "Norfolk gentleman," to take out three thousand pounds' insurance, and then disposed of the man to revenge himself upon the insurance companies. Also, it was rumored that he had an affair with a married woman in Calais, and removed her when she became serious. We know that Wainewright spent six months in a Parisian prison after strychnine had been found on his person, but the motivation behind his arrest was never revealed. It was believed that he lived in luxury in Paris, and it was believed that he lived in poverty. Once he wrote his friend Proctor for a loan, stating simply: "Sir, I starve."

Meanwhile, his forgery on the Bank of England had at last been detected. A warrant was issued for his arrest. Had he remained in Paris, he would have been safe. He chose to return to London, to follow a new love. "He knew that this forgery had been discovered," wrote Oscar Wilde, "and that by returning to England he was imperilling his life. Yet he returned. Should one wonder? It was said that the woman was very beautiful. Besides, she did not love him."

He reached London safely, and took a room on the ground floor of a hotel in Covent Garden. One morning he heard a noise in the street. He pulled back his curtains and peered out— at the precise moment that a Bow Street runner, Forrester by name, was passing. The detective recognized him at once. "That's Wainewright, the bank-forger!" Wainewright was arrested and immediately placed on trial at Old Bailey. The Bank of England agreed to waive discussion of murder, and not to press for the usual death penalty for forgery, if he pleaded guilty. He pleaded guilty. He was sentenced to the penal colony of Tasmania for life.

Shortly after, as Wainewright sat in Newgate awaiting transportation, Charles Dickens, Macready, and Forster arrived to make a tour of the prison in quest of fresh material. They were strolling past the cells when, as Forster recalled it, "They were startled by a sudden tragic cry of 'My God!

there's Wainewright.' In the shabby genteel creature, with sandy, disordered hair, and dirty moustache, who had turned quickly round with a defiant stare at our entrance, looking at once mean and fierce, and quite capable of the cowardly murders he had committed, Macready had been horrified to recognize a man familiarly known to him in former years, and at whose table he had dined."

He had little remorse for his crimes. One day an insurance official visited him, and remarked that his misdeeds had been a poor speculation. Wainewright was philosophical. "Sir," he said, "you City men enter on your speculations and take the chances of them. Some of your speculations succeed, some fail. Mine happen to have failed, yours happen to have succeeded. That is the only difference, sir, between my visitor and me. But I will tell you one thing in which I have succeeded, to the last. I have been determined through life to hold the position of a gentleman. I have always done so. I do so still. They pay me great respect here, I assure you. They think I am here for 10,000 pounds, and that always creates respect. Yes, sir, even in Newgate I am a gentleman. It is the custom of this place that each of the inmates of a cell shall take his morning's turn of sweeping it out. I occupy a cell with a bricklayer and a sweep, but they never offer me the broom!"

He was sent from Portsmouth to Hobart Town, Tasmania, on a ship called the *Susan*, in the crowded company of three hundred other convicts—"country bumpkins," he disdainfully called them. After he arrived in Tasmania, he was confined to the penal-colony hospital. Twice he tried to poison his nurses, and twice he failed. His hand had lost its cunning at last. He took to opium, and to sketching. A self-portrait in pencil he captioned: "Head of a convict: very characteristic of low cunning and revenge." In 1847 Lady Blessington received from a brother in Tasmania an oil of a young girl done by Wainewright. Forster saw it and thought that Wainewright had "put the expression of his own wickedness into the portrait of a nice kind-hearted girl."

(295)

Befriended only by an elderly cat, Wainewright died of apoplexy, at the age of fifty-eight, in 1852. In London, the literati he so admired were still reading of his terrible exile in Edward Bulwer-Lytton's popular *Lucretia*, in which Gabriel Varney faced the sentence of transportation with abject fear: "The idea of the gibbet lost all its horror. Here was a gibbet for every hour! No hope—no escape . . . The hour-glass was broken up—the hand of the timepiece was arrested. The beyond stretched before him, without limit, without goal—on into Annihilation or into Hell."

Just ten years after Wainewright's death, there was published in London what T. S. Eliot has called "the first, the longest, and the best of detective novels." This was William Wilkie Collins's *The Moonstone*. Collins spun an exciting story about the theft of a sacred Hindu diamond from the forehead of the Moon-God, in India, by a violent Englishman known as Herncastle. The diamond, which a dying Brahmin predicted would bring disaster to its owners, was eventually inherited by the Englishman's niece. At a birthday party, the precious stone disappeared. An inspector from Scotland Yard was summoned. He deduced that fresh paint, on a dressing-room door, would have come off on the culprit's nightdress. The inspector's hunt for the stained nightdress proved one of the highlights of the novel, which, after much suspense and some tragedy, ended happily with the diamond mysteriously returned to the Moon-God in India.

The story was satisfying, but in its gallery of characters there was one figure who caught the public fancy. The figure was that of Sergeant Richard Cuff of Scotland Yard. Collins's first description of the sleuth was unforgettable. He was "a grizzled, elderly man, so miserably lean that he looked as if he had not got an ounce of flesh on his bones in any part of him. He was dressed all in decent black, with a white cravat round his neck. His face was as sharp as a hatchet, and the skin of it was as yellow and dry and withered as an autumn leaf. His eyes, of a steely light gray, had a very disconcerting trick, when they encountered your eyes, of looking as if they expected something more from you than you were aware of yourself. His walk was soft; his voice was melancholy; his long lanky fingers were hooked like claws. He might have been a parson, or an undertaker, or anything else you like, except what he really was." He was a detective, one of the pioneer eccentrics of mystery fiction, who grew roses, pared his nails with a penknife, consumed Scotch by the bottle, and contended that "human life . . . is a sort of target—misfortune is always firing at it, and always hitting the mark."

He was also quite real. For Wilkie Collins had found the model for Sergeant Richard Cuff in a much-maligned yet brilliant detective of Scotland Yard named Inspector Jonathan Whicher, who was still alive and in retirement when *The Moonstone* first appeared. But the literary road that Wilkie Collins had traveled before he conceived Sergeant Cuff and *The Moonstone* had been a difficult one.

Wilkie Collins, whose father was a painter, was born in London during 1824. At seventeen he was apprenticed to a company engaged in the importing of tea. Among the tea leaves, perhaps, he first saw his destiny. He began to write. Then, by happy circumstance, his younger brother married the sister of the celebrated Charles Dickens. In 1851, when Collins was caught between the law and authorship, he met Dickens, and his destiny was confirmed. He wrote eleven books before he struck upon *The Moonstone*.

Like so many writers before him, Collins often obtained his best inspiration from fact. *The Woman in White*, published in 1860, was the product of an actual occurrence. There are two versions of the novel's origin. In the more romantic version, Collins was out walking one evening when he heard a feminine scream. A beautiful woman, attired in a flowing white robe, dashed out of a dark mansion, where she had been held prisoner under hypnotism. Collins, a bachelor with an affection for unattached females (one paramour of five years gave him three illegitimate heirs), rescued the lady in distress, took her for a mistress, and retained her story for his first successful book. In the more prosaic version, Collins found his woman in white while reading about a half-century-old French law case. In 1787 the Marquise de Douhault had traveled to Paris to recover from her black-sheep brother some properties left her by her father. Kidnapped by her brother, she was kept drugged and imprisoned for years, until a secret note smuggled to friends brought about her release.

If there were two versions as to the origin of Anne Catherick in *The Woman in White*, there was only one as to the inspiration for Sergeant Richard Cuff in *The Moonstone*. During 1860 the London press had been filled with accounts of detection done by Inspector Jonathan Whicher in the horrifying Road Hill murder case. Also, Charles Dickens's *Household Words* magazine had published a series of articles on Whicher's career, though the magazine had changed the detective's name to Sergeant Witchem. As a result of these stories, it was thought, Collins probably made Whicher's acquaintance.

Collins saw a fine fictional detective in Whicher, and he saw an intriguing plot in what he knew about the supposed curse of the actual Kohinoor diamond. He put the two together, and wrote the first installments of *The Moonstone* in Paris. The novel was more than a year in the writing. Half-blinded by an eye ailment, suffering intensely from rheumatic gout, Collins dictated much of the story from bed, under the influence of opium, while several male secretaries and finally a young woman, who became his mistress, set his words down on paper.

The first installment appeared in Dickens's *All the Year Round* on January 4, 1868. It increased the periodical's circulation even more than had Dickens's *Great Expectations*, which provoked Dickens to snidely remark that the tale had "a vein of obstinate conceit in it that makes enemies of readers." The nine hundred pages of *The Moonstone* were issued in three volumes by William Tinsley of London, who feared that the novel might not sell. When the initial edition of fifteen hundred copies was sold out at once and the London *Times* praised the work, Tinsley took heart and printed new editions. The novel became a classic in its field. As Dorothy L. Sayers remarked: "*The Moonstone* set the standard." Sergeant Cuff became one of the first to show what a professional detective should be in fiction—just as, in real life, Inspector Whicher was the model of the perfect investigator.

We know nothing of Jonathan Whicher's early years. We know only that he joined the Metropolitan Police in London, and that his intelligence and imagination enabled him to rise rapidly in the ranks. He was a quiet, dignified, decisive man of middle age when, in 1860, he was thrown into the highly publicized, extremely controversial Road Hill mystery. He had solved several important cases before, but none had brought him the fame or vilification that were his lot in the investigation of the surly Miss Constance Kent.

The arena for Jonathan Whicher's greatest challenge was a stately three-story residence called Road Hill House, located near Towbridge, in Wiltshire. The master of the great house was Samuel Saville Kent, son of a carpet-manufacturer, who was a government factory-inspector. A considerable portion of Kent's energies, it is apparent, went into his family life. In his first six years of marriage, his wife, Maryanne, gave him four children, three of whom survived. After the fourth birth, Mrs. Kent lost her sanity. She destroyed her husband's library. She lost her way in her own home. When a knife was found beneath her pillow, it was thought that Kent would do well to confine her to an institution. This he refused to do. He took charge of his mentally disturbed spouse himself, and apparently with unwholesome affection. For in the next ten years the insane Mrs. Kent gave birth to six more children. The first four of these died within a year of birth. Two survived. One of these, born in February 1844, was Constance Kent.

In the two decades before Mrs. Kent passed on, her five children were raised by a faithful governess named Mary Pratt. A year after Mrs. Kent's death, which occurred in 1852, the master made his children's governess the second Mrs. Kent. In seven years Mary Pratt gave Kent four more children, three of whom survived. One of these was a delightful boy, Francis Saville Kent, much admired by his prolific father.

By the summer of 1860, Kent had his enormous household well under control. On the second floor he kept his second wife, who was pregnant again, and her three children, attended by a young nurse named Elizabeth Gough. On the third floor he kept his four children by his first wife: sixteen-year-old Constance, her two sisters, and her younger brother (the older brother had died three years before). More than the others, Constance chafed under this arrangement. She had resented her stepmother from the first, especially because her stepmother had tried to send her off to boarding-school when she was twelve. A year after, Constance had tried to run away from home. With her eleven-year-old brother in hand, she had stolen outside to a privy or closet in the shrubbery, dressed her brother and herself, clipped her hair short, and hiked ten miles to Bath. There she was picked up by police and returned to the third floor of Road Hill House.

The Friday night of June 29, 1860, was a night like any other in the busy Kent household. The ménage was put to bed early. Before midnight, as was his habit, Kent locked the windows, checked the doors, and went to sleep. The house lay quiet in the night. There were footsteps, and there was savagery, but not one person was disturbed from the night's rest.

It was five in the morning when Elizabeth Gough, nurse of the second brood of children, woke and glanced over at the crib. The four-year-old boy, Francis Saville, was missing. The nurse was not concerned. She assumed that he had gone to join his mother. Miss Gough went back to sleep, only to awaken again at six thirty. The crib was still empty, its covers neatly laid aside. Miss Gough made her way to the large bedroom and softly knocked. The Kents did not awaken. Miss Gough returned to her room, woke the girls, said her prayers, and returned to the bedroom to knock again. She was told to enter.

"Please, ma'am, have you got Master Saville?" she asked. Mrs. Kent replied: "No, we have not got him. Where is he?" The terrible Road Hill case had begun.

Swiftly, Kent and his servants searched the house. There was no sign of the boy, but a window and door were found open. Certain that a kidnapping had occurred, Kent drove his carriage the five miles to Towbridge to summon the police. Meanwhile, neighbors had been alerted. They helped the family canvass the estate for clues. One neighbor opened the privy in the shrubbery, and there lay the missing four-year-old boy. He was wrapped in a blanket. His throat was slashed from ear to ear, so that his small head was almost severed from his body. "Is he murdered?" shrieked Mrs. Kent. "Good God, it is someone in the house who has done it!"

The bumbling local police had another theory. They felt that the house had been entered by someone, a factory worker perhaps, seeking to revenge himself upon Kent. Neighbors, and the sensational press, thought otherwise. They pointed the finger at the nurse, Elizabeth Gough, and ventured the opinion that she had been found entertaining a lover by the awakened boy. Fearful that he might speak, she had killed him. In some quarters it was thought that the lover had been Kent himself.

Since the investigation had reached a dead end, a local magistrate appealed to Sir Richard Mayne, Commissioner of the Metropolitan Police in London. At once he assigned his star detective to the widely publicized case. On July 14 Inspector Jonathan Whicher arrived at Road Hill House. In two days he announced that he knew the criminal, and in six days he made his arrest.

His suspicions, from the first, were directed toward the dark-haired, phlegmatic Constance Kent. She was self-reliant, and she had used the privy in the shrubbery once before in her flight from home. When a schoolmate had remarked, shortly before the crime, that it would be fun to return home for the holidays, Constance had snapped: "It may be to your home; but mine's different."

The most important clue of all was that of the missing night-gown. The murder had been committed at night—and one of Constance's three nightgowns was curiously missing. After examining her garments, Whicher summoned Constance for questioning.

"Is this a list of your linen?" he asked.

She said that it was.

"In whose writing is it?" he asked.

"It is my own writing," Constance replied.

Whicher held up the list. "Here are three nightdresses. Where are they?"

Constance replied: "I have two. The other was lost in the wash the week after the murder."

Whicher promptly questioned Sarah Cox, the maid in charge of the laundry. She remembered that three days after the murder, Constance had left her soiled nightgown and other clothes in the wash basket, as was the custom. Whicher pressed further. Was that all Constance had done? Not quite, Miss Cox recollected. "Miss Constance came to the door of the lumber-room after the things were in the basket, but I had not quite finished packing them. She asked me if I would look in her slip pocket and see if she had left her purse there. She then asked me to go down and get her a glass of water. I did so."

Whicher had what he wanted. He theorized that Constance, attired in a nightgown, had murdered her hated stepbrother, and had stained her garment in the process. She then burned it, wore another to soil it, left it with the maid for the wash, then got rid of the maid on the pretext of wanting water, recovered her nightgown, and insisted that it had been lost in the laundry.

In a private letter to the Police Superintendent of Bristol, Jonathan Whicher outlined his theory in detail:

"My opinion is, in the first place, that the fact of there being two families, or rather a stepmother and a family by that stepmother, was the primal cause of the murder; and that the motive was jealousy towards the children of the second marriage. The deceased was the favourite child, and spite towards the parents, the mother in particular, I believe to have been the actuating motive of Constance Kent. The reasons for my suspicions are as follows:

"Miss Constance possesses an extraordinary mind, which I think is proved by what she and her brother did on a former occasion. The two medical men mixed up in the present case believe her to be a monomaniac. Now, nothing happens to the child while she is at school, but on the fourteenth night after her arrival in the house the child is murdered, and by someone in the house. Now, who was there in that house likely to entertain any bad feeling toward the deceased but the person in question?

"Again, whoever did the deed doubtless did it in their night-clothes. When Constance Kent went to bed that night she had three night-dresses belonging to her in the house. After the murder she had but two. What, then, became of the third? It was not lost at the wash, as it was so craftily endeavoured to make it appear, but was got rid of in some other way. . . . This is my theory, and if a more reasonable one can be adduced I will most willingly bow to it, but until then I cannot alter it, although I know it is not the prevailing one."

With this theory in hand, Whicher issued a warrant for Constance Kent's arrest. He knew he did not have enough evidence to convict her in court, but he was certain she would break down and confess. He underestimated his suspect completely, and her icy calm in court almost ruined his reputation. When Whicher took her off to jail, she wept and cried: "I am innocent." During the entire trial she did not deviate from this plea—or from her earlier impassivity. Her defense made much of her youth, insisting that the crime was too vicious for so innocent a girl. As for Whicher's case: "There is not one tittle of evidence against this young lady—not one word upon which a finger can be laid to show that she is guilty. Where is the evidence? The sole fact—and I am ashamed in this land of liberty and justice to refer to it—is the suspicion of Mr. Whicher, a man eager in pursuit of the murderer, and anxious for the reward which has been offered, and it is upon his suspicion, unsupported by the slightest evidence whatever, that this step has been taken."

This carried the day. Constance was released for lack of evidence. The press, almost without exception, fell upon Inspector Whicher. The *Annual Register* lashed him as "absurd and cruel" and called his theory "childish." Within three years Whicher was hounded into disgraced retirement.

Still the Road Hill case remained a mystery. Elizabeth Gough was tried and acquitted. Kent was followed by crowds who shrieked: "Who killed the boy?" In despair, he moved his family to Wales, though without the company of Constance. In 1861 she entered the Convent de la Sagesse in France. Three years later she was back in England, serving at the St. Mary's Home in Brighton. She was wonderful with little children, and close to God, and in April 1865 she confessed the murder to her superior.

At her own request, she was placed on trial in July. Her confession of the crime, as reported by her doctor in *The Times*, was a gruesome one:

"She left her bedroom and went downstairs and opened the drawing-room door and window shutters. She then went up into the nursery . . . took the child from his bed and carried him downstairs through the drawing-room. She had on her nightdress, and in the drawing-room she put on her goloshes. Having the child in one arm, she raised the drawing-room window with the other hand, went round the house and into the closet, lighted the candle and placed it on the seat of the closet, the child being wrapped in the blanket and still sleeping, and while the child was in this position she inflicted the wound in the throat. She says that she thought the blood would never come, and that the child was not killed, so she thrust the razor into its left side."

Everything was precisely as Jonathan Whicher had deduced —the motivation of deep resentment, the blood spots on her gown, the recovery of the gown from the clothes basket. Whicher was in the courtroom when the judge put on his black cap and passed the sentence of death, a sentence later commuted to life imprisonment. Constance Kent was twenty years at Millbank Prison before her release in 1885, at the age of forty-one. It is thought that she then entered an Anglican convent and died shortly after.

Though fully vindicated, and regarded again as a detecting genius by all classes, Jonathan Whicher remained in retirement. He emerged only once, to help save the respectable Tichborne family from a monstrous hoax.

In 1854 the slim, youthful Sir Roger Tichborne, traveling from England to Jamaica, was thought to have drowned off Brazil. His mother refused to accept his death and spent a fortune advertising for the lost heir. After twenty years a semi-literate, 280-pound claimant appeared out of Wagga Wagga, Australia, and announced that he was the missing Tichborne. The old lady accepted him as her son. The rest of the Tichborne family fought the intruder's claim and retained Whicher to investigate him.

Whicher did a remarkable job. He learned that on Christmas Day, 1866, the claimant, before revealing himself as the heir to twenty-five thousand pounds a year, had gone to Wapping to look up his real family. His name was actually Arthur Bull Orton, and his profession was that of butcher boy. After a 102-day trial the case was dismissed, and Orton was tried again, this time for perjury. After a second trial of 188 days, he was sentenced to fourteen years' hard labor. Thereafter, he made his livelihood lecturing in music halls, and on his coffin he had inscribed: "Sir Roger Charles Tichborne."

On a note of triumph, Jonathan Whicher went back into retirement, and there remained until his peaceful death a short time after the Tichborne affair. Constance Kent and Arthur Orton were his memorials—unless one wishes to remember him as Sergeant Richard Cuff of *The Moonstone.*

. . .

In complete contrast to those prototypes who were involved in the field of crime, we have their more sedentary relatives—the professional intellectuals. By professional intellectuals I mean those heroes and heroines of the drawing-room whose knowledge was broad, whose ideas were advanced, whose conversation attracted circles of famous personalities, and whose livelihoods were dependent on an extraordinary ability to comprehend, reason out, and communicate stimulating opinions.

Since their lives were largely cerebral, it might seem that the intellectuals had little to offer as models for fiction. Yet literary history proves otherwise. Ideas, on paper or in speech, can be as provocative as physical activity. And men and women of ideas can be as colorful as men and women of adventure. Certainly Nathaniel Hawthorne believed this when he pilloried Sarah Margaret Fuller in print in 1852. "Would that Miss Margaret Fuller might lose her tongue!" Hawthorne once exclaimed. But had she lost her tongue, he might have been one heroine less. For it was Miss Fuller, feminist, critic, lecturer, gadfly, who gave him the stimulus for the creation of the energetic Zenobia in *The Blithedale Romance*. Miss Fuller, a prodigy who knew Latin and read Shakespeare before she was eight, edited a literary quarterly with Ralph Waldo Emerson, wrote a best-seller on the emancipation of women, and bore an Italian nobleman his child out of wedlock in Rome, was an aggressive, shocking, erudite, and ambitious woman. Hawthorne, who came to know her at the Brook Farm Institute, an ideal experimental community where he was a shareholder for a year, disliked her intensely. He was repelled by her pushiness, her frankness on the subject of sex, and her influence on his new wife. Two years after her drowning off Fire Island, Hawthorne satirized her unmercifully in his third and most unsuccessful novel.

Certainly, too, Marcel Proust believed in the cerebral prototype when he met that insolent and vain dandy, Count Robert de Montesquiou-Fezensac, in 1893. Montesquiou, an aristocratic descendant of the original D'Artagnan, an intimate friend of

Hardly Coincidental

D'Annunzio, Whistler, Verlaine, and Oscar Wilde, was a pervert and a poet and an arbiter of fashions in clothes and in conversation. His seven volumes of verse and three volumes of memoirs were forgotten after his death in 1921, but his dazzling snobbery inspired Proust to use him as Baron de Charlus in *Remembrance of Things Past* and encouraged Joris Karl Huysmans to portray him as Des Esseintes in *Against the Grain*.

Other intellectuals, with perhaps more solidity and accomplishment than Montesquiou or Miss Fuller, have served novelists as well, if not better. Perhaps the very best example of the mental prototype was the prolific writing man who inspired a notable character in *Bleak House*.

Just a year after Hawthorne avenged himself upon Miss Fuller, thereby alienating her vocal following, Charles Dickens performed the same literary crucifixion of an intellectual in London, and stirred up a similar controversy. In Dickens's case, however, the dissection was more painful, for it was performed on a victim still alive. The victim was none other than the highly regarded, sixty-eight-year-old Leigh Hunt, poet, essayist, critic, editor, discoverer of Shelley and Keats, promoter of Lamb, collaborator with Lord Byron. And the character he inspired Dickens to create was the irresponsible, parasitical, pathetically juvenile Harold Skimpole of *Bleak House*.

Between 1839, when the twenty-seven-year-old Dickens first met the elderly Leigh Hunt, and 1851, when he first determined to cruelly caricature him, the author came to know his model quite well. In those years between, Dickens gained financial stability. His father had been in debtor's prison, and he himself had worked at the grimy task of labeling blacking-bottles and toiling as a court reporter. Out of this poverty and drudgery, he produced *Pickwick Papers*, *Nicholas Nickleby*, *A Christmas Carol*, and *David Copperfield*, and his fortune was made. Leigh Hunt, on the other hand, was neither so talented nor so fortunate. In his old age, he remained the darling of the intelligentsia and the liberals, and the bane of his numerous creditors.

From all evidence, the two men liked each other. Leigh Hunt

thought Dickens's face had "the life and soul in it of fifty human beings." Dickens, for his part, admired Hunt for his charm, conversation, and journalistic ability. He sent Hunt copies of his novels, he invited Hunt to his children's birthday parties, and he hired Hunt to write for his *Household Words* magazine at "the highest rate." When the perennially poor Hunt was in his most desperate straits, Dickens told friends that the old man deserved "some enduring return from his country for all he has undergone and all the good he has done," and then proceeded to do something about it. To raise money for Hunt, Dickens staged, and appeared in the prologue of, a benefit play presented in Manchester and Liverpool.

Yet, for all this mutual affection, Charles Dickens could not resist, when the creative urge was upon him, exposing Leigh Hunt as Harold Skimpole.

David Copperfield had been in the bookstalls a year when Dickens sat down to his writing-table, dipped quill pen into blue ink, and began the writing of *Bleak House* in November 1851. The composition of the 380,000-word novel occupied the better part of two years. Its central plot was based on an actual legal case, the Jennings case, which revolved about a man who had left a fortune of 1,500,000 pounds but had designated no heir. The case was steadily in the English courts from 1798 to 1915, without determination, though legal fees mounted to 250,000 pounds. Using this factual springboard, Dickens invented the lawsuit of Jarndyce *versus* Jarndyce for a satire on the English judicial system and an indictment of the society of his time. In the story, human beings fighting for an inheritance were ruined and destroyed by the delays of the old Court of Chancery.

Dickens published the novel as a serial in *Household Words*. It appeared monthly, and regularly, from March 1852 to September 1853, helped inflate the periodical's circulation to thirty-five thousand copies, and, according to the jubilant Dickens, succeeded in "beating dear old Copperfield by a round ten thousand or more. I have never had so many readers." Beyond enriching Dickens's bank account and his reputation, the publication of the novel also succeeded in forcing a reform of the Court of Chancery and in deeply wounding Leigh Hunt. For in the second installment of his tale, Dickens had introduced the foppish, idle, and amoral knave Harold Skimpole, an old friend of Mr. Jarndyce of Bleak House.

Skimpole entered the narrative a minor character, but emerged a major scandal. "He was a bright little creature, with rather a large head; but a delicate face, and a sweet voice, and there was a perfect charm in him. All he said was so free from effort and spontaneous, and was said with such a captivating gaiety, that it was fascinating to hear him talk. . . . He had more the appearance of a damaged young man, than a well-preserved elderly one. There was an easy negligence in his manner and even in his dress (his hair carelessly disposed, and his neckerchief loose and flowing, as I have seen artists paint their own portraits) which I could not separate from the idea of a romantic youth who had undergone some unique process of depreciation."

He was a professional borrower, a barnacle, and airily arrogant about it. "Every man's not obliged to be solvent," he liked to say. "I am not. I never was. I have not the power of counting. Call it four and ninepence—call it four pound nine. They tell me I owe more than that. I dare say I do. I dare say I owe as much as good-natured people will let me owe. If they don't stop, why should I?"

This was Leigh Hunt laid bare, just as Skimpole's wife—who "had once been a beauty, but was now a delicate high-nosed invalid suffering under a complication of disorders"—stood plainly recognizable as Marianne Hunt. Dickens did not deny his prototype—in private. In a letter to Mrs. Richard Watson, dated September 25, 1853, Dickens wrote: "Skimpole—I must not forget Skimpole—of whom I will proceed to speak as if I had only read him and not written him. I suppose he is the most exact portrait that was ever painted in words! I have very seldom, if ever, done such a thing. But the likeness is astonishing. I don't think it could possibly be more like himself. It is so awfully true that I make a bargain with myself 'never to do so anymore.' There is not an atom of exaggeration or suppression. It is an absolute reproduction of a real man."

It was this "absolute reproduction" that John Forster feared when he first read *Bleak House* in galley proofs. He begged Dickens to modify the character, and Dickens obliged by changing several of Skimpole's outward mannerisms. Further, the artist selected to illustrate the novel was warned not to sketch any resemblance to Hunt, so that Dickens was able to tell Forster: "Browne has done Skimpole and helped to make him singularly unlike the great original."

Superficial camouflage was not enough. Readers of *Bleak House* saw through it at once, and Hunt's friends were beside themselves with rage. At first, ineffectually, they tried to prove that the selfish, idle Skimpole bore no similarity to their generous, hard-working idol. When this did not take, they hit out at Dickens. As for Leigh Hunt himself, we know that he was badly hurt. He penned a defense of himself for insertion in a revised edition of his autobiography, but was talked out of publishing it by Forster. After that, Hunt remained publicly silent, though he apparently made accusations directly to Dickens. He continued to invite "dear Dickens" to his home, since he needed him as an editor-publisher, but apparently Dickens frequently avoided him out of embarrassment. In 1855, after receiving an invitation from Hunt to come calling, Dickens jotted his acceptance with the provision that "I hope you will not think it necessary to renew that painful subject with me."

Two months after Hunt's death, in 1859, his friends rallied to renew the painful subject. One sent a batch of American reviews of *Bleak House* to Hunt's son with a note reading: "When your father so feelingly complained of 'the great blow' which came so unexpectedly and so staggeringly upon him, ought not Mr. Dickens to have told the world that it was never aimed?"

At last, four months after Hunt's death, Dickens made his public apology. The revised edition of Hunt's autobiography had just appeared, and Dickens used this occasion to publish, on the day before Christmas, 1859, an elaborate explanation in the pages of *All the Year Round* magazine.

"Four or five years ago, the writer of these lines was much pained by accidentally encountering a printed statement 'that Mr. Leigh Hunt was the original of Harold Skimpole in *Bleak House*,'" Dickens began. "The writer of these lines, is the author of that book. The statement came from America. . . . Since Mr. Leigh Hunt's death, the statement has been revived in England. The delicacy and generosity evinced in its revival, are for the rather late consideration of its revivers. The fact, is this:

"Exactly those graces and charms of manner which are remembered in the words we have quoted, were remembered by the author of the work of fiction in question. Above all other things, that 'sort of gay and ostentatious wilfulness' in the humouring of a subject, which had many a time delighted him, and impressed him as being unspeakably whimsical and attractive, was the airy quality he wanted for the man he invented. Partly for this reason, and partly (he has since often grieved to think) for the pleasure it afforded him to find that delightful manner reproducing itself under his hand, he yielded to the temptation of too often making the character speak like his old friend. He no more thought, God forgive him! that the admired original would ever be charged with the imaginary vices of the fictitious creature, than he has himself ever thought of charging the blood of Desdemona and Othello, on the innocent Academy model who sat for Iago's leg in the picture."

Actually, Dickens had used much of Hunt, but not the best of him. For the best of him was not in his manner or speech or financial attitude, but in his foresight and activity and talent. True, like Margaret Fuller, he had only a half-talent, but it was enough—and considerably more than Harold Skimpole possessed.

It is odd to learn that James Henry Leigh Hunt, so closely identified with English literature, was almost born an American.

His mother was a native of Philadelphia, and his father an attorney educated in New York. However, when his father, Isaac Hunt, was persecuted for loyalist sympathies, he transferred his allegiance to England and his profession to that of clergyman. As a consequence, Leigh Hunt was born in Middlesex, England, instead of Philadelphia or New York, during October 1784. He was a delicate boy who grew to maturity with a stammer and a flair for composition. His first book was promoted by his father, who badgered a number of parishioners and celebrated folk (among them the Earl of Cardigan, the Archbishop of Canterbury, Charles Lamb) into underwriting it. The volume appeared in 1801 and was entitled *Juvenilia; or, A Collection of Poems. Written between the Ages of Twelve and Sixteen, by J. H. L. Hunt.* Surprisingly, it went into four editions, and Leigh Hunt's future was cast.

After brief excursions in London as an attorney's clerk and an employee of the War Office, Leigh Hunt, at the age of twenty-four, joined his brother John Hunt in establishing a Sunday periodical called *The Examiner*, which would persist for thirteen years and earn both proprietors fame and notoriety. *The Examiner* was a liberal sheet, crusading for freedom of speech, for tolerance, for reform. It was this editorial policy that attracted Percy Shelley to Hunt. The poet came calling one day with several verses. "He was then a youth," Hunt remembered, "not come to his full growth; very gentlemanly, earnestly gazing at every object that interested him, and quoting the Greek dramatists." Hunt rejected Shelley's offerings, but their friendship was founded and grew firmer through the years.

Hunt's determination to remake England for the better, which so attracted Shelley, was the factor that precipitated one of the two most publicized episodes in his career. Hunt was twenty-eight when, in a fit of indignation over "the Regent's breaking his promises to the Irish," he published an article called "Princely Qualities" in *The Examiner* dated March 22, 1812. In the article he characterized the Prince Regent—later King George IV—as a "corpulent man of fifty . . . a violator of his word, a libertine over head and ears in disgrace, a despiser of domestic ties, the companion of gamblers and demireps."

Hunt and his brother were promptly brought to trial for libel. They were sentenced to different prisons for two years apiece and each was fined five hundred pounds. Hunt was incarcerated in two rooms of the Horsemonger Lane prison infirmary. He was permitted to furnish his cells as he wished. He moved his wife of four years, and his children, into the two rooms, and soon the cells were domesticated by the addition of rose wall-paper, pianoforte and lute, bookcases, flowers, and busts of the great poets. Charles Lamb visited the cells and thought there was "no other such room except in a fairy tale." Open house was held until ten o'clock every evening, and celebrated visitors came with fresh fruit and eggs for the journalistic martyr. Besides the Lambs, Leigh Hunt entertained Shelley, William Hazlitt, Cowden Clarke, Jeremy Bentham, and Thomas Moore. It was Moore who informed Hunt that Lord Byron was an admirer. Immediately, Byron was invited to attend a jail dinner of fish and vegetables. The noble lord came bearing a gift of books, and returned for several more visits.

During most of his two years in prison, Hunt was ill. Nevertheless, he continued to edit and publish *The Examiner* from his incredible cell. When at last he was released, in February of 1815, he faced the bustling outside world with hesitancy. "The whole business of life appeared to me a hideous impertinence," he said. "The first pleasant sensation I experienced was when the coach turned into the New-road, and I beheld the old hills of my affection standing where they used to do, and breathing me a welcome."

His notoriety had established his reputation with many of the most promising writers of the day. A rising young poet, John Keats, observed Hunt's freedom with a verse:

> *What though, for showing truth to flatter'd state,*
> *Kind Hunt was shut in prison? yet has he,*
> *In his immortal spirit, been as free*
> *As the sky-searching lark, and as elate.*

Hunt was soon able to repay Keats. *Blackwood's Magazine* printed its infamous slander, "The Cockney School of Poetry," signed by "Z." The scurrilous piece reviled Hunt. "His poetry resembled that of a man who has kept company with kept-mistresses. His muse talks indelicately like a tea-sipping milliner girl." But the article's attack on "Johnny Keats" was even more virulent. Hunt lashed back, and at every opportunity praised Keats. It was Hunt who brought Keats and Shelley together in his living-room and inveigled them into a contest of creating, with him, impromptu poems on a given topic. While Shelley took to Keats at once, Keats remained too shy, and too sensitive of being patronized by those of higher birth, to reciprocate.

Hunt continued his involvement with other writers. He published Charles Lamb's "The Inconvenience Resulting from Being Hanged." He hired John Forster as an assistant on *The Examiner.* He defended Lord Byron after the scandal of the separation from Lady Byron. And he predicted great things for Shelley in his *Young Poets.*

Yet, even among those he admired most, he made enemies. Shelley never wavered in his friendship, but Mary Shelley thought Hunt too "contrary." As for Keats, he confided to a friend that Hunt "is certainly a pleasant fellow in the main when you are with him—but in reality he is vain, egotistical, and disgusting in matters of taste and morals. He understands many a beautiful thing; but then, instead of giving other minds credit for the same degree of perception as he himself professes—he begins an explanation in such a curious manner that our taste and self-love is offended continually. Hunt does one harm by making fine things petty and beautiful things hateful."

It was not only his intellectual superiority that irritated. There was also his attitude toward friends and finances. He borrowed from one and all as if it were his due. Of all his friends, Shelley alone did not complain. And, finally, there were his wife and seven children.

From all reports extant, few households were more curious

or more repulsive. Hunt had wedded Marianne Kent in 1809. She gave him seven children and a life of hell. She was often incapacitated, spitting blood. She was sharp of tongue. She was addicted to drugs and drink. Long after her death in 1857, her physician, Dr. George Bird, revealed that most of Hunt's troubles had come from his wife. "In my opinion, she was mendacious, self-indulgent, and incapable of controlling her household. When I first knew her, about 1851, she was an intemperate woman and sodden from drink. How much Leigh Hunt knew of this infirmity I do not know. One day he said to me, 'Isn't a bottle of brandy a day, which I hear you have ordered my wife, too much?' As her doctor I had ordered abstention from spirituous drinks. Going one day into her room, Leigh Hunt kicked over a bottle of foaming beer, partly hidden under the bed. 'It's milk, my dear,' said Mrs. Leigh Hunt, and he accepted the explanation, with what reservations of his own I cannot tell." Lord Byron disliked Mrs. Hunt, but detested her children even more: "They are dirtier and more mischievous than Yahoos. What they can't destroy with their filth they will with their fingers . . . six little blackguards." Thomas Carlyle, while less vehement, was similarly impressed. Visiting the Hunt family, he noted: "nondescript, unutterable! Mrs. Hunt asleep on cushions; four or five beautiful, strange, gipsy-looking children running about in undress, whom the lady ordered to get us tea . . . an indescribable dream-like household."

In May 1822 Leigh Hunt embarked upon the second great adventure of his life. Shelley, who was in Italy with Byron, had written that Byron "proposes that you should come and go shares with him and me in a periodical Work, to be conducted here, in which each of the contracting parties should publish all their original compositions, and share the profits."

After a two-month journey, Hunt, accompanied by wife, children, and furniture, arrived at Leghorn, Italy. He placed his brood in an inn and hurried to the Casa Lanfranchi to visit his patron and partner. "Upon seeing Lord Byron, I hardly

knew him, he was grown so fat; and he was longer in recogniz-
ing me, I had grown so thin. He took me into an inner room,
and introduced me to Madame Guiccioli, then very young as
well as handsome." Later, Shelley arrived by boat to welcome
Hunt, and one of the Hunt boys remembered "the shrill sound
of his voice, as he rushed into my father's arms." After Shelley
had established the Hunt family in the ground floor of Byron's
Casa and taken Hunt to see the Leaning Tower of Pisa, he
borrowed a copy of Keats's latest verses and departed by boat
into a storm. Hunt did not again see him alive.

Together, Hunt and Byron carried on their project. The first
issue of *The Liberal* appeared in September 1822. Among other
items, it carried a poem by Byron, a translation from Goethe
by Shelley, and an article on Pisa by Hunt. Seven thousand
copies were printed and four thousand sold, and one London
critic called it an "atrocity." After three more issues, Byron
became bored and backed out—and the Hunts were left
stranded and broke in Italy.

Hunt remained two years in exile before an English publisher,
Henry Colburn, offered to bring him home if he would deliver
a book on Italy. Hunt agreed, and in October 1825 he was
safely back in London. However, instead of giving Colburn a
book on Italy, Hunt gave him a 500-page volume entitled
Lord Byron and Some of His Contemporaries. Almost a third of
the book was devoted to exposing the frailties of Lord Byron.
There were constant references to Byron's tippling. "It is a
credit to my noble acquaintance, that he was by far the pleasant-
est when he had got wine in his head." Or: "Lord Byron, who
used to sit up at night writing Don Juan (which he did under
the influence of gin and water), rose late in the morning."
There were references to his vanity. "In his hand was a tobacco
box, from which he helped himself occasionally to what he
thought a preservative from getting too fat. Perhaps, also, he
supposed it good for his teeth."

Except for that volume, and his autobiography, and the poem
"Abou Ben Adhem," Leigh Hunt added little to his stature as

a writer in his last years. In 1840 he produced a play, *A Legend of Florence*, in Covent Garden, which Queen Victoria saw several times. Encouraged, he wrote more plays, but none was ever staged. By 1847 he was pensioned by the Queen—two hundred pounds a year—"in consideration of his distinguished literary talents," though actually the pension was an apology for his unjust jail sentence thirty-four years earlier. And in 1852 he was publicized as Harold Skimpole.

Seven years later he was dead. Edward Trelawny and Joseph Severn, who had known Shelley and Keats as Hunt had known them, were at his funeral. Over his grave William Allingham carved his epitaph—words truer, and better remembered, than Dickens's belated apology:

> *These words, methinks, Leigh Hunt, from thine own pen*
> *"Write me as one that loves his fellow-men."*
> *That loves, we say, not loved; a man like thee*
> *Is proof enough of immortality.*

A NOTE ON THE TYPE

The text of this book was set on the Monotype in JAN-SON, a recutting made direct from the type cast from matrices made by Anton Janson. Whether or not Janson was of Dutch ancestry is not known, but it is known that he purchased a foundry and was a practicing type-founder in Leipzig during the years 1600 to 1687. Janson's first specimen sheet was issued in 1675. His successor issued a specimen sheet showing all of the Janson types in 1689.

His type is an excellent example of the influential and sturdy Dutch types that prevailed in England prior to the development by William Caslon of his own incomparable designs, which he evolved from these Dutch faces. The Dutch in their turn had been influenced by Garamond in France. The general tone of Janson, however, is darker than Garamond and has a sturdiness and substance quite different from its predecessors. It is a highly legible type, and its individual letters have a pleasing variety of design. Its heavy and light strokes make it sharp and clear, and the full-page effect is characterful and harmonious.

This book was composed, printed, and bound by KINGSPORT PRESS, INC., Kingsport, Tennessee. Paper supplied by S. D. WARREN COMPANY, Boston. Typography and binding design by WARREN CHAPPELL.